BILL MANLEY is an Egyptologist, university lecturer, museum curator and best-selling author. He teaches Egyptology and Coptic at the University of Glasgow, and is Co-Director of *Egiptología Complutense*. Honorary President of Egyptology Scotland and an Honorary Research Fellow at the University of Liverpool. He was formerly Senior Curator for Ancient Egypt at National Museums Scotland, and continues to work with archaeological projects in Egypt. His specialist output includes books, catalogues, articles and exhibitions covering such diverse subjects as ancient texts, the history of Egyptology, gold jewelry, the archaeology of Palestine and the world's earliest philosophy.

Thames & Hudson world of art

This famous series provides the widest available range of illustrated books on art in all its aspects.

To find out about all our publications, including other titles in the World of Art series, please visit **www.thamesandhudsonusa.com**. There you can subscribe to our e-newsletter, browse or download our current catalogue, and buy any titles that are in print.

1 View of the burial chamber
of the mayor of Thebes Sennefer
(see p. 119).

Bill Manley

Egyptian Art

274 illustrations

 **Thames & Hudson** world of art

Now, there is a law written in the darkest of the Books Of Life, and it is this:
If you look at a thing nine hundred and ninety-nine times, you are perfectly safe;
if you look at it the thousandth time,
you are in frightful danger of seeing it for the first time.
G. K. Chesterton, *The Napoleon Of Notting Hill* (1904) I.1

To JEB, for the gift of new eyes

pp. 8–9: Schist dyad of Menkaura and a queen (see p. 51).
pp. 62–63: Ostracon showing a female dancer or gymnast (see p. 256).
pp. 128–129: The Great Sphinx at Giza (see p. 135).

Egyptian Art © 2017 Thames & Hudson Ltd, London

First published in 2017 in paperback in the United States of America by
Thames & Hudson Inc., 500 Fifth Avenue, New York, New York 10110

www.thamesandhudsonusa.com

Library of Congress Control Number 2017945801

ISBN 978-0-500-20428-3

Printed and bound in China by Lion Productions Ltd

Contents

2 Personifications of the Nile
Valley (left) and a temple estate
presenting their produce as
offerings at the 'Red Chapel'
of the female king Hatshepsut
(see p. 222).

PART I   ART & CREATION

3 Calcite statue of king Amenhotep III and the god Sobk-Ra. Found near Gebelein. 2.57 m (8 ft 5 in.) high. 18th Dynasty.

Chapter 1 'Giving Stone to Its Lord': Offerings and Monuments

This book is about the visual art produced in Egypt when the land was ruled by the god-kings, whom we have come to call the 'pharaohs' (albeit the word originally meant 'the palace'). Consequently, it covers thousands of years from the first pharaohs, roughly about 3000 BC, until pharaonic authority dissolved in the national conversion to Christianity, between AD 300 and 350. Visual art, of course, may mean any crafted or decorated objects or surfaces we could sensibly understand as art, which in regard to ancient Egypt includes monumental painting, reliefs and sculpture, as well as smaller items of jewelry, furniture, decorated tiles, dishes and the like. Such artworks were fashioned in wood, ceramics, faience (glazed composite) or glass, and metals, including bronze and gold. Most of all, however, ancient Egyptians worked using stone of many kinds and qualities.

The subject may seem too vast and disparate for a single book, and in points of detail it certainly is. However, even a quick survey of ancient Egyptian artworks reveals how the majority come from a handful of contexts, principally tombs and temples. These are contexts we may characterize as sacred places, where humans attended gods, the living considered the dead, and where minds contemplated the eternal. Of course, there is art from other places that must also be considered, especially art from domestic contexts. However, we have surprisingly little, as we shall see in Chapter 14. Moreover, some contexts where we would expect to find art are mostly not relevant to ancient Egypt, including art from public spaces or official buildings. Even the wealth of jewelry surviving from pharaonic times on closer inspection turns out to have come down to us in burials. So we may begin by suggesting that ancient Egyptian art – at least as it survives today – is a subject brimful of antiquity but more modest in scope.

Initial observations

The finest art of ancient Egypt may fairly be described – even in our modern, sophisticated age – using words such as beauty, elegance and grace. To take an example, in 1967 a human-sized, calcite statue of the god Sobk-Ra was discovered by accident among the remains of his temple, near modern Gebelein in the deep south of Egypt [3,4]. The statue shows the massive, crocodile-headed god embracing the relatively diminutive, yet solid and elegant, figure of the once mighty pharaoh, Amenhotep III (c. 1390–c. 1353 BC). Despite the god's reptilian face, there is neither horror nor disgust in the composition, but serenity. The god has a human body, and is able to embrace the king like a proud father posing for a photograph. Although there is no sparing the outlandish details of his face, each individual tooth finely scored in the stone helps form the half-smile of the Mona Lisa. The king smiles likewise, and his arms have settled upon his kilt in a gesture of greeting (to us?). He is evidently not intimidated by his companion, and, we may note, his face is as handsome as the other's is monstrous. Individual barbs in the god's high-plumed crown, the folds of the king's iconic headcloth (or *nemes*) and the ever-present coiled uraeus-cobra on his brow, even the lines of his make-up, have been worked distinctly into the soft-stone surface. The god's solid knees and legs are shapely and muscular, and give the impression he may stand up at any moment, so fluid and precise is the modelling. The waxy stone has been carved into forms so plastic as to seem lifelike, and almost flawless after three and a half millennia.

What does a statue so beautifully carved tell us? Undoubtedly the relationship between the two characters – god and pharaoh – is crucial, intimate, and presented in human terms (family, serenity, touching, welcome). We see the crowned king, but beside him the god – more massive and enthroned – holds still greater authority. Both of them look towards the viewer, revealing no specific attitude nor emotion, though the confrontation is not hostile. As we look at the king, whose height the sculptor has arranged to meet our eye-line, the god's gaze remains slightly above the engagement. What does this engagement have to do with the function of the statue? Who was its intended audience?

Looking more closely, we see how the god's far hand is pressing the ancient hieroglyph ♀ reading 'life' onto his companion – in fact raising it to his face. His crown carries the same coiled uraeus-cobra as the king's, so whatever the uraeus represents ('domination', actually) applies to both of them. His throne takes a simple form, barely more than a cube with a step for the base and a back pillar rising to support the massive plumed crown, and it is covered at the sides with hieroglyphs that elaborate on the subject of the statue. In fact, where the statue is now on display, in the Luxor Museum of Ancient Egyptian Art, it is possible to walk round and see that the back too is formally plain but

4 Close-up view of the king in [3].

entirely covered with columns of clearly cut hieroglyphs. Through them, Sobk-Ra is made to speak to the king (not us) and state that he is, indeed, Amenhotep's father and he does, indeed, love him. Specifically, he has made his son's 'perfection', given him the festivals of kingship a million times over, and established him in the world according to the pattern of the Sun in the sky, so he may rise in splendour each day and endure until the end of time.

Accordingly there is so much in this image that seems recognizable, human and accessible, but there are also ideas and beliefs far from our own. Gather your thoughts for a moment, and the statue reverts to a crocodile-headed monster embracing a pint-sized 'king like the Sun'. In other words, we may respond to the humanity, beauty and even authority of the art, but we will not truly understand it until we appreciate specific ancient values, such as the eminence of kings and gods, the functions of statues and the meaning of crowns, gestures or hieroglyphs.

The challenge of ancient Egyptian art
However exotic the ideas and however bizarre the god's form, the statue of Sobk-Ra is first and foremost a thing of beauty. Art from the time of the pharaohs has captivated Western imaginations since Classical times, and has become familiar to

5 Scenes of guests at a sumptuous meal with musical entertainment, from the tomb chapel of Nebamun. West Thebes. Painted plaster. 0.61 m (2 ft) high. 18th Dynasty.

museum-goers all over the globe, from Australia and Japan to America. In AD 130, the Roman emperor Hadrian became only the latest Westerner to drink in the sights along the grand highway that is the River Nile, while more recent emperors in thrall to the art of the pharaohs included Maximilian of the Germans and Napoleon of France. Small wonder perhaps that, when scholars of a modern, critical bent comment on the imagery of the pharaohs and ancient gods, the words used are often measured, utilitarian words, such as 'convention', 'fiction' and 'propaganda'. It is as though a sophisticated eye must beware, because it is liable to be enchanted by a deceit – the deceit that an ancient, African culture could offer modern audiences substance along with style, and meaningful ideas wrapped in bizarre, 'old time' religion.

At the heart of this disquiet is a seeming paradise of images, populated mostly by human subjects with sublime, serene faces, for whom the wisdom of the ages seems allied to eternal youth. It is commonplace to find gaiety, excitement and colour in their artworks, and it is found most of all in their tombs. A lively party from the tomb of Nebamun – a man who probably lived during the reign of Amenhotep III – is a fine example [5]. Perhaps this is the nub of our fascination: the tension that exists between analysing the remains of a 'primitive' ancestor in critical terms, on the one hand, and on the other a nagging suspicion that their art is addressing problems so 'big' they still evade us today. They are problems of meaning, ideals, beauty, faith and death in the story of humanity. Any critical comment on the statue of Sobk-Ra or Nebamun's party seems bound to miss the point, since modern thinking can barely countenance bright colours in death, or the embraces of gods, or the nearness of ancient history, can it?

The challenges we face in making sense of ancient Egyptian art are of various different kinds. There are obvious, practical matters, such as finding out how artists went about their business, what tools they used or who their patrons were. As noted above, there are also matters of use and context: where and when did ancient Egyptians resort to art, which audiences might have experienced it, what changes became apparent through the centuries? Not least, however, are questions of meaning: what are they trying to say in their art, and could we possibly learn from it?

The king and the gods

Let us begin by establishing one basic use of art in pharaonic Egypt. Readers of this book no doubt identified the statue of Sobk-Ra as being 'ancient Egyptian' immediately because something about its style is distinctive and familiar. Similarly, a scene of the pharaoh Sety I (c. 1290–c. 1279 BC), who reigned two or three generations after Amenhotep III, is also quintessentially 'ancient Egyptian' [6]. The scene covers one wall of an entire temple that Sety I commissioned at Abydos in Middle Egypt. As we may expect, the figures are human in form, though once again there is an animal-headed oddity among them, and they are engaged in some esoteric performance presumably connected with the ancient life of the temple. The king, who is on the right, leans across a tall vase of flowers, evidently to present or offer something: on closer inspection, this is a bowl holding a woman wearing a feather in her hair ⌐ which in turn is a hieroglyph reading 'truth'. A caption written beneath the bowl confirms that Sety is 'giving Truth to the lord of Truth'. Before him a line of gods is seated in a kiosk topped off with more rearing uraeus-cobras. First among the gods – literally by position – is Osiris, king of the dead and lord of Abydos, seated on a throne, as befits his status in this, his home temple. He is holding a crook and a flail, while a goddess reaches out to him in the suggestion of an embrace. Appropriately, the hieroglyphs tell us she is his wife, Isis, and her right hand is raised in a gesture of greeting to the pharaoh. Behind Osiris and Isis, the falcon-headed deity is their son, Horus (so, however we explain his monstrous head, he is not simply the unnatural offspring of a human and a bird). Each character in the scene is distinctly visible, as though they are standing in a row, and each is distinguished by a crown or headdress, with horns and snakes among the more improbable millinery.

However mystifying aspects of the scene may be, the whole is attractive precisely because it is elegant, recognizably human and beautifully crafted. The limestone surface has been smoothed into delicate relief, until the contours of the king's knees appear as though seen through linen so fine as to be transparent. Despite such delicacy, the physical mass of a stone wall in the grand setting of a temple brings immense authority to the characters and the ritual, and to the throne of Osiris. Yet, this area of the temple has no windows, so the true scale of the wall is hidden from view and the scene has to be revealed bit by bit by lamplight. Evidently this monumental work of surpassing craftsmanship was intended for the darkness, which at least adds to the sense that we are in the presence of mysteries. Every wall of each room of the temple is decorated in the same fashion, so there are more scenes here than any visitor could hope to scrutinize, even if electric lighting were provided.

6 King Sety I worshipping the gods Osiris, Isis and Horus on a wall in his temple at Abydos. Limestone relief. 19th Dynasty.

Returning to the relief itself, though the pharaoh is present, again he is not the one enthroned. Instead, he is doing the work, making an offering, and he stands apart from the gods, outside their kiosk. Literally, he is taller than they are because he has his feet on the ground while they are on a platform, yet each figure in the scene attains the same height. In terms of composition the artist has arranged for all the faces to meet on the same eye-line. So whoever drafted the scene was not concerned to show the relative sizes of characters in a real-world sense (after all, what is the real size of an Egyptian god?), but to illustrate their interaction and to do so in human terms. It would make less sense, and no doubt be less decorous, to have the king tower over Osiris, or oblige Isis to pat her divine consort on the top of his head. Instead, the standing figures assume proportions that put them on a level with the seated god. Cleverly, this 'discrepancy' is not allowed to intrude into our viewing – we might not even have noticed it. (Looking back to the statue of Sobk-Ra, imagine how the king would tower over the seated deity, if they maintained normal human proportions. Instead, the sculptor has incorporated the necessary 'discrepancy', then adapted the result to present the pair as father and son.) So here is an important principle of ancient Egyptian art: that the artist puts more stock in presenting recognizable characters and their interaction than in creating representations of the world as it seems to the eye. After all, the finished art may be consigned to darkness. Look again at the relief-scene: is Isis 'really' standing behind Osiris as she embraces him, or is she standing beside him?

Of course, a king is a king, and away from the gods may be expected to take the throne himself. Accordingly, Ramesses II (c. 1279–c. 1213 BC), son of Sety I, is presented in a life-size sculpture carved from near-black diorite [7]. We can be sure this is Ramesses II because his identity is stated in hieroglyphs, which the sculptor has conveniently inscribed along the tie-band of his kilt, at front and centre of the statue. Ramesses sits upright, looks straight forward and his eyes meet ours. His face is clean,

7 Diorite statue of king Ramesses II with his queen. Presumably from Karnak. 1.9 m (6 ft 4 in.) high. 19th Dynasty.

smooth and lifelike despite the hard stone, whereas the pleats of his clothing are worked in extravagant detail, with one sleeve even billowing. He is wearing the same crown as his father does in Abydos, and here Ramesses has not only the throne but also the crook previously held by Osiris. This illustrates another principle of pharaonic art: that the artist frequently employs standard forms and typical poses, with stock clothes and regalia that devolve from one character to another in different scenes. Just as Osiris was embraced by Isis while Horus stood nearby, so Ramesses is flanked by his own wife and son, though we may not even notice them. The relative scale of the figures reduces their embraces to an incongruous clasp of his legs. Even less apparent are the bound enemies incised in the statue base, at ground level beneath the king's feet. Again, scale does not imitate the real world, and the relative size of the king and the others is a function of their relative importance within the composition. So, here is a third principle: that a composition is clearly organized, divided into distinct areas of information, and expresses abstract ideas directly, through iconography (such as regalia, headdresses), relative scale, hieroglyphic writing, or by whichever means. Nonetheless, the abstract compositions bring the different elements together in arrangements that remain acceptable to the eye, and seem as though they are 'real-world' forms at first glance.

Imagine yourself as part of the three artworks we have been discussing: a mighty king, Ramesses II, sits in front of you on the throne, impassive, his wife and son too, seemingly waiting for … what? Amenhotep III, in the company of a god, has stepped down from the throne, but still he stares straight at you and makes a gesture of greeting, as though expecting you to come forward and … what? Finally, on the temple wall Sety I pays you no attention at all because he is approaching a god, who sits enthroned with his family (you have no part in this two-dimensional scene, which exists in darkness). What is the pharaoh doing? He is making an offering. So what do you suppose the statues are waiting for you to do?

This is the context in which we shall begin our journey through ancient Egyptian art: temples and offerings. Almost every statue sits or stands frontally posed – erect, immobile, inscrutable – precisely because it is waiting, inviting you to approach and make an offering of some kind. As we have seen, the king may stand when in the company of gods, then sit when in front of a human audience. Likewise, in the presence of gods the king may be the one to make the offerings, while in the presence of humans he (as a statue) is liable to expect the offerings. The hierarchy — from the gods down to people, with the king in the middle — is obvious. That said, we are going to see later how statues and other images of mortal men and women are also intended to receive offerings (see Chapter 9). As a final note here, at the very heart of Sety's temple at Abydos is a line of seven chapels designated for offering to each of seven gods: Horus, Isis, Osiris, Amun-Ra, Ra-Horakhty, Ptah and, not least, Sety I himself.

Monuments as offerings

Of course, we are discussing religious art. Having noted at the outset that most of the art that has come down to us from ancient Egypt is from sacred contexts, religious subjects are no surprise. However, we may now realize that ancient artists were addressing specific artistic problems. For example, how to illustrate gods? More specifically, how to illustrate the ways in which gods interact with the world? One artistic solution is that gods are given human bodies so they can embrace, greet, kiss or perform other meaningful human acts. They are also given the human faculty of speech, their words being inscribed on the artwork in hieroglyphs (a later, Greek word that means 'sacred images'). That gods are not actually human is apparent from the occasional monstrous head, just as it is obvious from their authority over the king. That the king is like the gods in some sense is apparent from the intimate, familial relationships he has with them, and also the ways in which he may take on their regalia, and so on. Perhaps the question arises, how do the rest of us interact with the king and the gods? Presumably by making offerings as well, if we follow the model of the king; not least because, as the statues indicate, he exists among the gods.

This 'symbiosis' between art and offerings in pharaonic temples is explained in a two-dimensional scene created for Ramesses II in the largest temple of all, the temple of Amun-Ra at Karnak in Thebes (modern Luxor) [8]. The king is standing, gesturing a welcome to two great gods, Amun-Ra, with the twin high plumes, and behind him the mummified figure of Ptah. Amun-Ra responds with a speech, 'To you I have given all life, stability and authority, all health, all pleasure' (Ptah says something similar but the words are mostly now lost). On the ground between the king and Amun-Ra is a representation of the temple reduced to a gateway so small it barely reaches the tops of their legs. Beside it a caption states that Ramesses is 'giving stone to its lord'. So the gods give the pharaoh authority over the world,

8 Ramesses II worshipping the gods Amun-Ra and Ptah, from the temple of Amun-Ra at Karnak. Limestone. 12th Dynasty.

along with the tools for peaceful, civilized existence. In fact, the apparent 'sceptre' being handed to the pharaoh in Amun-Ra's forward hand is actually a composite of the hieroglyphs writing ⌐ 'authority', ♀ 'life' and ⏚ 'stability'. Ramesses, meanwhile, reciprocates by creating the stone monuments of Egypt, so the art we are looking at here – the very temple itself – turns out to be his offering to the gods. Strikingly, although we are looking at a massive wall in the temple, the pictorial scale remains determinedly human, and the relationship between the king and the gods literally dwarfs the picture of the temple.

Masterpiece
The Narmer Palette

9 Schist palette decorated on both faces with images of Narmer, the first king of Egypt. From the temple of Horus at Hieraconpolis. 0.65 m (2 ft 1½ in.) high. 1st Dynasty.

A slice of slate or black schist about 65 by 25 centimetres (25½ by 10 inches), inscribed on both sides, memorializes Narmer, the first historical king of Egypt, about 5,000 years ago. As such, the palette has become an icon of the sudden switch from the long silence of prehistory to the more recent chatter of the historical record. Although its original function is unknown, the palette was discovered at Hieraconpolis in a temple dedicated to Horus – son of Osiris and the god most associated with Egyptian kingship (see p. 34). Specifically, the palette was found in or near a dump of redundant, old items cleared out of the temple during new building work, apparently in the early 2nd millennium BC. In other words, the Narmer palette is just about the earliest example of a stone monument offered by a king to the temple of a god, and in many ways genuinely does establish the artistic template for the monuments of later kings.

Ostensibly it has the form of a mineral-grinding palette for making paint or cosmetics, though it seems too big and fancy to have been used as such. Moreover, large schist palettes were characteristically placed in burials during the last century or so before the first dynasty of kings, an era that we accordingly label 'pre-dynastic' rather than simply 'prehistoric' (see Chapter 8). Typically they were shaped as animals or boats, though this example is shaped more like a ceremonial knife-blade (see pp. 136–37, 140–41). Also, in the decoration there are animal images well known in pre-dynastic art, so the palette may be understood in the context of artistic themes developing in Egypt for decades or more before Narmer.

The decoration has been worked in shallow relief, and the modelling of the king – the details of his anatomy, regalia and make-up – are almost as detailed and accomplished, on a relatively small scale, as the reliefs in the temple of Sety I, though the palette is maybe 1,700 years older. The scenes on either side have been divided into separate registers using horizontal lines, which in turn serve as the ground or baseline for each register (the raging bull on the reverse, and the official standing behind the king on the face, even have their own 'personal' baselines). Registers will be employed as standard in two-dimensional art for the rest of the pharaonic era (see Chapter 6).

By the same token, it is striking that so many images on this palette remain standard in later representations of the pharaoh. These include his crowns, and also the bull's tail trailing between his legs, which every subsequent king will be seen to wear; the same tail is worn by Sety I in Abydos and Ramesses II in Karnak above. The oldest, and in all eras the most important, festival of kingship was named the *heb sed* or 'tail festival', and this will crop up repeatedly in this book. Narmer's name is written in hieroglyphs at the top of the palette on both sides, within a distinctive rectangular frame whose shape is that of the royal palace (see p. 34). His name is flanked by a pair of cows' heads, which may well represent a goddess, either the obscure Bat or maybe Hathor, who in later times is regularly identified with the queens of Egypt (see pp. 58–59).

Dominating one face of the palette is a motif of Narmer twisting the hair of his enemies with his forward hand, while raising a stone mace to crush their heads. Much later, from about 1450 BC in the New Kingdom, this so-called 'smiting scene' had survived to become the typical monumental decoration on the pylon gateways to every Egyptian temple (see Chapter 11). Although Narmer strikes a dynamic pose, his feet are fixed firmly on the baseline, so in fact his movement is conveyed only by the implication of violent action plus the slight dip of his shoulders, which insinuates the line from his mace down to his victim's skull. Beneath his feet are more victims, like the enemies under the feet of Ramesses II, marked as foreign by their nudity and long, trailing hair. Their broken bodies occupy a separate register, where they lie awkwardly crushed by the king's weight. Behind the king, 'the king's servant' carries his sandals, as though he ought not to soil them in enemy blood (though perhaps this vignette means to emphasize that he is wearing sandals). In front of him, the falcon with human arms must be the equivalent of the falcon-headed Horus in the scene at Abydos. Here, in Horus' own temple, the ferocious bird adopts the disembowelling pose of a bird of prey but, in fact, is dragging a human-headed emblem or cryptogram by the nose, as though delivering more captives to the king.

On the reverse, the central pan or circular depression formed from the intertwined, distended necks of big cats must be a conceit, assuming the palette was never actually used for grinding minerals. Many commentators have noted a profound resemblance between this big-cat motif and contemporary images from Mesopotamia (an area of ancient Syria and Iraq), in which case it bears witness to the fact that Egyptian artists at this early date were already working in a wider world of ideas (see pp. 141, 142–43). In Egyptian terms, a brace of panther heads forms a hieroglyph writing 'strength', which is consistent with the violent imagery of the rest of the decoration. Be that as it may, the ferocious animals being either tamed or goaded form the centre around which have been assembled images of the pharaoh's worldly authority and the physical demise of his enemies. At top, the crowned king walks in procession to survey the ranks of beheaded dead, followed once again by his sandal-servant and preceded by a priest with the standards of four districts or gods' shrines. The dead are not laid across a field in perspective but arranged in rows, as though viewed from above, in order to make clear what we are looking at. The king stands tallest, his head at the top of the register, level with the standards. At the bottom of the palette the raging bull is trampling a man and destroying the walls of his city; from now on, the 'strong bull' is going to be a standard metaphor in art and literature for each and every king who wears the bull's tail.

10 The reconstructed 'White Chapel' of Senwosret I from the temple of Amun-Ra at Karnak, near Luxor. Limestone. 12th Dynasty.

Chapter 2 'See My Perfection, My Son': Offerings and the King

Appreciating the fundamental relationship between art and offerings helps to explain the character of many, if not most, ancient Egyptian monuments and the artworks associated with them. To take an example from the long centuries between Narmer and Ramesses II, the beautiful 'White Chapel' was erected in the temple at Karnak for the 'tail festival' of Senwosret I (c. 1920–c. 1875 BC). Like Narmer's palette, it was discovered by archaeologists after being broken up in ancient times to make way for new building. Accordingly, though its original location is not known, the reconstructed chapel is effectively the oldest part of the grand temple of Amun-Ra still standing [10].

Despite its elegant proportions, the limestone chapel is a simple truncated cube, with a 6.5-metre (21 feet 3 inches) square base. Four rows of four rectangular pillars form the principal structure, and those round the outside are connected by a stone rail except where a pair of ramps forms the entrance and exit to the raised interior. In other words, there is a designated walkway straight through the middle of the chapel, though the whole building is carved with exquisite decoration. The fine decorative work is closely comparable to the best contemporary monuments elsewhere in Egypt, which no doubt confirms that the king had first call on the most skilled artists available. The scenes round the outside of the chapel have been worked in sunk relief, which ensures the cutting can be seen as internal shadows in the bright intensity of the Egyptian sunlight. By contrast, the interior decoration is worked in a high raised relief, which remains visible however the shadows edge across the interior surfaces throughout the course of the day.

Of course, 'White Chapel' is a modern tag: its ancient name was 'Horus' place of raising the crown', which not only associates the king with Horus once more but also identifies the chapel principally with the king, rather than Amun-Ra, the god of the temple. Perhaps Senwosret I sat on his throne here during the 'tail festival', waiting for a procession of Amun-Ra to leave the main temple. Perhaps he was first crowned here, who knows? However, a granite altar was added to the centre by a later king

11 Detail of a doorway of the 'White Chapel' [10] showing the king, together with a personification or statue of his spirit (identified by his Horus name), entering the presence of the cult statue of Amun-Ra.

in Senwosret's dynasty, so the chapel undoubtedly remained in use beyond its first festival. Which raises the question, what was it used for?

In profile, the White Chapel is reminiscent of the gods' kiosk shown in Sety I's wall relief at Abydos (p. 17), and the images on the pillars present the chapel as the same kind of meeting place. As though we are being allowed a glimpse of what went on here, Senwosret I is led by different gods into the presence of Amun-Ra, who is shown at the top of one ramp waiting to greet the king [11]. The king makes the expected offerings to various gods, and receives life and authority in exchange. Occasionally even connected episodes of activity are implied in the art while moving from one pillar to the next, as when the king is 'offering the cake' in one scene and nearby is 'crumbling the cake'.

In what sense is this a meeting place? First, the tell-tale ramps are indicative of a procession, and one doorway even illustrates a statue of the king on a sledge in procession. The structure of the chapel allows us to appreciate how statues on sledges or other vehicles (typically, in fact, boats slung on carrying poles) were dragged or carried up the central ramp by priests using the flanking steps. Eventually they would exit by the far ramp without needing to turn round or negotiate corners. The later granite altar is marked for the holiest statue of Amun-Ra, brought out of the main temple during the king's 'tail festival' and other processions. As the stand's size indicates, such statues were not massive but small wooden carvings, kept inside a gilded wooden box. Presumably the holiest statue of Amun-Ra at Karnak took the arresting form illustrated on the pillars, that of a man holding his erect penis. Although most of the decoration shows Amun-Ra, with his high twin plumes, in standard 'human' form greeting the king and speaking, occasionally he too is illustrated as a statue in the control of priests. In other words, the encounter between the king and Amun-Ra, as human onlookers might have seen it with their eyes, involved a wooden statue and the king – or even two statues. Nonetheless, the artist has illustrated not the sight but the meaning of the encounter, which is the loving welcome of a divine father for his royal son.

Today the area around the central shrine at Karnak is essentially decorated with scenes and monuments from the reign of Thutmose III (c. 1479–c. 1425 BC), erected as part of the building work during which the White Chapel was pulled down in the first place. However, several of Thutmose's monuments exemplify the same encounter between king and god by quoting the very words of Amun-Ra to the pharaoh:

> Welcome to me, and rejoice to see my perfection, my son and my protector, Menkheperra [= Thutmose III], living for all time. I light up for love of you, and my wish is fulfilled in your perfect visits to my estate. My arms enfold your body with protection and life. How nice is your amulet against my breast, when I hold you in my sanctuary.

Modern minds are bound to be sceptical of such matters, but in this ancient account the divine father hugs his royal son so tightly the king's pectoral amulet presses into him.

The palaces of kings
At Karnak, Amun-Ra welcomes his royal son to what is a god's house. We might suppose that the pharaohs too lived, as well as conducted their ceremonies, among such grandiose settings. However, as we know, stone monuments are their offerings to the

gods. In fact, surprisingly little in the way of statues or monumental art originated in the living spaces or working areas associated with kings of Egypt, still less (if any) in the public spaces of towns and villages. Most of what we know about their palaces is a matter of texts and 'dirt' archaeology rather than art history, and even the rare glimpses we do get in pictures emphasize a functional, working environment. In fact, the king of Egypt must have spent much of his time travelling from temple to temple, celebrating festival after festival, away from whichever grand residences he might have had. Akhenaten (c. 1353–c. 1336 bc), son and successor of Amenhotep III, recorded at Akhetaten a visit to a new city where he stayed 'in the matting tent made for his person'. ('His person' is the traditional euphemism for the physical presence of the pharaoh.) A walled encampment built for his father outside Thebes was obviously a substantial settlement but also relied on tented accommodation for some of the king's followers at least. Presumably, the king often made do with sleeping near the moorings or even on board the royal 'falcon boat', in which he was seen to travel like the falcon-god Horus (see [57]).

Nonetheless, archaeologists have excavated a handful of settlements directly associated with the accommodation of the royal family and the king's palace officials, though they are mostly from the New Kingdom and mostly at Thebes. Such 'palaces' were built principally using mud brick, timber and other organic materials, rather than stone. In addition, they were generally too small to accommodate a large community for long periods, so must have been used for limited times and particular purposes. Some would have been occupied only during certain festivals, including those known to have been built specifically for a given king's 'tail festival', while others were occupied by specific groups, such as the principal queen and her followers. Of course, still others must have been occupied at times for the purposes of government, whether the king were present or not. More to the point, most (perhaps all?) of the known palaces were initially developed as an element within a temple complex, or else added to an older temple site. One such was Giza, where several palaces grew up during the 18th Dynasty, more than 1,000 years after the Great Pyramid and Great Sphinx were first erected there during the 4th Dynasty. Likewise, such evidence as has survived from the Old Kingdom, including the extensive settlement at the Heit el-Ghurob (Wall of the Crow) in Giza, indicates that already back then the palace community moved through various residences, with different buildings of different layouts and sizes dotted in

12 Scene from a decorated floor in the palace at Malqata, showing water fowl in the marshes (see [78]). Painted plaster. 0.52 m (20½ in.) high. 18th Dynasty.

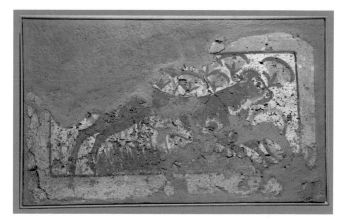

13 Scene from a decorated bench in the palace at Malqata, showing a bull leaping in the marshes (see [77]). Painted plaster. 0.50 m (20 in.) high. 18th Dynasty.

and around the royal temple complexes (see pp. 70–73). Like the White Chapel, but on a larger scale, palaces provided first and foremost for the king's attendance at the gods' festivals, and let him both see and be seen during ceremonies.

Where fragments of palace decoration have survived, they share common themes with the decoration of temples. 'Smiting scenes', like the one on Narmer's palette, were painted on pillars at Memphis in the palace of Merenptah (c. 1213–c. 1203 BC), son and successor of Ramesses II. More generally we find familiar scenes of the king in the company of gods, while bound foreigners on brightly glazed floor-tiles [14] are obviously counterparts to the enemies inscribed beneath the feet of the

14 Floor-tiles from the palace of Ramesses III at Tell el-Yahudiya, with stereotyped representations of the traditional enemies of the pharaoh. Glazed composition. 19th Dynasty.

enthroned Ramesses II (see p. 19). The tiles were laid to form specific walkways through the palace chambers so the king would tread on enemies as he went, adhering to the ancient template of kingship and art established by Narmer. Elsewhere, as in a palace of Amenhotep III at Malqata near Thebes, we glimpse delicate fragments of plaster brightly painted with water-fowl or calves at large in the marshes, which may seem suitably bucolic for a relaxed domestic setting [12, 13]. No doubt they were intended to create an attractive, restful environment and they are certainly colourful, but they are also themes otherwise common in funerary art and temple decoration, and serve to connect the remaining traces of palace decoration with the world of art we see in temples and tombs (see pp. 124–27). Consequently, the king is not only a central subject in the art of ancient Egypt – because he was central to the practice of offering to the gods – but he also lived and conducted his daily business in buildings adorned with the same images, and presumably the same ideas. To put this another way, perhaps we should recognize that the pharaoh built for the gods a monumental stone interpretation, or counterpart, of the perishable, organic art and architecture he occupied in life.

The tombs of kings

There is a final point to make regarding the relationship between the monuments of gods and the earthly residences of kings. From the beginning of history there was a place where the king too was accommodated in a stone-built monument. This was his tomb. At the king's tomb we find the crux of his relationship with the land of Egypt as much as with the gods, and also, throughout the pharaonic era, another prolific context for art. In life, the upkeep of the palace – the king, his family and officials – fell on the local districts of Egypt as a sort of common national activity. Another common activity came in the form of offerings for the festivals of the gods. For example, the exterior decoration of the White Chapel on two sides is actually a written inventory of the agricultural potential of each of the districts of Egypt, while the other two sides have corresponding pictures of the fertility of Egyptian agricultural land. In other words, offerings made by the king at the White Chapel represented the common wealth of the nation. The same common purpose is evident in the tombs of even the earliest kings, which were filled with huge quantities of offerings of many kinds – furniture, clothing, foods, wines and beers, oils and ointments – often labelled as contributions from named officials or estates around the country, thereby revealing the great congregation of production as well as labour involved in the interment of a king.

The cemetery of the earliest kings takes us back to Abydos but out in the desert, away from the main temple of Osiris, towards a far valley where the Sun sets in a natural gash through the western cliffs. The tombs here were built, using mud brick, imported timber and monumental stone, round a vast chamber (or multiple chambers) excavated from the rock floor [15]. Here the actual interment and offerings would be deposited, before being covered, probably with a solid, rectangular tumulus with an elaborate internal structure but no chambers as such. Such solid tumuli with a rectangular plan are usually referred to as *mastabas*, from an Arabic word for a plain bench. The whole site of the tomb was enclosed by a wall.

The best-preserved examples indicate that the royal tombs at Abydos had the same general form as the early temple of Horus at Hieraconpolis where the Narmer palette was discovered. Although the original form of the temple has been much obscured by later development, its distinctive features were a rectangular wall enclosing a massive, mud-brick-lined mound, on top of which the early shrines developed. As we have seen, to be king in ancient

Egypt was a sacred office insofar as a king exercised 'all authority' given to him by the gods, which he reciprocated by making offerings and building monuments as well as by governance. Hence he was the sole source of earthly authority at the heart of a regime encompassing the entire land and all its temples. The authority of other priests and officials was delegated from this spiritual centre, and they were empowered by enacting the king's will. Consequently, the graves of many of these priests and officials also surround the king's person in death, in what will be another template for future behaviour (see Chapter 9). The fifth king, Den, had about 136 such graves in the immediate vicinity of his tomb, while the third king, Djer, had more than 300 burials round him.

In the courtyard of the king's tomb, in front of the tumulus, a pair of free-standing stone markers, or *stelae*, simply stated his name [16]. These are among the earliest examples of the formal name identifying the king with Horus, as though each mortal king were a new incarnation of Horus, and the 'Horus-name' would now be used by every pharaoh, virtually without exception, across more than 3,000 years. Typically the name is written within a graphic enclosure called, in Ancient Egyptian, the *serekh*, perhaps meaning 'he who is made known'. The serekh is a representation of the palace as well as the temple of Horus, and on top perches the oversized falcon, watching for even the tiniest disturbance in a field of wheat, which would be his signal to strike and kill. In Ancient Egyptian the name Horus means 'the one above', a name consistent both with the highest authority in the land and also the coruscating, soaring falcon, for whom, to quote Ted Hughes,

15 Partially reconstructed burial chamber in the tomb of Den, cut 6 m (19 ft 8 in.) into the desert and exposed by the total loss of the covering tumulus [see also 23]. The floor was originally paved with red and black granite. Umm el-Qaab, west of Abydos. 15 x 9 m (49 ft 2½ in. x 29 ft 6 in.). 1st Dynasty.

16 Inscription at the top of a stela showing the king's Horus name written within the serekh, surmounted by the god Horus. One of a pair from the tomb of king Djet, west of Abydos. Limestone relief. 0.65 m (2 ft 1½ in.) wide. 1st Dynasty.

'It took the whole of Creation / to produce my foot, my each feather: / now I hold Creation in my foot ... I kill where I please because it is all mine.' According to the serekh the king is a heavenly presence within the earthly palace – the magnificent predator, by turns serene and vicious. Such is the oldest statement of the king of Egypt – a monumental palace marked for the divine falcon in death, surrounded by the offerings of his land, and the graves of his priests and officials.

Still, there is more, because the royal tombs did not stand alone at Abydos. Opposite the entrance to the main temple of Osiris, at sites much more convenient to visit than the remote royal tombs, are their monumental counterparts [17]. Not much of these 'other' buildings has survived apart from their once massive mud-brick enclosure walls, which have the distinctive niched appearance characteristic of both palace walls and the serekh of the royal Horus-names [18]. However, the best-preserved example, built at the end of the 2nd Dynasty for Khasekhemwy, has a once-impressive gate-complex leading into a grand courtyard, where the pitiful remains of what was once another tumulus stand at the north end. In other words, Khasekhemwy's temple has the same general form as the temple of Horus and, therefore, as the royal tombs. Analogy with later practice suggests that these counterpart buildings are mortuary temples, that is, temples intended for ongoing – probably daily – offerings for the spirit of each dead king.

Just outside the wall on the east side of Khasekhemwy's temple, at least fourteen full-size boats had been buried in a row in brick-lined pits [19]. In a sense, boats epitomize the peripatetic nature of the king's earthly office, and conversely the unity of the kingdom brought together by the king's travelling. Moreover, because the River Nile was the pre-eminent Egyptian highway, most journeys, literal or metaphorical, were evoked in art as boat journeys, so in a funerary context boats may symbolize both the king's leadership through life and the journey everyone must take to follow him into the next life. Be that as it may, in artistic terms boats certainly evoke the festivals of gods and one specific image

17 Mud-brick enclosure wall and outer perimeter wall of the mortuary temple of king Khasekhemwy, beside the main temple of Osiris at Abydos. 137 x 77 m (450 x 253 ft). 2nd Dynasty.

18 Detail of the northeast of the enclosure wall in [17] showing niched panelling consistent with the serekh in [16].

well known from later days: the image of the Sun forever sailing the heavens in the cycle of day and night, life and death, beginning and end (see Chapter 11).

Osiris, Isis and Horus

The relevance of the Sun-god's endless sailing is inextricable from Abydos as the location of the royal tombs because both lead us to the well-known myth of Osiris. Every ancient Egyptian account of the origin of the world begins from the belief that there is a Creator, who brought the world into being intentionally. The Creator himself is given countless names across the numerous shrines and temples of the land, and in art the intense Egyptian Sun (or Ra) is frequently used as a symbol of his overwhelming presence within the created world. Equally, however, he may simply be named Atum, literally 'he who is not' – that is, the one who is present without 'being' because the very possibility of anything 'being' depends upon him and begins with him. According to an account of Creation ascribed to the Old Kingdom and consistent with the oldest religious texts from Egypt – though sadly none has survived from as early as the 1st or 2nd Dynasty – Atum's original act of Creation was to speak the names Shu ('light' or 'energy') and Tefnet ('matter'). Hence the world comes about through the physical interaction of Shu and Tefnet, first of all taking the form of the sky arching over the earth to create the arena for our lives [20]. Meanwhile, the Creator sails in the firmament of 'Potential' (in Ancient Egyptian, *nun*), defining the form and the limit of the world. Everything we know and experience emerges from Potential in accordance with forms

19 View of the excavations that revealed fourteen burials of boats, each 18–21 m (59–69 ft) long, on the eastern side of the mortuary temple of king Khasekhemwy. 2nd Dynasty or earlier.

and principles intended by the Creator, so 'what comes from the heart takes the shape of Atum, and what comes from the tongue takes the shape of Atum'. To put this another way, our own intentions flourish or fail to the extent to which they conform to reality as it is intended, not as we prefer it to be (see p. 277).

Now, the very first child of the earth (Geb) and the sky (Nut), hence the first creature of our world, was Osiris himself, who had two defining characteristics: first, he was a king, and second, he was mortal. The presence of a king before there was anyone to rule emphasizes that the world is governed by elemental principles, which precede humanity and include authority and morality as surely as they include space, time and gravity. Nonetheless, Osiris was murdered and dismembered by a second child, his unruly and ambitious brother, Seth. Their sister, Isis, bound Osiris' fractured body with linen, buried him at Abydos as a king, and breathed new life into him. Thus the first mortal to die became the first to be born into the next life, which is termed 'Adoration' (duat) – the same condition in which the gods of the temples necessarily exist when we bring them offerings.

Death was doubly defeated in this mythological account when the faithful Isis was able to conceive Osiris' son, Horus. As such, the template for the legitimate transfer of royal authority was set at the beginning of the world, when, according to the same account of Creation, 'Osiris became as the earth in a palace' and 'his son, Horus, appeared as king'. In mythological terms, Horus grew up to vanquish Seth and reconcile whichever violence or rebellion may seek to transgress the elemental principles of the world (see p. 285); then 'a reed and a papyrus-flower were placed on the double doors of the temple of Ptah, which mean Horus and Seth pacified and united'. In historical terms, every pharaoh stood in this line of succession, and his authority was spiritual and universal rather than the temporal authority of a political leader (in modern terms, the pharaoh was more akin to Pope than President). Mythologically, Horus of Hieraconpolis was son and successor of Osiris of Abydos; historically, the new king buried his predecessor in a tomb, which was a monumental interpretation of his palace, and provided offerings for the late king as he would for a god. This too became one more template for pharaonic conduct until the throne of Egypt was handed to the Roman emperors some 3,000 years later.

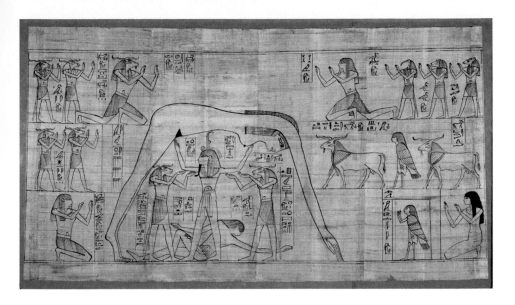

20 Illustration from a Book of the Dead showing the god Shu, with upraised arms, forming the vault of the sky over the earth. The formless space beyond is populated with the souls or 'forces' of the gods and the dead. 47 cm (1 ft 6½ in.) high. 21st Dynasty.

Masterpiece
Label from the tomb of Den, the fourth king of Egypt

21 Ebony label from the tomb
of king Den. 5.5 cm (2 in.) high.
1st Dynasty.

This slice of ebony, just 5.5 centimetres (2 inches) high, once labelled a jar of oil deposited in the tomb of Den, so the hole at top right is for a linen tie. Den was only the fourth king of Egypt after Narmer, but the scale of his burial at Abydos and the wealth of offerings there and in the tombs of his officials are duly impressive. Meanwhile the composition on this label offers a miniature encapsulation of pharaonic rule, along with another early example of artistic themes and techniques that will go on to be used repeatedly throughout the pharaonic era.

Chief among those techniques is laying out the whole composition plainly, dividing the pictorial information into separate sections, if need be, so that nothing is obscured from plain sight across the two-dimensional surface. The curved device at the right edge of the composition ⌠ (but reversed because we are reading from right to left) is a hieroglyph marking one year in a reign. Accordingly each scene on the label may be a statement of a different event in a single year, which together may stand as historical illustrations of the king's authority – as well as perhaps recording the vintage of the jar's contents. The whole is divided into two main areas by a vertical line down the centre, though this division is obscured at the top of the composition, where a depiction of the king on his throne sitting prominently alongside his Horus-name, written in the usual serekh enclosure, immediately identifies the subject.

The area to the right of the central line has been divided into three horizontal registers, mostly occupied with scenes known from many later examples. In the top register, the pharaoh sits in a kiosk with a stepped entrance, like that of the White Chapel. He has both the crowns worn by Narmer, but here they are shown together as a 'double-crown'. Another typical technique of the artist is repeating the subject in the same scene. Hence, in front of the kiosk the king is running round two groups of three stelae or markers, which symbolize the boundaries of his domain. At first glance we may doubt that the king could be watching and running as well, but the 'runner' is still holding the flail and still wearing the double-crown. While running he is (appropriately) stripped down to a kilt, whereas he seems to be wrapped in a full-length cloak on the throne (see p. 130). This scene is an illustration of the king during the actual 'tail festival', and the narrative juxtaposition of episodes speaks to the meaning of this crucial event.

In the central register, the king stands slightly left of centre wearing a crown and holding his crook and flail in one hand, but also manipulating a digging implement in the other to perform an

22 View across the tomb of king Den showing the outlines of some of the 136 surrounding tombs. West of Abydos. The entire complex measures about 53 x 40 m (173 ft 10½ in. x 131 ft 3 in.). 1st Dynasty.

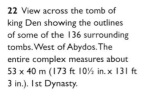

23 View showing the mass of mud brick and imported timber surrounding the burial chamber of king Den, partially reconstructed in both ancient and modern times. Some features are constructional, others part of the elaborate internal structure of the tumulus originally covering the burial.

agricultural ceremony beside the dykes of a named settlement. The inscription says he is dredging irrigation canals to promote the crops. Behind him is the title of the god of a local temple, which may well be the king's own mortuary temple at Abydos. The broken bottom register (or possibly two registers) seems to be an inventory of some kind, perhaps lists of produce or of victories, both subjects known in these very early royal artworks.

To the left of the central line is a statement of the jar's original contents, namely finest quality 'Libyan oil' made from the newest growth on a named estate in the royal domain. Such oil was used in purification ceremonies, so had a funerary significance as well as being part of an elegant toilet routine. The donor is named as the 'king's seal-bearer', Hmaka. While it may be unexpected to see a king performing agricultural ceremonies, here Hmaka is also given the title 'canal-cutter', which is well known among other early officials of Egypt. The royal officials formed such a small community that one of only a handful of grand tombs of this early date to have survived elsewhere at Abydos is the very tomb of this Hmaka himself (see pp. 146–47).

24 View of the principal temples against the Theban hills at Deir el-Bahri, illustrating the ramps and terraces that stand at one end of festival procession routes. The 18th Dynasty temple of Hatshepsut is in the foreground, the earlier mortuary temple and tomb of Montuhotep II prominent behind it. West Thebes.

Chapter 3 'The Risen Earth': Creation in Art and Architecture

The account of Creation summarized in Chapter 2 highlights a fundamental principle of pharaonic belief, which the Egyptians termed 'Truth'. We have seen Sety I offering Truth to Osiris as 'the Lord of Truth' (see pp. 16–17). Before 2300 BC Ptahhatp, vizier of Egypt and the world's earliest known philosopher, was teaching that '*the essence of Truth is its constancy*' and that '*a person grows by accepting Truth*'. In his account, Truth is the principle that the world exists because it is intended, and has form and meaning as a result: form, because it is not randomly happening; meaning, because it is here for a reason. How else could we ask questions? Because the world is Truth-full, so the elemental principles include not only laws of physics but also mathematics, aesthetics, justice and so on. If we appreciate beauty, sport or poetry, then we are responding to the elements of Creation, according to this point of view. As Ptahhatp urges, '*find the meaning for yourself in every event until your conduct becomes exemplary*'.

In keeping with the belief that things do not 'just happen', the original locations of many ancient Egyptian sacred sites seem to have been determined on the basis of meaningful features in the landscape, to which builders over time simply added a refined architectural form. Certainly, like the temple of Horus at Hieraconpolis, several early temples developed on the site of natural mounds of various kinds, while the famous Great Sphinx at Giza is one of several prominent monuments carved out of a distinctive natural outcrop. The interplay is such that many temple sites seem to grow naturally out of the landscape, and the architects' respect for the natural setting is obvious [24]. Nonetheless, the issue of origins almost always has to be inferred because the sites of most temples have been so thoroughly developed and redeveloped, then disturbed, in ancient as well as modern times. On the other hand, we can be certain that mathematics was intentionally employed to determine the appropriate forms of temples and, in religious terms, acknowledge and praise a higher authority. Evidently this is a principal reason for the significance the ancient Egyptians attached to ideal geometric shapes in architecture, including, of course, pyramids.

25 Shrine in the tomb chapel of the governor and priest of Hathor, Ukhhotep III. The typical form of a shrine was a box or a niche for a statue, approached on steps within an enclosed rectangular space. Meir. 12th Dynasty.

Similarly, the aesthetic proportions of the White Chapel were valued not because they *seem* pleasing to the human mind but because they *are* pleasing, and thereby celebrate the inherent meaning of forms.

To emphasize, the use of mathematics is not simply a matter of inference from architecture. The handful of mathematical texts surviving from ancient Egypt, which are essentially practical documents, include calculations for determining different geometrical properties of architectural forms, such as a pyramid or a truncated pyramid (in other words, a mastaba). Several hieroglyphic inscriptions survive to explain the layout of temples and state their architectural forms in ideal terms, using specific proportions and arithmetical sequences. The mathematical sequences in turn are related to knowledge about the temple's divine subject, just as we now relate mathematics to knowledge about the essential nature of the universe. Accordingly the temple was laid out as a microcosm of the world, and the word 'true' may even be written with the hieroglyph ⬛, which is the precisely cut plinth of a monument or the casing block of a pyramid [25].

The same inscriptions sometimes show the original site of the temple being measured and laid out on the ground by '*stretching a cord*', though not by surveyors as such because this is presented as the work of the pharaoh and his priests. Once laid out, the undeveloped site is purified in various ways, mostly using water, natural minerals and animal sacrifice, until the resultant ground is said to be made up of '*the spit of Shu*' – that is, a formless product of the energy of Creation. The building site may be given a temporary name as '*Horus' place of raising*', which also happens to be a variation of the name used for the White Chapel (see p. 27). At least from the mid-2nd millennium BC onwards, the laying-out ceremonies then entailed a ritual run by the king (or perhaps a run on his behalf) driving four calves along to trample in seed, a ceremony described as '*treading the grave of Osiris*'. Out of ground prepared in this way, the temple would literally rise up to become what the texts call ta tjenen, 'the Risen Earth', '*which has given birth to the gods, and from which every thing has emerged – foods, crops, offerings, and everything perfect*'.

The Inundation and the 'emergence'

'The Risen Earth' is a simple, iconic image used in myths and hymns to identify the very 'place' where the Creator stands. More literally it evokes a natural phenomenon that is definitively Egyptian, insofar as it is a feature of life along the lower reaches of the River Nile. To take an example, the so-called 'Colossi of Memnon' are actually statues of Amenhotep III, which once stood either side of a gateway in his mortuary temple, though time has removed almost all of the rest of the temple. Nowadays the Colossi stand several hundred metres from the river but in ancient times (before modern dams were built farther south) the Nile began to rise every year in late June, until it reached a peak in August typically 8 to 10 metres (26 to 33 feet) higher than it began and not unusually up to 14 metres (46 feet) higher. With such an overwhelming volume, the so-called Inundation swept floodwater and organic debris right through the temple and far beyond, to the desert cliffs [26]. The fundamental transformation of the Egyptian landscape by the Inundation was embodied in the three seasons of the ancient calendar, namely *akhet* ('inundation'), *peret* ('emergence') and *shemu* ('harvest' or 'dry season'). Consequently, at the beginning of the new agricultural year essentially the whole land was a single body of water, bringing the potential for life wherever it reached, while anywhere beyond remained desert. Dotted about in the floodwater were peoples' homes, workshops and farm buildings on patches of high ground, described as 'baskets', as though they were bobbing about until the water finally retreated by late October. Thereafter the promise of the flood was realized in the 'emergence' of a rich, fertile soil, out of which 'emerged' the crops that made Egypt's farmers the envy of their contemporaries [27]. *'For, these days, these folk collect their harvest with less trouble than anyone,'* claimed Herodotus, the great historian of the Greeks.

26 Archive photo showing the Nile Inundation swamping the 'Colossi of Memnon' in West Thebes. Quartzite. Originally over 18 m (59 ft) high. 18th Dynasty.

27 Scene of a wine-press from the tomb chapel of the governor, Pahery. El-Kab. Painted limestone relief. 18th Dynasty.

Thus in mythical terms out of the fluid Potential came the Risen Earth, and out of the Risen Earth the immanent seeds generated life in abundance. The ancient temples not only celebrated this annual cycle but were intended to become part of it through seasonal festivals and offerings, and even by welcoming the Inundation inside. A text of king Sekhemra-Usertawy Sobkhotep from Karnak during the 13th Dynasty commemorates '*his person's procession to the hypostyle hall of this temple so that the Highest Inundation would be seen. His person came just when the hypostyle hall of this temple was filled with water*'. This may refer to an exceptional event, of course, but Sobkhotep's procession, like the photograph of the Colossi of Memnon, at least demonstrates the proximity of most temples to the floodplain and the reach of the Inundation. Certainly some temples include ancient drains as part of their architectural foundation and, if a temple were flooded, it would also rise again during the 'emergence'.

Corridors of stars, courts of the Sun
If an ancient Egyptian temple is laid out as a microcosm, then the built architecture of the temple is bound to embody the myth of Creation implied in the Risen Earth. This is undoubtedly true of the grand temples of the New Kingdom and later, including those built by Amenhotep III, Sety I and Ramesses II, which we will return to in Chapter 11. However, other instances will already be apparent – namely the tumuli common to the tombs of the earliest kings at Abydos and apparently all the temples associated

with them at Abydos and at Hieraconpolis. We can no longer be sure what form the tumulus took in each case, but no special leap of imagination is required to connect these artificial mounds with the iconic pyramids of Egypt. Pyramids consistently featured in the tombs of the pharaohs and their queens, beginning in the 3rd Dynasty with Djoser's Step Pyramid at Saqqara [28] and continuing until the burial of Queen Tetishery, back at Abydos, during the reign of Ahmose (c. 1539–c. 1514 BC), first king of the 18th Dynasty.

In the context of the Risen Earth, Djoser's Step Pyramid is a clear development of the earlier royal tombs and temples. Djoser was probably the immediate successor of Khasekhemwy, and the Step Pyramid complex as a whole bears close comparison to Khasekhemwy's 'mortuary temple' at Abydos (see pp. 35–36). Of course, the scale of Djoser's tomb is greater still and the form of the tumulus is now unequivocally a pyramid, but there is also much that is familiar. The niched enclosure wall has been retained, though now modelled in stone, to enclose more than 15 hectares (37 acres) of ground. Once again a gate-complex at the southeast corner leads into a vast court open to the Sun on the south side of the tumulus. In Djoser's complex this court has clearly been laid out as though for the 'tail festival', incorporating the stelae or markers illustrated on Den's label (see pp. 40–43), though a smaller court alongside was perhaps the actual stage for the ceremonies with the vast court as its monumental counterpart.

At the centre of the site is the pyramid itself, underneath which the king was buried. Formally Djoser's pyramid bears close

28 Reconstructed 'dummy buildings' beside the south court of Djoser's Step Pyramid at Saqqara. Limestone. 3rd Dynasty.

comparison to the royal tumuli at Abydos, being built by first excavating a suite of burial chambers from the desert floor, with multiple adjoining galleries to stockpile offerings. Areas of these galleries were decorated as though the walls were covered with reed mats, though the 'mats' were actually modelled in faience and consequently survived in good condition into modern times. Above these chambers, the engineers constructed a mastaba presumably corresponding (in more elaborate form?) to those in the royal cemetery at Abydos, but subsequently the mastaba was wholly enclosed in a solid pyramid with four steps, later increased to six steps. Notably, this reverses the construction of several older tombs at Saqqara built for high officials, where a stepped tumulus was built first, then wholly enclosed by a mastaba (see p. 147).

The enclosure wall of the Step Pyramid has fourteen dummy gates, which has raised the suggestion that the complex is not simply an interpretation of the palace so much as a model of the largest Egyptian city, Memphis. No doubt the proximity of Memphis in the valley below Saqqara was part of the inspiration for moving the royal cemetery, and perhaps the stepped form of the outer tumulus had some local significance at Memphis. That said, inside the complex are large-scale, solid models of specific chapels for the gods of about thirty districts, as well as kiosks, other buildings and the aforementioned 'tail festival' courts, around which several statues of the king were discovered. So the variety and character of the 'dummy' buildings may indicate that the Step Pyramid complex is not a model of any specific palace or city, but rather an invocation of all the temples of Egypt. Perhaps similar buildings originally featured in the mortuary temples of the earlier kings at Abydos, but there had been modelled in mud-brick, reeds and other perishable materials. Perhaps the fourteen gates at Saqqara also relate to the number of boats beside Khasekhemwy's mortuary temple. On the north side of Djoser's pyramid, the complex is now terribly reduced and harder to fathom, though it had a different layout, relying on enclosed statue-chapels opening off a central court open to the Sun.

During the next dynasties, the step pyramid was replaced by other forms for the tumulus, most notably the 'true' pyramids, but the royal tomb complex still remains recognizably a development of what had gone before. From the 4th Dynasty, a valley temple – a feature already present in the Step Pyramid – acts as the principal gate-complex and also as a quay on the Nile not only for the king (and, presumably, eventually for his burial procession) but also for the statues of gods making their

29 Schist dyad of Menkaura and a queen, from his valley temple at Giza. 1.39 m (4 ft 7 in.) high. 4th Dynasty.

festival processions. The principal path through the valley temple makes use of hypostyle halls, which are roofed chambers with far more columns than are required for structural reasons. The columns are there to manage the influx of light while approaching statue-chapels. In other words, the chapels themselves were maintained in total darkness, until such time as a priest or officiant introduced an artificial light of some kind (see pp. 95–97). Exiting the valley temple the next transition is mediated through an enclosed, dark causeway with a star-covered ceiling, which climbs upwards, often hundreds of metres, to a mortuary temple on the summit of the cliffs overlooking the Nile floodplain.

Entering the mortuary temple through a hypostyle hall, the covered path leads into a court, suddenly and dramatically open to the intensely bright Egyptian daylight. On the far side of this Sun-court stood another hypostyle hall, reducing the light before entering an area of five or more chapels, each with an

enthroned statue of the king. Not surprisingly, the valley temples and mortuary temples of the pyramid complexes are the original source of many of the celebrated statues of the Old and Middle Kingdom pharaohs [29]. Interior walls were decorated with images of the fecundity of the land, as well as images of the 'tail festival' and the beneficence of the king [30, 31]. In many instances the columns are shaped as marsh plants, consistent with the Risen Earth as a concept, though there was no possibility of the Inundation reaching such a height. As we may expect, the king's tomb complex also contains subsidiary burials, mostly for his queens with their own smaller pyramids, while immediately around and about were the interments of his officials, sometimes laid out in what seems like street upon street of mastabas.

Of course, whether visitors arrived at the valley temple or stood in the Sun-court of the mortuary temple, their view would have been dominated by the pyramid itself. The model for the true pyramid form is the obelisk that stood at the heart of the temple of Ra-Horakhty, a god whose name means 'the Sun is Horus in the Horizon'. His temple was on the east bank of the Nile at Heliopolis, and the scant remains suggest it once covered an area as large as any temple ever constructed in Egypt. By the 4th Dynasty not only the royal pyramid itself but the enclosure wall, the causeway and other external features of the tomb complex had replaced the niched palace façade with a smooth exterior finish of the finest white limestone, from the Tura quarries near modern Cairo, intended to play with the rays of the rising and setting Sun. In ancient times the rising Sun reflecting on the Great Pyramid at Giza and many other royal pyramid complexes would have been visible from the temple of Ra-Horakhty on the far bank.

Although the temple of Ra-Horakhty at Heliopolis is now all but lost beneath Cairo, its form during the Old Kingdom may well be reproduced in the 5th Dynasty Sun-temples on the west bank of the Nile at Abu Ghurob [33]. In turn, the layout of these temples is analogous to the royal pyramid complexes beside which they stand, though the Sun-temples also feature an oversized calcite altar shaped to form the hieroglyph ⌂ 'offering' as the centrepiece for ceremonies conducted in front of a massive obelisk. At this altar – and presumably at Heliopolis too – verses from hymns to the Creator (addressed as Atum or as the Sun) were sung every day at daybreak and sundown, while at the same time offerings were presented in the neighbouring pyramid complexes to the enthroned statues of kings. A chapel beside the platform of the obelisk celebrated the fecundity of the land through the cycle of the seasons with brightly coloured images [32], comparable to the decoration in royal palaces at a later date (see p. 31).

Traditionally, changes to the particular form of the royal tumulus have been explained in evolutionary terms, as though the ancient engineers were making gradual progress towards a desirable outcome that was too advanced for them to know yet. In this scenario, the step pyramid form is an intermediate stage between a mastaba and a true pyramid, while the 'bent' pyramid form (in which the angle of the sides changes partway up) and other shapes for royal tumuli are disparaged as experimental mishaps, which the builders were nevertheless obliged to complete for some reason. If this were so, Snofru, first king of the 4th Dynasty, completed at least three of the largest pyramids ever built in order to get one in the shape he wanted. Without doubt some innovations were required by the developing technology of pyramid building, especially the engineering innovations that deal with relieving the increasing weight of the ever larger (and always solid) tumulus above the subterranean chambers. Nonetheless, a more sympathetic interpretation of events is that there was change and development during the 3rd and 4th Dynasties because meaningful choices were still being made regarding the appropriate form of the tumulus to be used in royal tombs. For example, successive kings introduced the step pyramid form, the bent pyramid form [34], successfully added internal chambers to the pyramid itself, and even reverted to the mastaba form, though these innovations were all subsequently abandoned.

32 Scene from the 'Chapel of Seasons' showing the Nile Inundation at top, and below men trapping water-fowl while a cow and calf come down to graze. The two figures at top are bent to their activity and have exaggeratedly large heads. From the Sun-temple of Nyuserra at Abu Ghurob, near Saqqara. Painted limestone relief. 0.72 m (2 ft 4½ in.) high. 5th Dynasty.

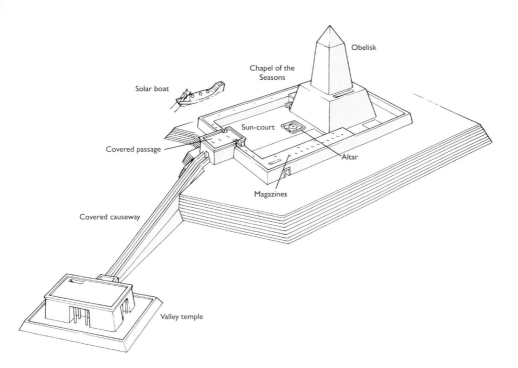

Obelisk

Chapel of the
Seasons

Solar boat

Sun-court

Covered passage

Altar

Magazines

Covered causeway

Valley temple

33 Reconstruction of a Sun-
temple built for the 5th Dynasty
king Nyuserra at Abu Ghurob,
whose layout is analogous to
that of a royal tomb complex but
centred on a monumental obelisk
rather than a pyramid.

Probably the form of the obelisk in the temple of Ra-Horakhty explains some of the innovation during the 4th Dynasty. The central obelisk of the Sun-god was named *benben* and featured a pyramidal pinnacle, possibly gilded, called the *benbent*, both words based on the indigenous word for 'rise' (as in 'sunrise'). Now, Snofru's 'bent' pyramid at Dahshur has the form of the benben, whereas his 'true' pyramid at the same site is based on the shape of the benbent specifically. At Meidum Snofru's oddest-shaped pyramid – which has been made to look even odder by later plundering for cut stone – may be a bold attempt to reproduce the shape of the whole obelisk including its platform [35], just as the whole obelisk was reproduced on a smaller scale in the temples at Abu Ghurob. The pinnacle of the Meidum pyramid in its present condition is stepped, though we cannot be sure whether the step pyramid was originally the intended outer shape, or the steps were meant to be encased in a different outer form. In the end, however, during the 5th Dynasty the straightforward, elegant and stable form of the true pyramid (that is, the shape of the benbent), rising as steeply into the sky as the solid mass of each pyramid easily allowed, became established as the

34 The 'bent' pyramid of Snofru at Dahshur. 4th Dynasty.

35 The pyramid of Snofru at Meidum. 4th Dynasty.

appropriate form of tumulus for royal tombs, and henceforward was retained at least until the royal burials moved to Thebes in the 11th Dynasty (see pp. 180–81).

If only for the sake of variety, change trumps continuity in any discussion of architectural and artistic development, so the changing form of the royal tumulus during the Old Kingdom tends to dominate accounts of early royal tombs in ancient Egypt. Nonetheless, the central fact of the tumulus – embodying first the Risen Earth and eventually also the 'risen' Sun in the benben – is constant, as are the inclusion of the Sun-courts, the placement of subsidiary burials round the king and so on. In many instances, the burials of full-size boats are still known to feature until at least the 12th Dynasty, and obviously this is a quite specific phenomenon that recurs from the beginning of royal burial in Egypt. In the same vein, the early royal burials moved from Abydos to other cemeteries, including Saqqara and Giza, which were already in use and dotted with the mastabas of high officials of the earliest kings (see pp. 74–77). This is not to say that the changing shape of the royal tumulus did not have specific relevance to the site of a given tomb, nor that the shifting choice of location was devoid of significance. Quite the opposite. The clear connection between the sites of many 'true' pyramid burials and the temple of Ra-Horakhty at Heliopolis has been noted. However, even the name Ra-Horakhty incorporates the name of Horus, and acts as a link back to the earliest kings and the mythology of Osiris, Isis and Horus. Likewise, the interplay of light and darkness in the hypostyle halls and Sun-courts round the pyramids is a constant theme, which recalls the Creator's first act upon 'the Risen Earth' – to speak the names of 'energy' and 'matter'.

As a final note, at the end of the 5th Dynasty the earliest ancient Egyptian funerary texts begin to be inscribed in the royal tombs (hence they are prosaically named by modern scholars 'the Pyramid Texts'). The poetry of these hymns or speeches entwines three distinct but harmonious visions of the immortal and eternal, each of which may be recognized in the built architecture of the royal tombs. First is the endless procession of stars through the night sky, particularly the circumpolar stars, which never set nor come and go with the seasons. Second is the myth of the dead father, Osiris, and the living king, Horus, in which birth and death are the scheme whereby all things have a beginning, a lifetime and an end, so the meaning of things is revealed in time ('not all at once', as Einstein is said to have remarked). Third is the perpetual boat-journey of the Sun-god through the firmament, intentionally forming the world out of Potential. Hence, the Pyramid Texts are able to picture Egypt coming together at the king's funeral to address him in words such as these:

> The town of Pe is sailing upstream to you, and
> Hieraconpolis is sailing downstream to you. For you the
> mourner is wailing, for you the shrine-priest is robing.
> Yours is a welcome to your father. Yours is a welcome
> to the Sun. The doors of the sky are opening for you, and
> the star-covered ceilings are sliding back for you.

Masterpiece
Greywacke statue of Menkaura

The valley temple of the pyramid complex of Menkaura, of the 4th Dynasty, contained at least five greywacke statues, each of which shows the king in the company of the goddess Hathor and one of Egypt's districts or temples. As we may expect, the divine Hathor and the districts are each personified so as to appear in the ordinary company of the king. In addition, the face of Hathor here (left) also seems to be that of the queen, who is shown alongside the king in the near life-size statue from the same temple. This particular statue is about half life-size, and cut with a simple back pillar for all three figures, which keeps them grouped and also allows the sculptor to form the crowns of the figures in a way that is not prone to damage. Hathor is the figure on the king's right, with cows' horns and a Sun-disc on her head; the personified district on his left is Hiw, south of Abydos, and the standard on her head shows the goddess Bat (see p. 24). The plinth is used to identify the characters and give the typical words of the goddess to the king, 'to you I have given all life, stability and authority, all health, all pleasure' (see p. 20).

The central figure of the king is slightly striding, which reduces the static character of the composition, while adding the dynamic of 'approaching' consistent with the context of offerings. There is also movement implied in the tension of the king's detailed physique, and in the relative placement of the characters. Hathor stands slightly behind the king, adding depth to a composition that would otherwise seem utterly two-dimensional. Still, there is no suggestion that they are not together, and indeed she is holding his hand. Subtly, the three figures look in slightly different directions, adding a further axis of movement to the composition, though again this has been done so discreetly as not to be intrusive nor disrupt the cohesion of the group.

36 Greywacke statue from the valley temple of king Menkaura at Giza. 0.93 m (3 ft 1 in.) high. 4th Dynasty.

37 Schematic reconstruction of
a typical Old Kingdom pyramid
complex; compare the Sun-temple
complexes of the same era [33].

The king is wearing only a heavily pleated kilt, and his physique
is modelled forcefully. Without overmuch detail, the muscles,
tendons and bones are realized prominently using bold lines in just
a few key areas, especially in his torso and legs but also his bullish
face, which has exceptional, naturalistic detail in the eyes and lips.
The female figures are static by comparison, and modelled in such
a manner as to emphasize their naked torsos, most obviously by
exposing their navels and demarcating a 'pubic' triangle. At first
glance, there seems little reason to suppose they are clothed at all,
other than the hemlines across their shins. However, the dresses
would have been painted a brilliant white originally and the collars,
now barely visible, would have been polychrome, so the apparent
nudity would have been less intrusive (see p. 87). That said, the
dresses must be an artistic conceit because nothing so tight could
have actually been worn in life.

The proximity of the prominent, powerful king and voluptuous
female companions is blatant, especially if one of them really does
have the queen's face. This juxtaposition is characteristic of every
statue found in Menkaura's valley temple, though by no means
all of them put the king in the centre nor necessarily make the
female figures subordinate. Hathor is obviously smaller than the
king but in a proportion that seems consistent with men and
women in real life. The other female figure, whose oddly high
breasts conform to the pectoral line of the king, is taller than
the goddess and simply stands beside him as though she were
somehow a counterpart rather than his more intimate companion.
In any event, because the context is the king's tomb, the sexuality
can hardly be overlooked. First, there is the simple juxtaposition
of procreation to death, especially in reference to the myth of
Osiris, Isis and Horus. Second, and prominent in the context
of offerings for the dead king, there is the life-bearing fertility
of the districts of Egypt. Finally, since the laying out of a temple
presumably involved the pharaoh trampling in seed at 'the grave
of Osiris', with this statue we come full circle. Here the harvest of
the land may be offered at the dead king's tomb.

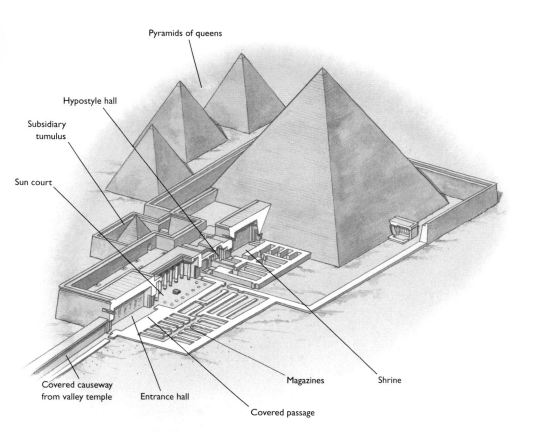

Pyramids of queens

Hypostyle hall

Subsidiary
tumulus

Sun court

Covered causeway
from valley temple

Entrance hall

Covered passage

Magazines

Shrine

PART II   ART & THE ARTISTS

Cairo Museum. Series B. No. 1. Splendid statue in
black granite, found at Karnak in 1901, it is the portrait
of Aménèthès (Amenhotep) son of Apoui, as an old man.
XVIIIth dyn. (B. C. 1600—1368).

38 Granite statue of Amenhotep, son of Hapu, with his arms in a gesture of greeting. He wears a traditional wig, and signs of old age are apparent in his face. From the temple of Amun-Ra at Karnak, near Luxor. 1.2 m (4 ft) high. 18th Dynasty.

39 Diorite statue of Amenhotep, son of Hapu, seated as a scribe. He wears a wig characteristic of his time, and indications of corpulence are visible in his torso. From the temple of Amun-Ra at Karnak, near Luxor. 1.3 m (4 ft 3 in.) high. 18th Dynasty.

Chapter 4 'All The Craftsmanship was Under My Attention': The Artists

Amenhotep, son of Hapu, was the most distinguished man of his age, recognized in his lifetime as the king's most effective and reliable official. In the context of this book we may best appreciate him in his office as 'chief of all the king's works' for Amenhotep III, a role to which he was appointed at the height of his powers after service as a scribe, a priest and a community leader. As we evaluate the monuments of Amenhotep III, we have here the official who – his statues assert – was ultimately responsible for ensuring that they *came into being according to the will* of his namesake, the king. The stature of Amenhotep, son of Hapu, among his fellow Egyptians is shown in the marvellous statues of him [38, 39], mostly from the temple of Amun-Ra at Karnak, but especially in the reputation he held for centuries after his death as someone of exceptional understanding, even able to cure sickness in response to prayers. The statues seem to show him at different points of his career, and specific details include clothing and wigs characteristic of the end of the 18th Dynasty. Hence he is shown up to date, as a man of his time. Yet the basic form of each of his statues is based on a different Old Kingdom model from 1,000 years or more earlier, as though he were not only appropriating ancient archetypes but also knew all about them. Indeed, the temples and cemeteries of Abydos and Saqqara and other such places must have been familiar to the great man, because he did not obtain his models in galleries, museums or public spaces.

If we presuppose a modern interpretation of the artist as a creative *individual*, we may object that Amenhotep, son of Hapu, was more bureaucrat than artist, even though his funerary inscriptions mention specific monuments and statues for which he was responsible. In which case, we simply turn to his contemporaries, a father and son named Men and Bak, who have left a joint funerary inscription on an outcrop at Aswan in the far south of Egypt, beside the quarries for the black and red granite used in some of their artworks [40]. Men is shown at an altar in front of a colossal seated statue of Amenhotep III on the right, while Bak stands in front of a figure of the next king, Akhenaten. Bak is also offering at a great altar so, by analogy with his father's scene, the royal figure is not Akhenaten himself but a monument, perhaps one of the great boundary stelae at Amarna (see p. 223). The so-called 'Amarna style', which became an important revision of the usual royal style during Akhenaten's reign, has been used here for Bak's scene but not Men's. In other words, father and son are shown in the one composition working with two different art styles, and this may be, as close as we are likely to discover, a first-hand record of a couple of ancient Egyptian artists at work at one moment in history. It is impossible to point to any particular monument and say Men made this or Bak made that – however tempting it may be to attribute, say, the 'Colossi of Memnon' to Men (see p. 47). Still, we do know who the two men were and what they did for a living, and we can surmise that Men's boss was Amenhotep, son of Hapu. These are only three men, but many other names could be added to the roll-call of pharaonic artists and their supervisors from almost every era of pharaonic history, from the venerable Imhotep of the 3rd Dynasty down to Senusheri, who erected monumental statues in the temple at Coptos for Ptolemy II Philadelphus (285–246 BC).

Even the happy outcome of linking an artist to a specific artwork is not always beyond our ken. For example, at the beginning of the 18th Dynasty, a scribe and official at Karnak

40 Rock inscription showing Men (right) and Bak (left) offering in front of monuments of their respective kings. Aswan. 18th Dynasty.

41 The calcite shrine of Amenhotep I built under the direction of Ineni. From the temple of Amun-Ra at Karnak, near Luxor. 4.5 m (15 ft) high. 18th Dynasty.

named Ineni set up an inscription in his tomb at Thebes, in which he recorded the time he spent directing the masons and artists who carved and decorated a distinctive chapel using the finest native calcite from Hatnub ('the golden mansion'), '*and all the craftsmanship was under my attention*'. The chapel he is talking about was commissioned by Amenhotep I (*c.* 1514–*c.* 1493 BC) to house the holiest shrine of Amun-Ra at Karnak, and may still be seen nearby today [41]. Moreover, possibly the first of the towering pylon gateways characteristic of later temples was built at Karnak for king Thutmose I (*c.* 1493–*c.* 1481 BC) – with a pair of magnificent granite obelisks in front of it – and this work was also supervised by Ineni. The pylon and one of the obelisks are still standing. On top of all this, Ineni built king Thutmose's tomb in the Valley of the Kings, '*alone, none seeing, none hearing*'.

So the artists of ancient Egypt are not so anonymous as may be expected after thousands of years. In fact, if we wish to study village life in pharaonic times, it turns out that the best-known communities are actually communities of artists. Every bit of evidence indicates that artists were highly respected and well supported by the nation through the provisions of the king and his highest officials; they are well known precisely because so much attention was paid to them and so much material provision made in support of their activities. Of course, all this support and provision was thoroughly recorded, so official documents can be added to the archaeology of their artworks, homes and workplaces. Despite the popular impression of slavery in ancient Egypt, with pyramids piled up at the tip of the lash, in recent years we have learned how well looked after were the builders of even the grandest of the pyramids, as demonstrated by the towns they settled at the Heit el-Ghurob at Giza and not least by their own well-appointed tombs.

Back in the 20th century, it used to be customary to discuss the development of Egyptian art in evolutionary terms, as though watching our simple ancestors trying to make sense of what art may be, and what can be done with it. In the new millennium we may be increasingly inclined to view the extraordinary transformation of the human landscape wrought by monumental art and architecture in terms of technological innovation, since the flavour of today is that each generation discovers new technological mindscapes. In that case, why not look for change and innovation in every generation of the ancient world too, and recognize the building of ever bigger and more sophisticated monuments as an end in itself? In truth, perhaps we ought to see more clearly how the advances of art in pharaonic Egypt are based upon social innovation. The eruption of monumental art in this culture during the early 3rd millennium BC was based upon professional specialization, as men were encouraged and supported to hone skills as painters, masons, sculptors, plasterers and so on. In turn, specialization depended on the emergence of the institution of kingship – in historical terms as much as mythology. Art in ancient Egypt – like the other extraordinary new technology, writing – evolved from the same nucleus as the king.

Working for the temples

Monumental art also needed the Nile Inundation. By virtue of the Inundation, Egypt was an exceptionally fruitful land, with a thriving agricultural economy common to all districts. The farmers grew a rich variety of produce, often obtaining multiple crops in any given year. As well as bringing water, the Inundation could be relied on to replenish the soil annually and cleanse the accumulation of salts, thereby eliminating the necessity to leave land fallow and rendering the vagaries of rainfall of little concern to Egyptian farmers, apart from the occasional destructive storm.

42 Scenes of commercial traffic from the tomb chapel of the governor Pahery. Painted limestone relief. El-Kab. 18th Dynasty.

Equally the Nile was a reliable highway connecting, at all times of the year, the various communities of Egypt, which seem far flung on a modern map but were rarely more than a few kilometres from the river [42]. The Inundation even brought desert areas, including building sites on the desert edge, within easy reach of boats for several months of every year. The constant flow of water northwards into the Mediterranean Sea is complemented by a constant, strong, south-moving wind, so travel on the Nile in either direction is usually straightforward for experienced pilots. Consequently quartzite from Gebel el-Ahmar, finest limestone from Tura, calcite from Hatnub, finest sandstone from Silsila, granite from Aswan or diorite from Toshka could be moved throughout the length of Egypt on barges, to supplement the basic limestone and sandstone bedrock of the Nile.

Because the Nile was a reliable highway for the exchange of people and goods, the larger towns were obvious focuses of economic and administrative activity for the smaller communities of each district, and typically also the religious heart of each district. Of course, the exceptionally dense settlement round Memphis indicates that this was an extended focus of activity for the nation as a whole, but away from Memphis and the large towns, settlements might dwindle to no more than a cluster of farms. Nonetheless, efficiently exploiting the Inundation for agriculture required collaborative efforts to construct the banks, dykes and canals necessary to move huge volumes of water to wherever they were needed and hold them there. In other words, efficient farming in ancient Egypt was beyond the capability of farmers acting individually and, already during pre-dynastic times, patterns of activity had been established involving organization on a community-wide basis, and centred on the towns. So, in effect, governing Egypt as a nation meant unifying the activities of Memphis and the larger towns, and the farmers who depended upon them – a cohesive process facilitated by the presence of a single common language, Ancient Egyptian. The priorities of government were those of the farmers, whose success was the foundation of the economy, and in turn their agricultural production was taxed in kind and made available to be redistributed in line with the hierarchies of authority (the more responsibilities you had within an institution, the more you received from it).

For example, each temple was endowed by the king with agricultural land from which to apportion offerings and also feed its staff and dependent communities, including those who built, decorated and maintained the fabric of the temple buildings. In addition to the offerings and legacies of private individuals, such temple endowments were often greatly supplemented by revenues obtained from foreign trade or tribute, and at times even military conquest by the king. As a result, temples actually became the principal administrative and economic institutions of Egypt certainly from the New Kingdom onwards, by which time we have detailed information. In this way the specialization of time and skills, and the organization of labour, required for monumental art became possible, and with it the building of monuments in the temples of every principal community. For earlier periods, the same detail in the documentary evidence does not exist but the sheer size of pyramid complexes is an obvious indication that they were institutions on a national scale, employing many thousands of people at any one time. They employed people, of course, to maintain and support those who operated the temple complexes, though the numbers directly involved in the original construction must have been many thousands at times. One authority, Dieter Arnold, has estimated that up to 4,800 people were employed on the building site itself during construction of the pyramid complex of Amenemhat III (c. 1805–c. 1760 BC) at Dahshur.

In this regard, the three (or more) pyramids of Snofru highlight two important points (see pp. 54–56). First, a pyramid, like a cathedral, was a place in which to bury a king but not necessarily a tomb (in the end Snofru could only have been buried in one of them). In our own culture, we recognize that Westminster Abbey is really a church and El Escorial a palace, college and monastery, though they are both appropriate places to bury monarchs. In the case of a pyramid complex, the concept of the Risen Earth undoubtedly lends itself to royal burial beneath the mastaba or pyramid but it does not require a burial. Which leads to the second point: the 'mortuary temples' of the early kings at Abydos or the Sun-temples of the 5th Dynasty at Abu Ghurob are not burial places either but they are products of the building process associated with royal tomb complexes. Indeed, we may surmise from the singular example of Snofru's pyramids that, during the earliest days of the pharaohs, there was always a royal complex being built somewhere, and possibly more than one, with huge implications for employment, taxation, and every aspect of the government of the land.

To turn this idea round, the temples of ancient Egypt, however huge and well provisioned, were not places of congregation; once built, they were places for offerings, where only a handful of priests might be required at any time. Nonetheless, a pharaonic temple has to be understood as a busy institution with a central core devoted to worship but a much larger area, physically and organizationally, devoted to other activities, including palace communities, as we have seen, but also the housing, factories and stores required by priests, masons, potters and numerous others. For example, the settlements at the Heit el-Ghurob were part of the operational fabric of the royal pyramid complexes at Giza – both while the pyramids were being built and afterwards, when they were in use as temples. Enormous areas of the grand temples of the New Kingdom and the Greco-Roman Period fit the same description, as operational complements to the sacred buildings. Book-keeping accounts that happen to have survived from temples at Abusir in the 5th Dynasty dovetail straightforwardly with comparable documents from the 13th Dynasty and the New Kingdom at Thebes to reveal patterns of behaviour consistent across more than a millennium among the temple staffs and dependent communities, which included full-time priests, part-time priests, craftsmen, scribes, watchmen, dish-washers, lamp-carriers, labourers, fishermen, traders and so on. According to these accounts, the daily offerings required in temples were held in the central stores and granaries of different temples, where teams of scribes – many of whom doubled as priests – kept tabs on what needed to go where, made sure each shrine was provided with offerings as and when required, and maintained inventories of whatever was still in store. So the business of a temple in one sense was to make offerings, but in another sense it was to build and constantly maintain the monumental infrastructure for these offerings.

Hence, the archaeological remains of temple granaries, as much as the written accounts noted above, indicate beyond doubt that many temples were so well furnished they could provide for dependent communities of many thousands of people. The pyramid town at the Heit el-Ghurob is in the desert, so the people who lived and worked there could not have grown their own crops, even if they were obliged to do so. However, the nearby temples at Abu Ghurob were able to provide their communities with more than 100,000 individual rations every year, according to the temple accounts. The villagers simply received food and other requirements as 'gifts' from the temples, with bread, beer and meat most apparent in the archaeological remains. The distinguished archaeologist Barry Kemp has calculated that, 1,000 years later, the granaries of the mortuary temple of Ramesses II – the so-called 'Ramesseum' at Thebes – once filled could have fed at least 3,000 'average' families for a year without being replenished, while the festivals of the gods accelerated the outlay for local communities and expanded to include 'festal' beer, fruit cakes and other luxury 'gifts'.

Another document, the 'Great Harris Papyrus' from the 20th Dynasty, addresses the same matter from a different perspective. This document – the only one of its kind to have survived – was compiled shortly after the king's death as a summary statement of the numbers of men whose service was reassigned to various temples during the reign of Ramesses III (c. 1187–c. 1156 BC). The numbers involved are so enormous that for a long time scholars assumed the scroll contained a statement of all the men in Egypt whose service was available to all the temples during the king's reign. In fact, only a small number of temples is listed. For example, the productive activity of 86,486 men and herdsmen, with the use of several ships, was turned over to the estates of Amun-Ra during Ramesses' reign, with another 13,000 for the estates of Ra-Horakhty, 3,000 for the estates of Ptah, and so on. Of these, however, more than 62,000 were assigned to the king's newly founded mortuary temple at Medinet Habu (see p. 199), and at least four other new temples are mentioned among a couple of dozen building projects. The figures can be understood in one of two ways: either these are the numbers of workmen who were resettled in order to build the new temples and the king's other new projects, in which case the average number of men available to each project was at least 3,500 (compare the figure of 4,800 men on p. 70); or else, given that 'herdsmen' and 'ships' are specified, they are the numbers of farmers whose production was being taxed and redistributed specifically to support the new building projects. If the latter interpretation is correct, then the men in question will not have moved from their own land, and might not even have noticed a meaningful difference in their lives. In either scenario, many might have been transferred from older temples that were now built or redundant, such 'transfers' presumably being routine during each new reign. Nonetheless, assuming many of these men were the heads of extended families and adding in the numbers of family members, it is clear how vast numbers of Egyptians – hundreds of thousands at least in a population of a few million – were immediately caught up in the constant commitment to building temples, whether paying taxes to them or actually working on them. As a final note, however, more often than not the families involved were specifically placed under the jurisdiction of the palace or local officials, which is to say that temples might tax or employ them but temples did not have unchecked authority to control their lives.

Masterpiece
The offering shrine of Ptahshepses

43 Architrave and offering panel
in the form of a niched wall from
the tomb chapel of Ptahshepses.
Painted limestone relief. Architrave
4.17 m (13 ft 8 in.) wide; panel
2.8 m (9 ft 2 in.) high. 5th Dynasty.

For much of the 5th Dynasty Ptahshepses was high priest of the god Ptah at Memphis. His tomb, at nearby Saqqara, was almost the archetype of a pharaonic official's tomb, a subject to which we will return in Chapter 9. Though measuring nearly 40 by 30 metres (120 by 100 feet) in plan, with an original height of at least 3.5 metres (11 feet) but probably significantly more, his mastaba was nevertheless a solid tumulus with almost no internal structure. Its mud-brick façade had the familiar niched appearance of early royal monuments, but otherwise the only external features were two brief statements of his titles and name, plus the architrave over a door. The text on the architrave is a request for offerings, and the door led into a single offering chapel built into the mass at the southeast corner of the tumulus. Nearby, but not accessible from the chapel, was a single vertical shaft, which actually dropped vertically through the roof of the mastaba into the subterranean chamber where Ptahshepses was finally interred.

As visitors passed through the door into the offering chapel, they would be directly facing the so-called 'false door', red-painted (to simulate granite, perhaps?) with blue hieroglyphs (to simulate faience inlay, perhaps?). Such a massive, decorated feature is obviously intended as a point of contact for the living and the dead, where offerings may be left but through which none may pass. Scholars regularly use the term 'false door' to describe any similar feature in an offering chapel, though clearly this example emulates a wall niche, not a door, and is 'impenetrable' even in a symbolic sense. Across the surface the hieroglyphic text recounts for the visitor who is making the offerings (at least, if they have brought a lamp) a life lived forty-five centuries ago, and built upon proximity and service to the pharaoh. As such, this is one of the earliest recorded biographies of an individual anywhere in the world.

Ptahshepses was born in the reign of Menkaura (see pp. 58–61), educated in the royal palace, and another king (probably Userkaf) later 'gave him the king's eldest daughter, Maatkha, as his wife because his person [the pharaoh] wanted her to be with him more than any man'. Ptahshepses devoted his professional life to following the king by boat or on land in all the king's festival appearances, while acting as 'the keeper of secrets for all the work his person wants doing'. As a result, 'whenever his person praises him on a matter, his person has let him kiss his foot, for his person does not let him kiss the ground'. Consequently Ptahshepses' false door is also a statement of pharaonic values hammered into the face of the rock, and his mastaba thus becomes a record of the advance of civilization and the king's authority across the world.

As high priest of Ptah, Ptahshepses bears the titles 'prophet of Ptah in all his places', 'prophet of Hathor in the same places' and 'prophet of Truth in the same places'. He was also 'greatest of directors of craftsmen', a title common to every high priest of Ptah, which implies the 'flow' of creativity from the Creator through the high priest to the working craftsmen. A modern, sceptical audience may assume a priest's association with crafts is a polite conceit, but other titles indicate that his priestly duties also extended to the king's valley temple and three of the Sun-temples at Abu Ghurob (whose names are given as 'Hieraconpolis of the Sun', 'Where the Will of the Sun Gathers', and 'The Consideration of the Sun'). These are among the handful of major monuments of the 5th Dynasty, so Ptahshepses was directly responsible for what are now huge archaeological sites. As such, he stands in the same relationship to the monuments of his age as does Amenhotep, son of Hapu, much later (see pp. 64–65). Whether Ptahshepses was responsible for building them or simply served among them as a priest is probably a moot point, given the expected relationship between priests and the foundation of temples. However, his professional concern was to realize the interests of his king, and the final statement of his biography insists that it is Ptahshepses *who inspires all craftsmen before the king*.

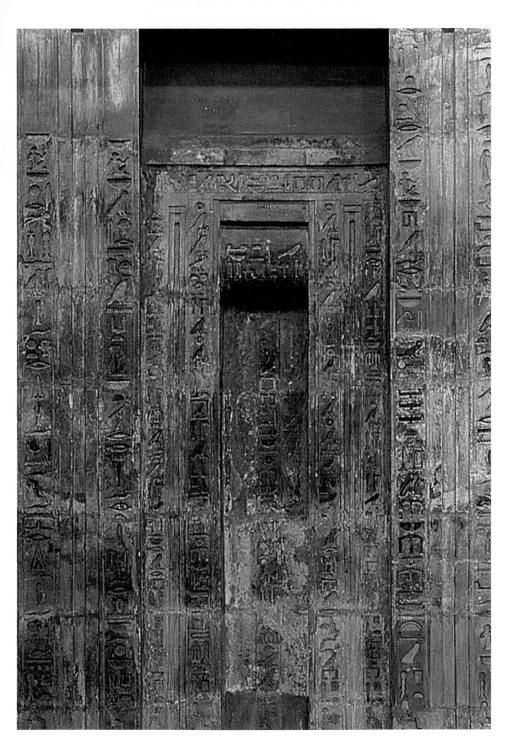

45 View of the New Kingdom
village at Deir el-Medina. West
Thebes.

Chapter 5 'Rejoicing in the Perfect Monument': The Artists at Work

Many different kinds of specialist communities under the supervision of temples in ancient Egypt are known to us, from priests to pig-farmers. However, most prominent among them is the village of the artists and masons who built and decorated the tombs in the Valley of the Kings at Thebes. During the New Kingdom, the Valley replaced the earlier royal pyramid complexes, and the men who worked there along with their families had their own exclusive village at Deir el-Medina, which lay on the desert edge because of the nature of their work [45]. Far from being isolated, however, the village was ideally located between a line of busy mortuary temples along the edge of the Nile floodplain and the men's workplace in the Valley. Like the villagers at the Heit el-Ghurob, the good folk of Deir el-Medina could grow nothing of their own so the pharaoh supplied all their food and textile needs from the stores of the nearby temples and equally watched over their security via palace officials. During the 13th century BC there were up to eighty households in the village, with dozens more in the near vicinity. Compared with most Egyptians of their day, they lived in houses which we could classify as nice or very nice, even though they are not the extensive villas of the grandest Egyptians. Some of the men's names are still painted on the front-door frames, and the first room in each house had a shrine for making offerings to the family's ancestors, which could perhaps be screened off to accommodate the birth of the next generation. However, the village was abandoned when the Valley of the Kings was closed down about 1070 BC and, lacking farmland, was never fully reoccupied. Consequently the houses of the villagers survive to this day, and the documents they left behind add so much detail to the archaeology that this village of artists is the best-understood community in the whole of the ancient world.

Under normal circumstances, the men of Deir el-Medina were expected to do no more than their principal task: build and decorate what they simply called 'the Tomb'. In this sense there was no 'art for art's sake' in the village, at least on the part of the individual artists. The commitment to art was on the part of the pharaoh through his temple-building, his tomb and the tombs of his officials. The villagers were employed as workers in an industry of art, part of the project to build what the German art historian Hans Gerhard Evers memorably described as 'a nation built out of stone'. Nonetheless, many of them were genuine artists in any sense of the word, and occasionally their little sketches bring to life the men at work – ancients who, to these artists, were simply neighbours [46]. Other compelling traces of the villagers have survived, including half-finished work in the Valley of the Kings, the administrative records of their business (including even records of absence), archives of family letters and, of course, their own tombs, which stand right next to the village in the shadow of the Theban hills (see pp. 102–104). Perhaps the most unexpected glimpse of their work is a detailed and annotated ground-plan of the subterranean tomb of king Ramesses IV (c. 1156–c. 1150 BC).

Deir el-Medina is an extraordinary community but still far from being the only place that allows us a meaningful glimpse of the artists at work. For example, from the 12th Dynasty a lively scene in the tomb of the governor Thuthotep shows a colossal statue being dragged by sledge from the calcite/alabaster quarries at Hatnub, in the Middle Egyptian desert, some 16 kilometres (10 miles) from the Nile [47]. The statue is said to be 13 cubits high (about 7 metres, or 23 feet) and 'the road on which it came was more difficult than anything'. Four groups of forty-two men

46 Limestone *ostracon* (rough flake of stone) showing a stonemason at work, notable for the unshaven face and muscular arms and neck. Presumably from Deir el-Medina. 14 cm (5½ in.) high. 19th–20th Dynasty.

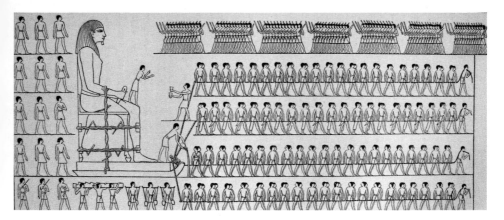

47 Drawing of a scene in the tomb chapel of Thuthotep (also known as Djehutyhetep) showing the transport of a colossus. Deir el-Bersha. 12th Dynasty.

each haul a rope, paired up so we understand they are standing on either side of the statue to pull, with a single overseer making calls at the head of the line. Captions tell us there are gangs of 'youths' from each bank of the Nile hauling on the outside ropes *'rejoicing in the perfect monument'*, while inside is a gang of 'recruits' and a gang of 'priests'. In spite of the hard work and desert conditions, men are running at top, waving branches, *'excited as they see what favour you* [i.e. Thuthotep] *have before the king'*. Beside the sledge more men carry a large, serrated board to help with traction when it threatens to get stuck, and others constantly bring water to wet the vehicle as it slides. Interestingly, the text confirms what we might have expected: that the stone was quarried as a block and transported to the town of Ashmunein in the same condition, though the scene seems to show a finished statue in transit. Once again the artist has illustrated what we know to be the case (the transport of a statue), not what we would have seen had we been there on the day.

A monumental block such as Thuthotep's was isolated in the quarry by channelling through the living rock to form crawl-ways for the quarrymen. Once the required size and shape had been isolated, slots were cut under the block and used to split the stone away with levers, or sometimes perhaps wooden wedges forced in tightly and wetted until they swelled. Creating channels and slots involved a lot of labour, even in the relatively soft limestone and sandstone that predominate in Egypt; but in hard-stone areas such as the Aswan granite quarries, the work – simply using pounders of even harder stone – must have been a grim, exhausting business at times. A block that cracked was liable to crack even more, if attempts were made to scavenge smaller blocks out of it. A successfully detached block then had to be hauled or rolled down a slope onto a sledge, which might have been the most problematic moment of the operation: a large block that missed its sledge would possibly be immovable after it hit the quarry floor.

Plentiful labour, however, was one thing the pharaonic system of organization could provide. Occasionally criminals were punished by being sent to work in the desert quarries, but much more often an expedition to the desert was organized, provisioned and dispatched under the leadership of senior officials, who were personally accountable for getting the important work done and, just as importantly, getting everyone safely home (see p. 252). In the reign of Pepy I of the 6th Dynasty, the courtier Weni was appointed to lead the expedition to quarry the king's sarcophagus and the capstone for his pyramid because he had successfully led five armies abroad on campaign. Another time, the king:

> sent me to Hatnub to bring a great altar of Hatnub-stone, and I brought this altar to him in seventeen days, cut from Hatnub. I had it sail downstream in this barge – I cut for it a barge of acacia of sixty cubits [about 30 metres, or 100 feet] in its length and thirty cubits in its width.

Weni notes with pride that he was able to move this mighty barge in the dry season, without waiting for the Inundation.

Blessed with plentiful labour, the artists and builders of ancient Egypt kept most of their tools and techniques simple and straightforward. For example, to begin building a pyramid they would simply excavate a T-shaped pit, whose 'leg' would become an access ramp, while the 'cross-bar' would become the basis for the suite of subterranean chambers. This initial layout has now been exposed in the royal tombs at Abydos, whose superstructures have been eradicated by time [15, 23]. In this way, the artists would be able to complete most of the decoration and masons set the king's stone sarcophagus in place before two lines of stone slabs were set at opposed angles to form a Λ-shaped roof over the chambers. The decorated rock-cut elements were then buried beneath the solid mass of the tumulus. The surface of the surrounding site need not be especially flat because the bottom of the tumulus could be 'fluked' using foundation layers of stones shaped or piled up to adapt to the rough-cut surface. Occasionally an uneven desert surface might even be cut into rough steps, then incorporated into the structure of the tumulus.

Temples nearer the floodplain were built on foundations of rough-cut heavy blocks laid directly in the ground on a layer of sand, which may seem dangerously precarious to us but the finished walls could be expected to hold together through sheer dead weight.

Then the walls were laid with courses of rough-cut rectangular blocks, dressed smooth only on the bottom, before the masons moved them into place using levers and a layer of mortar, or maybe using rollers for the initial blocks that needed to be positioned exactly. Adjoining faces of blocks would be dressed as the masons moved along the course, the top surfaces not needing to be dressed until the entire course was complete. An obelisk, a monolithic column or a colossal statue could be erected simply by hauling the rough-cut block base-first up a mud-brick ramp until it eventually pivoted down into a hollow formed above the intended plinth. As it pivoted, the massive block would be pulled upright and straightened using ropes, occasionally relying on a pre-cut slot in the plinth to keep the block square while guiding it into the final position. Likewise, different configurations of mud-brick ramps were used to haul blocks and stones to the required point in, say, a temple wall, and the bulk of the resultant scaffolding helped support and protect the partially built architecture [48]. Eventually the masons would bring the scaffolding down, and the artists gradually dressed and decorated the surfaces as they did so, but ancient scaffolding can still be seen conspicuously in situ in unfinished areas of Karnak and other temples.

48 Mud-brick scaffolding in situ behind the unfinished first pylon in the temple of Amun-Ra at Karnak, near Luxor. 30th Dynasty or later.

49 Scene of a sculptors' workshop, from the tomb chapel of the mortuary priest Kaemrehu. Note that the statue, which is destined for a tomb chapel, is shown as though naked (see p. 148). Saqqara. Painted limestone relief. 5th Dynasty.

A scene from the 5th Dynasty tomb of Kaemrehu at Saqqara shows artists at work in a studio [49]. A millennium later, the 18th Dynasty tomb of Rekhmira at Thebes shows artists in a studio that is recognizably the same in terms of organization, working practices and technology [51]. The tools they use while collaborating on a statue are a wooden mallet, a copper chisel and an adze, and such simple tools were sufficient for most of pharaonic history. Many examples have survived in the archaeological record, and Egyptian artists and masons seem to have been immune to the supposed 'advantages' of iron tools or mechanized equipment for many centuries after they were introduced to them. Various copper saws, a set-square with a plumb bob, a level for checking plane surfaces, along with different sizes of drills – used with copper drill-bits and an abrasive slurry of sand and water – more or less complete the principal toolkit in use throughout pharaonic times. A stone mortar and pestle would be on hand to grind charcoal, gypsum and minerals such as malachite and orpiment to produce a basic palette of colours: black, white, yellow, various reds and browns, and various blues and greens. (Such minerals are not chemically inert, and in many instances have changed colour markedly since ancient times.) The pigments were applied using a brush made of reeds or palm fibres – doubled over, lashed together, then chewed at one end – and a suitable medium, which might have been a soluble plant gum or even egg white, typically laid on top of a dry plaster wash (secco). In a studio such as the one illustrated in the tomb of Kaemrehu, many folk other than the artists would have been on hand in order to fetch water, sharpen tools, replace drill-bits and so on.

Masonry marks and other graffiti of the time reveal that the artists and masons who, for example, built the Great Pyramid at Giza were organized into gangs each named after a key area of a boat, namely prow, stern, port-side, starboard-side and cabin. A millennium later the men from Deir el-Medina working in the tombs in the Valley of the Kings were still organized into gangs labelled 'port' and 'starboard'. Hence, as in so many areas of life in ancient Egypt, the imagery of the work-gangs is based on that of boats making steady progress along the Nile, and the different groups of artists and masons belong together literally as 'a crew'. In the next chapter, we are going to see that forming a crew is only one of various practices intended to allow the artists and the workers round them to collaborate in sufficient numbers to build and decorate monuments as quickly as possible on whatever scale was required. In the meantime, the practice recalls a story from the Greek historian Diodorus of Sicily, writing in the 1st century BC. Two Egyptian artists, he says, were commissioned by Greeks to sculpt a monumental statue, whereupon one set to work on the island of Samos and the other in the city of Ephesus. Each completed one half 'and when the two parts were brought together they fitted so well that the whole work looked like it had been made by a single man'. Of course, the story may be apocryphal but it speaks volumes nevertheless about the reputed ability of Egyptian artists to work not as individuals, but as part of 'a crew'.

Masterpiece
Life-size statues of Rahotep and Nofret

This pair of life-size statues came from a 4th Dynasty mastaba, on the same scale as Ptahshepses' mastaba, built within sight of Snofru's pyramid at Meidum (see p. 56). Their eerie naturalism, evoked by well-preserved colouring and lifelike eyes inlaid with quartz and rock crystal, quite frightened the workers who uncovered them in 1871. Yet, oddly, their excellent preservation is largely attributable to the fact that they were found in a sealed chamber, hidden behind the niched outer façade of the mastaba; so they were no longer available to receive offerings, once the tomb had been completed.

In pharaonic art, pairing a man and woman (other than kings and gods) usually indicates that they are married, and the mastaba in this case had shafts for two burials, so the pair seem to have been interred alongside one another. However, the only relationships stated in the hieroglyphic texts are with the king: the woman is said to be 'the king's acquaintance, Nofret'; the man is Rahotep, 'a king's son of his body' as well as the chief priest of Ra-Horakhty at Heliopolis. Among his other titles he was 'the elder among artists', 'expedition leader' and 'overseer of haulage', as well as 'the carpenter of the royal sceptre (?)' and 'controller of the tent' (for the king's travels, see p. 30). So, Rahotep might have been a son of Snofru, beside whose pyramid he was buried, but perhaps he is the son of the previous king, Huni. Certainly his titles suggest that much of his career might have been spent overseeing the building and decoration of the Meidum pyramid complex, in which case Snofru would have been his contemporary and so his brother.

Both statues are cut with a simple plinth and back pillar, thereby retaining the original outline of the parent stone block as it was quarried. Nothing of the figures protrudes outside

50 Statues of Rahotep and Nofret.
Meidum. Painted limestone. 1.21 m
(3 ft 11 in.) and 1.22 m (4 ft) high
respectively. 4th Dynasty.

the matrix of the original blocks, though this simplicity need not be for lack of expertise [97, 100]. First, although each 'seat' and back pillar is no more than a plain rectangle of stone, as an artistic conceit they do allow the sitters the apparent dignity of a throne. Secondly, the statues were set against the far wall of what was, at some point, an offering chapel, so they adopt the usual frontal pose and have no need to be released from the stone. Moreover, the white-painted back pillars are an effective background against which to display their faces clearly, as well as a useful base for the hieroglyphic texts, which identify exactly who the two people are.

Rahotep's chair is wider than Nofret's, which, almost imperceptibly, allows a modicum of extra weight to him and, by contrast, greater elegance to her. Typically, the man's authority is expressed graphically in mostly physical terms, though the pendant painted round his neck is the king's seal. Otherwise he is clothed in no more than a brief white kilt, and his powerful body is modelled in just a few bold lines. In fact, particular attention to his knees – at the front of the statue – and his eyes creates the impression that there is more detail generally in the sculpture than there really is. His right arm, folded across his chest, evokes both strength and the authority of an official salute, though this is also a gesture of greeting at the approach of an offering-bearer. His left hand, at his side, is tightly gripped, which also evokes a dynamic tension, but this (quite typical) grip also implies the presence of something in his hand, perhaps an official's staff or sceptre, which could not otherwise be modelled without creating a dangerously fragile length of stone. Rahotep's moustache is characteristic of many officials during the middle part of the Old Kingdom, especially the 3rd and 4th Dynasties.

Because of the painting, it is apparent that Nofret is wearing a dress, whose straps are visible, under her wrap or cloak. Despite these layers her tightly wrapped limbs are still visible, and the prominent nipples draw attention to her breasts. In other words, once again her sexuality is made obvious, especially when juxtaposed with her partner's naked torso. However, it is also apparent that a skin colour was applied over her limbs before the brilliant white garments were layered on top, and the effect is to evoke the translucent quality of the finest linen (see p. 125), which, in tandem with her heavy wig and necklace of multi-coloured beads and blue-green pendants, says as much about fashionable beauty and affluence as it does about her physicality. Her pretty floral headband may be another conceit, imposing a false white background to highlight an elegant diadem, which was actually spun from metal wires (see p. 278).

The stark distinction in the skin colour of the two is an early instance of what will become another template in pharaonic art. Male figures tend to be painted with brown skin, while female figures are noticeably paler. Of course, the relative merits of tanned and pale skin are entangled in notions of beauty for many cultures, including our own. Arguably, in ancient Egyptian art, there is also an association between tanned skin and physical activity (in keeping with Rahotep's powerful torso), and between pale skin and domestic activity, including raising children. However, these ideas are not spelled out in writing by the ancients, and the two skin colours are not always applied rigorously on the basis of gender. Nofret's face is fuller and more rotund, and her eyes conspicuously narrower, than those of Rahotep, so perhaps there is a hint of corpulence to add to her affluent style and pale skin. These aspects together may paint a picture of a woman whose circumstances are of the most indulgent, and some men of that ilk will be encountered below. However, the imponderable question at this point is, how much of her appearance is simply an artistic device and how much is taken from life (see pp. 157–65)?

51 Scene of a sculptors'
workshop, from the tomb chapel
of the vizier Rekhmira, showing
men polishing and painting a
standing statue, a seated statue
and a sphinx. West Thebes.
Plastered and painted limestone.
18th Dynasty.

Chapter 6 'A Gateway to the Far Side of the Sky': The Principles of Art

It is worth taking a moment to recap some of the principles of ancient Egyptian art we have already encountered. For example, how the artist puts more stock in explaining the interaction between recognizable characters than in creating representations of the world as it appears to the eye (see p. 12). To that end, gods are often given forms consistent with the king's human body, and are shown to interact with him in human terms, though they may also have strange heads consistent with their divine characteristics to mark them as 'not-human'. Likewise, a scene is usually composed using distinct areas of information, and in particular baselines divide scenes into registers, and even into sub-registers within registers (see p. 118). The effect of these and other principles could be summarized by concluding that ancient Egyptian art is intended to seem clear, familiar and human, and in that sense both accessible and attractive. At the same time, it is resolutely abstract and, though this may create unfamiliar and off-putting outcomes, these are rarely allowed to intrude on our initial viewing. The fundamental value of abstract ideas is clearly not confined to pictorial art. For example, the recurring practice of burying full-size boats round royal tomb complexes only makes sense as abstract thinking or symbolism. The symbolism of the Risen Earth and the burial tumulus, whether a mastaba or a pyramid, became the basis for a whole genre of architecture expressed through another abstract idea – perfect geometric forms, which do not occur in nature. To put this another way, ancient Egyptian art is bound to be configured in accordance with the abstract meaning of a composition expressed in many different ways, whether in iconography (such as standard forms and typical poses, stock clothes and regalia), in the relative sizes of figures, in texts (such as speeches and captions), or whatever means are available.

Registers show how skilfully the artist may manipulate the two key ideas, namely that the art should be both accessible and abstract. For example, in the artists' studio depicted in the tomb of Rekhmira, men are shown working round two statues as though on scaffolding, one row above another [51]. However, in the space between the statues, men working on smaller objects are arranged in the same way, and we appreciate they are not going to be on scaffolding. Instead, we are being shown depth in the studio – the far scene shown above the near scene (or vice versa) – but in such a way that there is no obscuring or cluttering the view with perspective. The tall statues on either side frame the registers, so the sub-registers work attractively and efficiently within the same frame, and the treatment of each element of the scene is consistent. Once again, people are not scaled naturalistically but are shown interacting face to face, so subjects crouching have 'real-world' heights greater than those shown standing, but this is apparent only when the matter is consciously analysed. At first glance, everything seems natural.

We have already noted the implication of narrative in depicting a ritual at the White Chapel (see p. 28) or on Hmaka's label for king Den (see pp. 41–42). More straightforwardly, in a scene of grape-treading in the tomb of Pahery a gang of men and women (distinguished from each other by dress and skin colour) may simply pick the grapes but, as a consequence, an undulating, unbroken line is formed, which leads the eye to the wine-press (see [27]). This flow of activity is sufficient to illustrate the complexity of a process or the passage of time. A vintner collecting the juice in a 'real-world' sense seems to be hovering in the air. Of course, in artistic terms he has simply been removed from 'behind' the wine-press, where he would be invisible, and the artist has cleverly used a horizontal strut in the press as the baseline for the jars in the vintner's sub-register. Every composition in ancient Egyptian art is likely to disclose such artistic conceits and break down what would be complex for the eye into 'parcels' of clear and distinct visual information, to which may be added abstract information invisible to the eye. Of course, the cleverest aspect of this conceit is that it does not blatantly intrude into our viewing.

Literal meanings and abstract meanings
So, what is the relationship between the literal meaning and the abstract meaning of a scene? Let us take as an example the painted goose-count from the offering chapel of Nebamun, and consider what it tells us [52]. In truth, there seem to be innumerable ways to interpret such a deceptively simple scene – more or less literally, more or less symbolically.

First, we may assume Nebamun is wealthy to have so much at his disposal, though this assumption in turn speaks about his success in a hierarchical society where people supposedly benefit

52 Scene showing a count of geese, from the tomb chapel of Nebamun. West Thebes. Painted plaster. 0.71m (2 ft 4 in.) high. 18th Dynasty.

in proportion to their authority and responsibilities, and the king's favour likewise is spelled out in rewards (see [174]).

Of course, in a place of death the scene may speak about life and fertility and the seasons, which is perhaps the preferred antidote to death. More specifically, this is a scene of beautiful things and happiness. After all, what is more relaxing and nostalgic than a farm (if you are not working there), more handsome than a bird's plumage, or more charming than a gaggle of geese? What more poignantly removes the sting of death? As the poet Rupert Brooke asks, 'Say, is there Beauty yet to find? / And Certainty? and Quiet kind?'

Next, there are specific cultural references that an ancient Egyptian audience would surely recognize. For example, funerary art regularly employs marshland and water-fowl as a symbolic boundary – a liminal zone, neither water nor land, hence symbolically neither life nor death (see pp. 124–27).

Fourthly, and quite specifically, water-fowl are an epitome of the offerings asked for in funerary prayers, while offerings for the dead are a counterpart to offerings made to the king and the gods. In other words, on the decorated walls of a tomb, geese are bound to evoke offerings, and offerings are a reminder that we too may pass into the next life and enter the condition of 'Adoration', like the gods (see p. 38).

There seems to be at least one more line of interpretation. The 'tax man' at left, tallying the geese as they are counted in baskets, is tall enough to frame both registers behind him, while his two assistants are sufficiently tall to 'intrude' through the baseline of the upper scene. Hence we are encouraged not to treat the registers as separate scenes; the men at top and geese below somehow belong together. Now, the geese are a tax and the men kiss the ground or salute, so perhaps the scenes are two sides of the same coin: both tax and homage acknowledge authority, which is a cultural attitude; both fowl and adoration are aspects of offerings and the 'Adoration' due to the deceased, which is a religious belief.

Each of these interpretations seems to expand out of another, and each suggests that a picture of Nebamun's estate may speak about his situation in different senses – his success, his good conduct, his place in death and so on. A bucolic scene may illustrate his authority or his funerary offerings, or may be the model for his pleasant garden in the eternal hereafter ('paradise', as we say in our own culture). Obviously the interplay between literal interpretation and symbolic interpretation guides an audience towards understanding that Nebamun's goose-count is not a simple depiction of one episode from life. The meaning – or truth – of the artwork is developed in different directions, ostensibly by 'reading between the lines'. In fact, this method of understanding art was perfectly familiar in the ancient world. Classical philosophers, such as Xenophanes (c. 565–c. 475 BC) and Anaxagoras (c. 500–c. 430 BC), used this method to analyse Homer's poems, and the Egyptian scholars Philo (who died after AD 40) and Origen (c. AD 185–253) relied on it to make sense of the Old Testament. According to this method we recognize what is impossible in the composition when taken literally because this points us to other aspects of meaning, which ancient scholars believed would express the spiritual authority of the artwork. Of course, we should anticipate that there is spiritual authority in the art that concerns us in this book because, as we know, ancient Egyptian art is essentially religious (see p. 20).

The problem of the audience

There is another point to raise here regarding interpretation, which can be put like this: the problem of meaning in ancient Egyptian art is not necessarily a problem for an audience. Consider a celebrated statue of king Khafra [53]: statues are always frontally posed to face the priest or officiant in an offering

chapel, so clearly the falcon embracing Khafra's neck is covered by his wig and not at all visible to anyone who approaches from the front. Whatever information the falcon conveys (about the king's authority, or his divine protection, or his condition as the deceased) was simply not available to an observer – at least, not in the manner it is nowadays, while the statue is on display in a museum. Indeed the statue might well have been kept in darkness originally, so may be understood to 'embody' something essential but not for the benefit of an audience. Similarly, the statues of Rahotep and Nofret were bricked in when their mastaba was completed so, whether or not the chapel was ever in use, they were eventually put out of sight but not disposed of. Likewise many of the great temple scenes or even the grand inscriptions of the pharaohs were displayed in blackness – in high, windowless corridors and chambers, often with limited space to step away from a wall so that even a lamp could illuminate only a snatch of a face or an isolated phrase in writing. It seems as though

54 Granite statue of king Senwosret III, making a gesture of greeting. From the mortuary temple of his forebear Montuhotep II and presumably associated with offerings for the dead king. Deir el-Bahri, West Thebes. 1.22 m (4 ft) high. 12th Dynasty.

the meaning is to be found in the making of such art, not in the viewing – a celebration of saying, not seeing. As in a modern diary perhaps – but on a monumental scale – considerable time and attention has been spent in realizing ideas that may never be seen except by a few persons already in the know.

Appreciating the notable absence of an audience allows us to make sense of other characteristics of ancient Egyptian art, such as the absence of emotions in most subjects. Of course, ancient people had the same feelings as any man, woman or child in any age, and emotions may be shown as such [199]. However, a king such as Senwosret III (c. 1840–c. 1805 BC) is presented as a religious subject, and consequently the sculptor is concerned with spiritual qualities such as authority, eminence, dignity and even perfection, as we shall see later (see pp. 157–60) [54]. Consequently, emotions, which are specific distortions of the subject based on a moment in time, have no relevance. Perspective, likewise, reduces the subject to a particular viewpoint at a given moment, and confuses our view of the 'real' subject. Hence perspective is rarely shown, as was apparent in Rekhmira's painting of a studio, where clarity was preferred to any particular viewpoint (see p. 90).

Of course, the lack of an audience would tend to temper any ambition on the part of an artist to innovate or display individual skills. In their biographies, men such as Ptahshepses and Amenhotep, son of Hapu, claim success in terms of fulfilling to the best of their abilities what was expected of them, rather than realizing their own artistic visions. There might have been no-one for the artists to impress, beguile or entertain other than perhaps the king. In the modern world, we are so accustomed to discussing artefacts by reference to context, evolution, progress and change that we may be startled by the apparently limited and unchanging repertoire of the artists in ancient Egypt, where familiar forms and stock scenes get repeated over and over again for two, three thousand years. Consequently, a modern, critical analysis may pay too much attention to specific details and concentrate on matters that do change in preference to the preponderance of unchanging forms valued by the ancient artists themselves. For a modern audience, the details often become the epitome of the time and place in which the artwork was created; hence Senwosret's oversized ears, which are not present in statues of Old Kingdom pharaohs, have recently become both the essence of the statue and the Middle Kingdom zeitgeist (but see also p. 132). Modern scholars have gone so far as to interpret

55 Hieroglyphic inscription laid
out using a square grid in the tomb
chapel of the marine commander
Ahmose, son of Abana. El-Kab.
Limestone relief. 18th Dynasty.

Senwosret's ears in terms of governmental reforms – or even the
reinvention of kingship – during the reign of 'the listening king' par
excellence. This may be true, of course, but ancient Egyptian art is
not a primitive form of photography, nor a depiction of events the
ancients lived through: such historical information must be sought
elsewhere. Rather, ancient Egyptian art embodies the constancy
of the professional and spiritual values that artists maintained
throughout the entirety of pharaonic rule. So, when we compare
the statues of Khafra and Senwosret III, we do well to recognize
first of all what has *not* changed during the course of half a
millennium between those kings before we turn our attention to
whichever details happen to look different. After all, constancy
may be a sign of confident understanding rather than the inability
to develop: Johnny Cash's guitarist, Luther Perkins, when asked
why he stuck so assiduously to one simple style of playing, is said
to have replied, perhaps apocryphally, 'what everybody's looking
for I already found'.

Hieroglyphs and language

For artists faced with the conundrum of adding abstract
information to compositions that must also remain clear
and accessible, hieroglyphs were an invaluable tool [55]. Like
monumental art, the earliest writing in Egypt is associated with
the first kings, though the oldest connected texts explaining their
values and beliefs in detail actually come from the offering chapels
of their high officials as late as the 4th Dynasty. Subsequently
hieroglyphs remained in use, but only in sacred contexts, to the
end of the pharaonic era. The forms of hieroglyphs as pictures
were intrinsically attractive and often executed in as much
detail as any other imagery the artists worked upon. However,
hieroglyphs are not pictorial as such, and it is a common
misconception to suppose that hieroglyphs are picture-writing.
In fact, hieroglyphs are a device for writing the *sounds* of Ancient
Egyptian to add linguistic information to a scene in a manner
that enhances its visual attractiveness while clarifying its meaning.
The interplay may remain simple, as when a god hands a king
the sceptre which is not a 'real' sceptre but a composite of the
hieroglyphs ⌐♀⚏ (see p. 21). Likewise the god provides 'breath'
and, because the phrase for 'breath' in Egyptian is literally 'life-
wind', we have already seen Sobk-Ra wafting the hieroglyph ♀ 'life'
into the face of the king (see p. 12).

On the other hand, hieroglyphs add information to art so
efficiently that, some scholars argue, whole compositions may be

reduced to words and 'read' as though they were texts. In other words, we may analyse a composition by asking, what does the composition mean as a word (see pp. 93–94)? For example, the 6th Dynasty scene of Sabni fishing with a harpoon and catching birds with a throw-stick is typical of the decoration of a high official's tomb at any period and, as ever, we are confronted with the problem of how to interpret the composition, literally and symbolically [56]. In a literal sense, we may conclude that the deceased is healthy and having fun, despite the funereal setting. On the other hand, boats and marshes are likely to have symbolic associations in tombs, evoking the transition to death. Likewise, various incongruities suggest we cannot simply take the scene at face value. For example, in the sub-registers well-dressed people (family, servants?) are waiting on Sabni in the marshes. So what do we make of this? If we were to 'read' the scenes instead, we may discern that there is a pun on the words 'throw' and 'create' (that is, the two words sound the same in Ancient Egyptian); likewise, there is a pun on 'spear' and 'inseminate'. In either instance, we use the 'reading' of the scene to point us towards an interpretation that has more to do with procreation and new life than death and non-existence, an interpretation which may be appropriate to the tomb but is a long way from the actual activities of fishing and fowling. In an obvious sense, such an analysis seems too limited and reductionist because the vitality, dignity, happiness and contentment of Sabni as a man are apparent in the scene without having to reduce it to a couple of words. However, hieroglyphic texts are also integral to the composition, if only to specify what we are looking at and – crucially – *who* we are looking at, so we cannot simply dismiss this 'extra step' of specific language-based interpretation for being wholly far-fetched (see p. 126).

To take an example, the starry ceilings appearing in the royal pyramid complexes of the Old Kingdom become typical of the ceilings of all royal temples and tombs (see p. 51). As a hieroglyph a star writes the word 'adore', the very activity we associate with temples and tombs. So the starry ceiling of the tomb may well evoke eternity and heaven as an image and *at the same time* invoke 'Adoration', the very word that characterizes the eternal afterlife. If the possibility still seems far-fetched, then consider the following statement from the tomb biography of Ankhtyfy (whom we will see again in Chapter 10): Ankhtyfy describes his own tomb with the words, '*I have made a gateway to the far side of the sky / and its roof is heaven, its belly the sky. / It is covered in stars.*'

56 Fishing and fowling scene in the tomb chapel of the overseer of Upper Egypt Sabni. Qubbet el-Hawa, near Aswan. Plastered and painted sandstone. 6th Dynasty.

In the end, the use of hieroglyphs in ancient Egyptian art is always informative, and it also obliges us to recognize that a definitive and final interpretation of any particular theme or composition is beyond our ken. To take an almost silly example, did the pharaohs actually wear bulls' tails, given that they always do in art (see p. 22)? Quite possibly the tail is an artistic conceit but then, in an inscription from a temple of the god Montu, we read the following statement about Thutmose III: '*He slew seven lions by archery in the space of a moment, having taken the hides of twelve bulls in a single hour. Breakfast-time came and their tails were at his backside.*' So did Thutmose really wear their tails? Is this a case of art imitating life or vice versa?

Masterpiece
Sennedjem's burial chamber

In the matter of discerning symbolic interpretations of art, a masterful case in point is a dramatic painting at one end of the subterranean burial chamber of Sennedjem and his wife, lyneferti, who died a little after 1300 BC during the reign of Sety I. Decorated burial chambers in non-royal tombs are exceptional outside the village of Deir el-Medina and western Thebes. Usually any decoration in the tomb is reserved for chapels above ground, but here we are in the local cemetery of the artists who built and decorated the tombs in the Valley of the Kings, where Sennedjem and his neighbours possessed the requisite skills to decorate anywhere they chose. So, though we can never be sure of the reason for choosing this unusual location, we may have here an exceptional insight into how a privileged artist would choose to decorate his own final resting place. On the other hand, miniature versions of the same scene are used to illuminate the traditional funerary scrolls Egyptologists call the Egyptian Book of the Dead (see p. 262), so this may in fact be the usual, expected imagery of a burial but copied by an artist on a grander scale than usual.

At first glance the composition is just another agricultural scene, which adds a note of quiet and beauty to an otherwise bleak and sombre location. Still, surely Sennedjem had no expectation that the burial chamber would be visited or the painting be seen, once he and his wife were finally interred. More to the point, Sennedjem never spent a moment like this in his life. As a man of Deir el-Medina, he worked for the palace and spent his living and working days in and about the desert. Indeed, nobody ever ploughed and reaped wheat alongside his wife, both in their finest, whitest, most fashionably pleated clothes. As for his bare shoulders, Sennedjem would be burnt red raw in no time beneath the unrelenting Egyptian sunshine. So, once again

57 Painting at the west end of
the burial chamber of the tomb of
Sennedjem. Deir el-Medina, West
Thebes. Plastered and painted
limestone. 19th Dynasty.

incongruities collect as clues to a conceit that points us away from the literal meaning of the scene towards the type of spiritual interpretation acknowledged by the ancients. For example, the cycle of ploughing and reaping the land is shown encircled by a fluid waterway, edged with marshes – again, a liminal image – and the new life of the plants emerges directly out of the fluid Potential (*nun*). At top, the falcon-headed Sun-god is sailing the waterway in a boat, describing the arc of the sky (and the burial chamber is arched too). A pair of baboons adore the Sun-god and even speak, briefly saying, '*he is in the sky as life*'. Between the register of the solar boat and the earth being cultivated below lies a distinct area defined by two activities: at one end 'adoring' the Sun-god, at the other end burial – while the interval between them is traversed in a papyrus boat like Sabni's [56].

The only point of contact between these activities and the register of the Sun-god is a remarkable band of black and white stripes. Hence the ploughing and reaping, life and death, night and day are presented as pairs of opposites bound up by the sailing of the Sun-god. Through the entire scene a brilliant gold – the colour of the wheat and the Sun – illuminates land and sky alike, recalling for us perhaps the radioactive sky and the swathe of corn in Vincent van Gogh's *The Sower* [58]. In the Dutchman's deep-set, viscous landscape, images of death among life – sowing corn ahead of the harvest, crows preying on seeds, the cloying, underlying blackness – are illuminated by the radiance of Creation, while the man standing on the earth rises up to the sky. Likewise, Sennedjem and Iyneferti, alone together, are the apogee of Creation, their feet on the sprouting soil of the Risen Earth, their lives (and deaths) bridging the apparent separation between the world and its Creator.

58 *The Sower* by Vincent
van Gogh. Oil on canvas. 0.8 m
(2 ft 7½ in.) wide. AD 1888.

Chapter 7 'For Your Spirit – Have the Perfect Day': The Canon of the Human Figure

Insofar as ancient Egyptian art is intended to present recognizable subjects and abstract meaning in the same moment, then the characteristic treatment of the human figure in two dimensions is exemplary. Perhaps nothing is so characteristic of pharaonic art as the 'walk-like-an-Egyptian' pose adopted by most human figures. That said, the mere fact that their pose can be lampooned indicates how close to the reality of the human form it must be, else the pose could not be mimicked. Nonetheless, the affectation of the ancient figures is apparent, not least through the peculiar manner in which they look over their shoulders, and such peculiarity can easily be ascribed to limited technical ability or even a lack of understanding of human anatomy on the part of the artists. On the other hand, we would have to set such conclusions against the Egyptians' commitment to retaining this peculiar treatment across dozens of centuries. So, to make sense of their commitment, let us begin within our own culture using a familiar portrait.

Hans Holbein's portrait of Henry VIII with his father is a study for a lost mural in the Palace at Whitehall [59]. Henry's physical presence is as blatant as it is huge. He seems elegant and powerful – not merely big – because the shapely legs and slender face contrast with his bulky torso. Looking more closely, though, where do his arms disappear to beneath the heavy robes? How long must they be to reach his shoulders? To put this another way, how unfeasibly broad must his shoulders be to meet his arms? Is his waist at the level of his right hand and belt, as the codpiece suggests? If so, how short is his torso in relation to his legs? How long is his neck, and is it really so thickset as it seems beneath the beard? Does the top of his head really slope in line with the hat? On another matter, what precisely is his grim-faced father standing on and why? More to the point, if Henry is king, how is his dead father in the portrait at all?

These are genuine questions about the portrait but they are not especially troublesome. After all, the composition is plausible: recognizably human, attractive, acceptable to the eye even in the moment when it defies our expectations or our analysis and asks us to consider what we are actually looking at. If the implausible aspects of the composition point to a meaning

59 Preparatory study for a portrait showing King Henry VIII of England with his queen and parents, by Hans Holbein the Younger. Ink and watercolour on paper. 2.57 m (8 ft 7 in.) high. AD 1537.

deeper than a simple likeness of two men named Henry, we may well recognize a portrait of a king in legitimate descent from his father, who in turn is receding into the background – perhaps even ascending to heaven. Likewise, we may recognize the portrait as an expression of Henry's power and authority stated in physical as well as abstract terms, so that ultimately his massive 'torso' is no more than an artistic conceit inferred from the two-dimensional elements, which are all the artist has actually drawn. The physical body we infer (we cannot actually see his torso) befits the power of a man on whom hangs the voluminous regalia of authority. The fact that aspects of the scene are impossible does not indicate that nothing here is true, only that what is seen immediately may not be the real subject of the composition. For example, Henry might well have been a hefty man in real life, but this one scene alone would not be sufficient evidence of that. The scene is not re-creating his actual body as such: it is speaking in the abstract about authority and who rightfully holds it.

Analogous reasoning can be found in the portrait of a 6th Dynasty Egyptian, Ty [60]. As with Holbein, the style is plausible and acceptable to the eye, and Ty is immediately recognizable as a fellow human being. Moreover, a great deal of information is available to us in the first viewing. A youthful man of some dignity or stature sits at a table, and an analogous man stands in a separate register. The hieroglyphic texts tell us that both pictures show the same man, Ty, and that the table is filled with offerings. In each scene Ty wears the collar, wig and fine kilt of an Egyptian nobleman, and in the lower scene he also carries a staff (as a blatant statement of power) and a sceptre (as a symbol of legitimate authority). Otherwise, in both registers we see his body, naked and exhibiting the hallmarks of the ancient Egyptian treatment of the human form. It is this treatment of his body that does not stand close scrutiny as a depiction of what appears to the eye, but it is no less 'real' as a consequence. For example, his shoulders are shown from the front but his stomach and hips are in profile –his navel is visible at one side – so the form of his torso has to develop as a triangle from a slender (profile) waist to broad (frontal) shoulders. The result is unnatural but wholly attractive: after all, how desirable are broad shoulders and a trim waist in a 'real' man to this day? So the scenes are talking in the abstract about the 'real' Ty, rather more than they are 'showing him' as our eyes would comprehend him.

In fact, almost all of Ty's body is shown in profile, whereas the shoulders need to be shown from the front in order to be able to 'suspend' a pair of arms on the figure, rather than just

60 Stela from the tomb of the priest Ty. Probably from Dendera. Painted limestone relief. 0.56 m (1 ft 10 in.) high. 6th Dynasty.

61 Limestone *ostracon* showing various preparatory sketches. Presumably from Deir el-Medina. 0.42 m (1 ft 4½ in.) wide. 19th Dynasty.

one as would be the result were his shoulders in profile. This discrepancy between the view of the shoulders compared with the other elements of the body is essentially what creates the familiar 'walk-like-an-Egyptian' pose. On the other hand, why are the other parts of the body shown in profile? Because Ty's body has been assembled as a composite, and the artist is maintaining a single, distinctive view for each element of the body, avoiding unclear, overlapping or distorted forms. More often than not, the 'distinctive' view means the view of each body part in profile (or in outline, as we may say). So, there is no unified viewpoint for the body as a whole because this would introduce the visual distortion of perspective.

An *ostracon* (a rough flake of stone) presumably from Deir el-Medina has been decorated with various preliminary studies. For one, the artist has drawn a standing figure on the left, using exactly the same compositional technique as in the standing figure of Ty [61]. However, the hand holding the staff is 'the other way round' from Ty's, and looks as though it were drawn on backwards, until we realize that in two dimensions a figure only has hands, but neither right and left nor near and far hands. The hand here is simply 'grasping' a staff (which, in turn, is budding as a lotus) because this is the entirety of the meaningful role the hand plays in the composition. Above the standing figure is the head of a god, Ptah, shown in profile, while on the right is a column of hieroglyphs, which in pictorial terms is simply a sequence of things, each shown in a distinctive, unambiguous profile. Lastly, however, the centre of the ostracon is occupied by the study of a wooden box-shrine, used for housing a statue of a god, and the box is undoubtedly shown from the front, precisely because this is the most distinctive and recognizable view. From above or in profile the box would be no more than an indeterminate rectangle. Nonetheless, in this one study alone it is apparent that the artist's powers of observation are hardly deficient. Exceptional detail is involved in copying the carvings above the doors and rendering the doors themselves with a simple but effective reed-work (or bead-work?) pattern. The large standing figure has also been sketched (twice, facing both left and right) into the carving above the doors. So, whatever reasons the ancient artists might have had for rejecting a single, unified viewpoint in treating the human form, the explanation is certainly not that their eyes, minds or hands were defective or inferior compared with our own.

A canon of proportion

Because the human figure in pharaonic art is a composite, sometimes obvious indications of how the composites were put together are still preserved. For example, the female figure in the tomb of Sarenput II has been drawn on a grid of squares, something like the copying grids in modern children's drawing books [62, 63]. Using the grid as a guide, the artist has assembled her figure as discussed above, so the shoulders are shown from the front and everything else seems to be in profile. Although her navel is not visible, notice how the profile of her torso results in the appearance of a single breast, as though beneath her armpit.

62 Scene in the offering shrine of the governor Sarenput II showing a standing female figure with square grid in situ. Qubbet el-Hawa, near Aswan. Painted and plastered sandstone. 12th Dynasty.

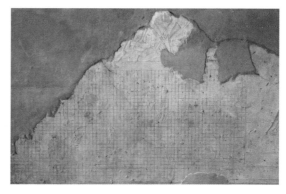

63 Wall in the tomb chapel of the governor Senbi prepared for decoration with monochrome background and red-square grid in situ. Meir. Plastered and painted limestone. 12th Dynasty.

There is a further discrepancy: the dress is shown frontally, so there are straps across both shoulders but neither covers her breast, so the top edge of the dress has been dropped below her breast to avoid highlighting this odd profile. Likewise, the woman has two feet, one shown as though looking across the toes, the other with the profile of the inside foot – only the big toe and arch shown. However, in 'real-world' terms the feet seem to be on the wrong legs (the 'near' foot on the 'far' leg). Again, what matters is that there are two feet, not that they correspond to any specific 'real-world' view and, of course, there cannot be 'near' and 'far' in two dimensions. Finally, we may notice one of the prominent characteristics of human figures in pharaonic art: the head is shown in profile but the eye is shown from the front, and seems to stretch from the bridge of the nose to the temple. Again, as in the treatment of Ty's torso above, the 'oversized' eye is both unnatural and wholly attractive. In fact, the unnaturally large eye is not disguised but accentuated with eyeliner to create a specific shape, which also happens to be the shape of a hieroglyph used to write the word 'beauty'. (Today, when anyone tries to look 'ancient Egyptian' they are likely to start with kohl around the eyes, though the characteristic 'Elizabeth Taylor as Cleopatra' appearance is more a function of art than a typical feature of life.)

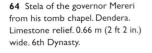

64 Stela of the governor Mereri from his tomb chapel. Dendera. Limestone relief. 0.66 m (2 ft 2 in.) wide. 6th Dynasty.

Already by the 1850s a pioneering surveyor of Egyptian monuments, Karl Richard Lepsius, had noticed how any human figure in pharaonic art is constructed on the basis not only of characteristic forms but also typical proportions, which scholars term a *canon* of proportions. The canon begins with a horizontal baseline – literally so, because, once a wall had been smoothed and covered with a plaster wash, a baseline for the composition had to be drawn first. To do so, the artists snapped a length of twine charged with red or black paint against the wall. Using the Old Kingdom figure of Mereri as an example [64], working from the baseline to the hairline (yellow), the canon determines that a line snapped near-halfway (blue) marks the junction of the legs and the torso at the curve of the buttocks. Three evenly spaced lines further divide the figure, marking the knees (orange) below and the inside of the elbows (red) above. A central line drawn at right angles to these provides the basis from which to take other vertical lines in parallel, including the upright posture of Mereri himself, as well as the column dividers for the hieroglyphic inscription. By the Middle Kingdom, this canon of proportions had been developed into the grid of squares shown in [62], using eighteen lines marked from baseline to hairline, and others at right angles to these. (The grid is drawn to the hairline rather than the top of the head because of the unpredictable variety of crowns, wigs and other items worn by royalty and gods especially.) Occasionally scholars have tried to equate the grid squares with 'real-world' dimensions so that, for example, one square = one fist. More likely, however, halves and thirds together simply generate sixths, while thirds and sixths produce the ninths and eighteenths of a whole figure. In fact, different grids based on different numbers of lines were used in certain periods, which seems to confirm that the original basis for eighteen-square grids is the practical convenience of a canon of proportions rather than specific dimensions.

Sufficient examples of such canonical grids have survived to allow us to determine how they were typically used, and indeed adapted to specific scenes. For example, in the case of the 18th Dynasty plastered writing board in the British Museum, a study of a seated figure drawn with the grid still in place has fourteen rows of squares from the bottom of the feet to the hairline, rather than eighteen [65]. A comparable figure in the tomb of Sarenput II has been marked up with the same fourteen-square grid to illustrate what is happening [67]. The top half of the man, from the line of the buttocks (blue) to the hairline (yellow) is entirely unaffected. The line of the elbows (red) remains at six lines below the hairline. Of course, the four missing rows correspond to the length of the upper leg, which is simply drawn at right angles to the buttocks along the line of the seat of the chair. Hence the line of the buttocks drops from line 9 above the baseline to line 5. The line of the knee (orange) remains at line 6 above the baseline, and as a result is now one line above the buttocks.

As we noted above, different grids were used as standard in certain periods, most conspicuously during a short-lived revision of art during the Amarna Period, to which we will return in Chapter 12. More importantly, from the 7th century BC the standard grid of squares was adjusted from eighteen rows, baseline to hairline, to become twenty-one rows from the baseline to the top of the eye. On the other hand, a limestone ostracon in the Louvre dating to this period shows the top of the knee at line 7 and the rear elbow at 14, so the canonical proportions remain

65 Plastered wooden board showing king Thutmose III on a 14-square grid. West Thebes. 0.53 m (1 ft 9 in.) wide. 18th Dynasty.

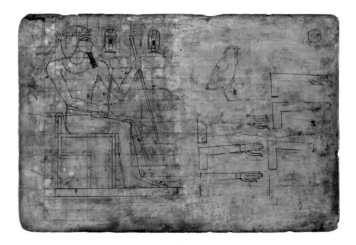

66 Limestone ostracon showing king Apries and another figure in the presence of a hawk-headed deity on a 21-square grid. Provenance unknown. 26th Dynasty.

67 Central scene in the offering shrine of the governor Sarenput II (see [135,136]). Qubbet el-Hawa, near Aswan. Plastered and painted sandstone. 12th Dynasty.

essentially the same as they were in earlier periods [66]. However, in this grid, which remained in use until Roman times, the upper leg tends to be relatively longer (to line 11 of 21 rather than line 9 of 18) so the torso is typically 'compressed' in later pharaonic art.

For a workmanlike artist, a canon of proportions and grid would have been a convenient means of working efficiently and in accordance with expectations. However, in the hands of a competent artist, their use need not be mechanical nor produce repetitive figures. Simple adjustments within the treatment of figures could make significant differences. For example, the woman in [62] has been drawn with the bottom line of her buttocks at line 10, one line higher than the usual: consequently she has longer, more elegant legs and a shorter torso. This explains her improbably slender waist, which must expand to the full width of the shoulders within the space of five lines rather than the standard six. How could we ever know whether this woman had an exceptionally slender figure in real life? In fact, drawing women with buttocks elevated on the grid relative to men is not unusual, and no doubt provides better evidence about ancient notions of beauty than about the specific appearances of individuals. Likewise, in male figures the shoulders often cover six squares and the full width of the torso reaches four squares, but this woman's shoulders are about one square narrower, so she appears more slender, which again is not unusual.

Obviously grids would be effective when laying out multiple human figures quickly and efficiently across decorated surfaces of any size, maintaining the desired proportions while varying the scale to fit whatever space might have been available. The figures on the drawing grids in the British Museum and the Louvre could easily be scaled up to serve as the model for a life-size image of the king on a temple wall, or scaled down for a decorative inlay in a box. If we think back to the statues of Menkaura [36] or Rahotep and Nofret [50], we can easily envisage how guidelines or grids drawn according to a canon of proportion on the front and the sides of a statue in three dimensions would help to lay out and sketch the subjects on the rectangular matrix. On the other hand, often wooden statues and occasionally metal statues were made in pieces and pegged together; the value of a canon in such cases would be to allow pieces to be crafted separately, by different people perhaps, before being assembled as a unit. A grid could also be used straightforwardly to align and lay out pictorial elements alongside human figures within a larger composition [68, 69]. With

68 Deteriorated scene from the tomb chapel of the vizier Ramose, showing standing figures and hieroglyphs while being cut in raised relief, with red-square grid in situ. West Thebes. Limestone. 18th Dynasty.

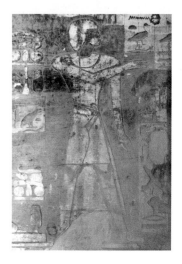

69 Scene from the tomb chapel of the marine commander Ahmose, showing standing figures and hieroglyphs while being cut in raised relief, with red-square grid in situ. West Thebes. Limestone. 18th Dynasty.

the hypothetical guidelines removed from the stela of Mereri, it is apparent that the artist has allowed the man's staff to act as one of the vertical guidelines for the hieroglyphic text [64], thereby breaking down any barrier between the image and the writing, which in turn adds crucial information to the image – not least the hieroglyphs isolated between the staff and Mereri's leg, which are the very ones that spell his name. Of course, his name and perhaps his face may be the only aspects of the representation of Mereri that are taken from life, not simply generated from the standard treatment of the human form.

In wall-painting the grid was typically applied in red before the actual figures were drawn freehand in black [63], though [62] illustrates the opposite practice. Not uncommonly superimposed lines survive to indicate corrections made by an overseer. Allied to the experienced eye of a single overseer, a canon of proportions would tend to generate consistency overall even within a monumental scene. A canon also allowed the 'crews' of artists to collaborate over large areas by developing co-ordinated guidelines or grids in predetermined spaces. In the tomb of Suemniut, the artist or artists have begun three smaller registers behind the principal figure, but not by extending the grid used for the principal [70]. Instead, the artists have divided the height of the principal figure into three parts, apparently by eye, and drawn baselines for three registers accordingly. Then guidelines drawn parallel to the baselines – but not separate grid squares – mark the lines of the knees, shoulders and top of the head, to establish the proportions of the minor figures. Because the lines have been plotted freely, there are inconsistencies between the registers in terms of how the figures have eventually been sketched (for example, the figure in the upper register does not even reach the guideline for the top of the head). Likewise, the hypothetical grid in [67] does not seem to extend to the smaller figure, whose height relative to the seated figure seems to have been determined by eye. In other words, grids may be a useful organizing device but they were not used slavishly in every aspect of a composition, and the artists using them were generally skilled and experienced at their business.

Once the scenes were sketched in and corrected, wherever relief work was required the artists used pounders and drills to cut the figures in sunk relief, or wear down and smooth the background to release the figures for raised relief, which was the more delicate medium preferred for interiors [6]. Thereafter details were modelled with bronze chisels. In decorating walls and columns cut from the living rock, Egyptian sandstone and especially limestone was soft and friable as often as not, so a layer of plaster was frequently applied and modelled as necessary. Likewise, mistakes were often 'fluked' by recarving or replastering, so where the plaster layer is now lost a scene may be entirely confusing to modern eyes. A skim of fine gypsum plaster would be the final preparation for the arrival of the painters.

70 Draft scene from the tomb chapel of the king's butler Suemniut. West Thebes. Plastered and painted limestone. 18th Dynasty.

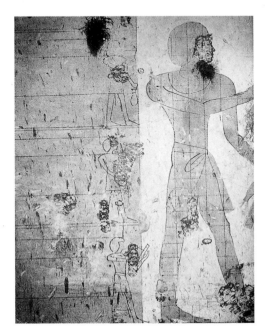

71 View of the burial chamber of the mayor of Thebes Sennefer. West Thebes. Plastered and painted limestone. 18th Dynasty.

People together

In a painting of the Mayor of Thebes, Sennefer – seated in his tomb with his (probably) first wife, Meryt – the table before them is laden with food, which the texts tell us is a funerary offering (see Chapter 9) [71]. As expected, the food is illustrated not in a naturalistic fashion but by building up a composite 'pile' of items, each of which is shown using a distinctive view. The items include a bowl of onions hovering 'impossibly', topped off with a bouquet of lotuses (for which, see below) because the artist simply prefers to let the meaningful elements fill the available space. Consequently the composition becomes filled with both colour and information, while no item is allowed to obstruct the view of another. The same is true, though, of the married couple, who have been drawn sitting in a line so both figures are clearly illustrated. Of course, this does not confuse the eye in the first viewing because they are 'obviously' sitting at the table together, while the wife is seen to embrace the husband (see p. 17). Because of the apparent position of Meryt's arms our eyes may tell us she is embracing Sennefer with her left arm, in which case she would be sitting on her husband's right and nearer to us than he is. However, her knees are tucked behind his bottom, which suggests she is on the far side of him – as though this were a visual puzzle by M. C. Escher. Of course, in two dimensions she can neither be nearer nor farther away and the artist is merely seeking to characterize their relationship through the embrace, while emphasizing their togetherness through the proximity of their legs. Their respective positions in relation to us, as viewers, are of no significance whatsoever. However, in order to hold the figures apart and still show the couple seated 'in tandem', the artist supplies a 'chair' for the husband to sit on. This conceit avoids confusing the eye by showing Sennefer's backside seemingly suspended in mid-air. On the other hand, repeating only part of the chair allows us to deduce (or simply suppose, without even noticing) that he does not have a chair separate from his wife's. Again, the artist is seeking to create forms that remain acceptable to the eye, while presenting the relevant information – both literal and abstract – as clearly and concisely as possible.

At Ramose's party each couple has been separated out, which creates the impression they are seated in rows, at least if we analyse the scene [72]. (At first glance, there is simply a

72 Scene of family guests in the tomb chapel of the vizier Ramose. West Thebes. Painted limestone relief. 18th Dynasty.

120

73 Detail of [5] showing musicians and dancers, from the tomb chapel of Nebamun. West Thebes. Painted plaster. 18th Dynasty.

large gathering of people.) The artist has also created the same improbable 'six-legged' chairs to suggest a single seat for each. The married couples are shown embracing, though the two men at the back of the scene overlap more conspicuously, partly because there is no embrace here to illustrate and partly because their bodies have the same gender, so the form of one may be deduced directly from that of the other. (Our expectation has to be that a human body in pharaonic art will adopt a standard, composite form, so one man obscured by his companion will probably have the same body form.) Specific information about who each figure may be is given only in the accompanying hieroglyphic inscriptions. Otherwise, the illustrations conform to expectations and the pictorial information is not specific to individuals. For each pair, one member holds a bouquet of lotuses, a plant whose daily flowering in ponds is a specific symbol of rebirth in pharaonic tombs, but the rest of the 'real-world' information in the composition is an illustration of subjects such as togetherness, beauty and love – which in itself is no mean testament.

On the other hand, parties and get-togethers are often the best examples we have – in the formal, sacred setting of most pharaonic art – that artists were not necessarily bound by such conventions as a canon of proportions or standard composite figures. For example, the parade of figures from the tomb of Ramose is immediately recognizable in Nebamun's party scene too, but here the vignette of musicians and dancers has a different character [73]. The faces and bodies of two musicians are shown from the front, while dancers beside them bend and twist in genuine profile in front of a rack of wine jars 'labelled' as such with grapes and garlanded with more lotuses. The dancers adopt dynamic forms – twisting away from the upright, while one kicks a foot up off the baseline – though they are scaled to maintain eye contact with the seated musicians. The musicians' braids also

74 Detail showing a serving girl, from a scene in the tomb chapel of the vizier Rekhmira. Plastered and painted limestone. 18th Dynasty.

75 Scene of a board game at the entrance to the burial chamber of the tomb of Sennedjem (see [57]). Deir el-Medina, West Thebes. 19th Dynasty.

'dance' conspicuously as their heads bob out of the upright and their pleated dresses sway.

In a well-known scene from the tomb of Rekhmira, a serving girl has her back turned fully towards us as she leans to pour drinks for the more formal figures [74]. As she does so her braids fall across her face and either side of her shoulders, creating depth for her torso and avoiding the static 'over-the-shoulder' pose characteristic of more formal figures. Her eye, though treated in the standard fashion, now glances from behind the braids and, as she pours the alcohol, she is 'speaking' the knowing words, *'for your spirit – have the perfect day'*. About her there is an obvious eroticism, her bare bottom visible through the sheath 'dress' – which is no doubt the usual artistic conceit – emphasized by a slender belt that has settled on her waist. We scarcely notice how the composite arrangement of her feet threatens to trip her up. However, we may recall the 'same' serving girl pouring drinks at Nebamun's party, breaking up the formal parade of men and women, adding a hint of licence and intoxication to the walls of a chamber of death. In these two scenes different artists have allowed themselves to manipulate attractive human forms to create dynamic and engaging poses and add alluring overtones, which are all the more powerful for how they contrast with our expectations of pharaonic art (see also Chapter 14).

76 Scene of a board game in the first chamber of the tomb of queen Nefertiry. Valley of the Queens, West Thebes. 19th Dynasty.

Amid so much togetherness, we leave this topic with a scene of Sennedjem and Iyneferti side by side, ready to play a board game, though confronted by a table of offerings [75]. In fact, this scene is not uncommon in the tombs at Thebes during the New Kingdom, to which we are going to return in Chapter 11. The same composition appears in the nearby tomb of Nefertiry, the Great Wife of Ramesses II, but her version of the scene obliges us to recognize that the deceased Sennedjem and Iyneferti are playing on the same side [76]. Who is the opponent? What are the rules of the game?

Masterpiece
Nebamun with his wife and daughter capturing water-fowl

77 Fishing and fowling scene from the tomb chapel of Nebamun. West Thebes. Painted plaster. 0.98 m (3 ft 3 in.) high. 18th Dynasty.

The scene of Nebamun with his wife and daughter capturing water-fowl in the marshes has been among the treasures of the British Museum since the mid-19th century. Originally, the scene had a counterpart showing Nebamun spearing fish, like the composition in the tomb of Sabni [56]. As in the previous Masterpiece, showing Sennedjem and Iyneferti ploughing, there is a beautiful – not to say captivating – aspect to the scene. Handsome young people, elegant clothing, a vivid landscape, exotic birds and butterflies, inflated, gawping fish and a playful cat are all irresistible in their own ways. The birds' naturalistic plumage is detailed, vibrant and downy; the cat's soft fur is dappled and sleek, his eye sparkling with gold leaf; and the artist has been able to render the fish under water with sharp, glassy colours. However, the reeds are so stark and impressionistic as to prefigure a modern graphic design, and – as with the scene of Sennedjem – there are other conceits that guide us away from the initial, literal interpretation of the scene towards a deeper meaning.

The man is dressed for the marshes in little more than his finest linen kilt, banded collar and beaded bracelets, as well as a wig whose bead-tipped braids exemplify the fashion of the late 18th Dynasty. His wife is drawn so small that her scale seems unlikely to represent their relative heights in life. More to the point, his wife's clothing is ridiculously inappropriate for hunting, and most resembles the clothing of the ladies at Ramose's party (see p. 120). Her pleated dress is so fine it barely conceals her body, while the conical daub of unguent on her head, suffused with the textures of the dress and hairband, tells us that she is perfumed. The fashionable details of her wig and hairband do not disguise an obvious comparison with the appearance of the lady Nofret, 1,000 years earlier [50]. She also holds a bunch of lotuses, and her daughter reaches out to grasp the lotuses flowering in the marsh with one hand, while the other grasps her father. If the daughter's scale suggests an infant, her physical form is that of a small adult, which is typical in the treatment of children.

If, once again, we allow ourselves to be guided away from the obvious by such inconsistencies, we see that Nebamun's pose is analogous to that of king Narmer [9], and he assumes the same dynamic line from his striking hand to the birds he has captured. While the birds round him seem to create a flurry of movement, in fact all is calm. The bottom of the papyrus boat has been fitted with an improbable wooden 'plank' to serve as the horizontal baseline, though the boat otherwise has a curved profile. The movement in Nebamun himself is implicit, his feet fixed on the baseline with only an ankle raised, while the birds in his grasp seem to glide in formation. The birds ahead of him are perching on the reeds. Only the golden-eyed cat seems genuinely active, disembowelling birds in front of Nebamun in the same way that the falcon disembowels enemies in the marshes in front of Narmer. Even the throw-stick in Nebamun's striking hand turns out on close inspection to be a conceit – a snake. We may be certain that Egyptian officials did not really throw snakes at birds, so what does this conceit mean? Perhaps it evokes the uraeus-cobra on the brow of each king? However, formally the snake seems more likely to be a specific hieroglyph [16], perhaps here spelling the word 'time'. If such an interpretation seems fanciful, then note the caption behind Nebamun, which tells us that he is *'enjoying seeing the perfect place from the position of an eternity of life happy and without sadness'*. So, the hieroglyphs do spell out the spiritual meaning of the scene, the deeper meaning urged on us by so many inconsistencies in any literal interpretation of a scene in which a family is simply hunting for birds.

PART III   ART IN CONTEXT

Chapter 8 'The First Instance': The Earliest Art of Pharaonic Egypt

Ancient Egyptian art belongs to sacred, contemplative contexts, especially to the temples and tombs that in turn become places of offering. Although the art itself often was destined for darkness or for spaces visited only by specific officiants, the act of making art (as well as the architecture it graced) organized, exemplified, instantiated and celebrated human relationships: relationships with one another, with authority, with divinity, with the fact of Creation, and with the meaning of things. As such, pharaonic art rarely belongs to the particular or to the moment, still less to the artist, but seeks to illustrate and invoke what is perpetual and eternal, not as ideals but as the key to making sense of lives and events — the archetype by which to comprehend the individual, and the individual by which to recognize Truth.

Of course, when discussing a culture as ancient as Egypt a fascinating challenge is to appreciate how fundamental, familiar and challenging ideas first emerge. Chapter 1 discussed how early dynastic art, notably the palette of king Narmer, already embodies templates for many images that typically appear later. On the other hand, there are also the little differences and discrepancies that occur when people first try to get things just right. Hence, Chapter 3 looked at how the shape of the tumulus in the royal tomb changed and developed as new thoughts and new inspirations were directed towards the nation's most sacred act, the king's burial, and equally as new knowledge was gained about practical matters such as building on a monumental scale.

Nonetheless, even in the broad historical sweep of pharaonic art, there is a ghostly prescience about the ivory figurine showing one of the earliest kings just as we may expect to see him at any period [79]. The figurine was discovered in an ancient cache of early dynastic material, and though recognizably pharaonic is also worn in interesting ways by the resourceful passage of time. Still, the veneer of antiquity must not be mistaken for the primitive or naïve because this piece was once finely detailed, brightly coloured and carved with aplomb. In its original condition it would not look out of place in a collection of royal images from Egypt in 250 BC or 1400 BC, let alone nearly 3000 BC, which is what its archaeological

79 Ivory figure of an early king. 9 cm (3½ in.) high. Probably 1st or 2nd Dynasty.

context requires. Woven stripes are marked in a heavy cloak draped round the king's shoulders, evidently the cloak worn by the king during the tail festival (see p. 41). His arms are suggested beneath the cloak, until the hands emerge to grasp one another and its hem trails out of his grip. Though the king's ears seem oddly distended at first glance, the weight of the tall White Crown upon them soon becomes apparent, though their intrusive, bovine appearance also recalls the disproportionately large ears usually associated with statues of Middle Kingdom pharaohs (see p. 97). His face – sullen or determined, according to taste – is consistent with the slight but conspicuous stoop of his shoulders, which may evoke responsibility or the wisdom of a grand age. This stoop – the slightest shift from the expected upright – and the tiny size of the piece indicate that it was not intended to receive offerings, though it might have been an element within an offering itself, after the manner of various other human-shaped ivories and ceramics deposited in temples and tombs of late pre-dynastic and early dynastic date.

In fact, this single figurine is not only an archetype of the pharaoh but also an epitome of kingship in Egypt as it will now be repeated through the coming millennia. Early in human history this may be, but values and beliefs known from later eras seem fully formed already in the 1st Dynasty. For example, the text of a label in the burial of Qa'a, last king of the Dynasty, reports various activities integral to the kingship in perpetuity, not least building temples, celebrating the festivals of kingship, and even building festival boats [80]. Earlier still, an ebony label from the tomb of Aha, the second king, includes images alongside the writing [81]. Clearly the king's Horus-name appears in the top register, facing the marked gateway to a rectangular enclosure, apparently a temple of the goddess Neith. Here a conspicuous tumulus or tent stands at the far right, beyond a walled courtyard, while a boat with a decorated cabin hovers above, as though ready either to emerge for a festival or travel the sky with the Sun. In the second register, a bull (the king?) is charging in front of a building or a tent marked with an indeterminate bird (the palace? the temple of Horus?). On the opposite side a human figure (a priest? the king?) is shown in Hieraconpolis presenting a bowl, above which are hieroglyphs seemingly writing 'authority' or perhaps 'electrum'. The third register shows boats sailing apparently to agricultural ceremonies (or temple foundation ceremonies?) at a pair of named towns or estates. Finally, a bottom line of hieroglyphs labels the offerings in the jar to which the label was originally attached. Once more, there is nothing here that cannot be interpreted

80 Ivory label for aromatic oil from the burial of king Qa'a, apparently dated to a festival of Horus at Hieraconpolis. Abydos. 1st Dynasty.

81 Ebony label for aromatic oil from the burial of king Aha. The last line of text seems to mention the temple at Coptos (see [85]). Abydos. 10 cm (4 in.) wide. 1st Dynasty.

straightforwardly in terms of later beliefs and practices. That being so, there is nothing apart from the king's name that precludes a different interpretation, a point to which we shall return below.

At such an early date ambiguity may also arise in purely historical terms: do we attach a special significance to the first occurrence of a particular image or scene? However repetitive a scene may seem to become in later ages, do we treat its first occurrence as a singular event – not licensed by simple convention and therefore authentically 'historical'? For example, a handsome ivory label from the tomb of king Den is another example of the 'smiting scene', the classic image of the king literally imposing his authority on the earth by crushing his enemies' heads [82]. Hence

82 Ivory label for sandals in the burial of king Den. Abydos. 5 cm (2 in.) wide. 1st Dynasty.

83 One of a pair of restored lions from the temple of Min at Coptos. Limestone. 1.33 m (4 ft 4 in.) long. Probably 1st or 2nd Dynasty.

the enemy is on his knees, and his land is a formless desert that constitutes a baseline only where Den treads. The king is not only wearing a bull's tail, he is specifically identified as 'the bull' (see p. 101). In fact, the principal text across the label apparently says '*the first instance of striking the east by the bull*'. Therefore the question may arise, is this scene commemorating the first such attack in Egyptian history or is it simply the first instance during Den's reign? Each reader's answer is likely to betray their preconceived expectations of what art is, and how history should be.

Lion kings

There is much else among the monuments of early kings we may recognize from later days, and may surmise would have had the same significance originally as we can establish with more certainty later. For example, two fragmentary lions found near the temple of Min at Coptos [83], possibly the oldest monumental sculptures that have come down to us, seem to recall elements of temples dating to two and three thousand years later, where sphinxes (of falcons, rams and other animals, as well as lions) often flanked entrances, and sometimes whole avenues of sphinxes lined processional approaches (see pp. 238–39). Although we do not know how the lions were originally employed at Coptos, a comparison with later practice seems straightforward. Likewise, the lions also evoke later poetry and hymns literally lionizing the king (see pp. 236–37). At first, the Coptos lions seem benign, grinning almost comically, their tails flicked onto their flanks. They may even be wearing muzzles, as do the oddly entwined 'big cats' on Narmer's palette. Nonetheless, the snarling lips, bared fangs and pendant tongues, presumably directed at anyone approaching a particular entrance, evoke imminent violence in a manner analogous to the predatory serenity of the royal falcon (see pp. 34–35).

Henceforth the leonine sphinx, often displaying the human face and headdress of the king, would remain a standard expression of the royal presence. Indeed, in modern imagination the Great Sphinx, beside the causeway to Khafra's pyramid, has become both the essence and the icon of the antiquity of Egyptian kingship (see pp. 128–29). During the New Kingdom, already 1,000 years after it was first sculpted, the Great Sphinx was named 'Happening-Sun-Creator-Horus-in-the-horizon', a boggling definition of the divine presence risen in the earth. To this day, he sits on guard at Giza, as formidably imperturbable as his primeval forebears once were at Coptos.

On the other hand, the violence of the royal lion is actually unleashed on the Battlefield Palette, which is one of a group of schist palettes (including Narmer's palette) decorated with violent images and dating to the moment of transition to the first kings. Typically, the obverse face of the palette has a central hoop [84], as though it were a space for mineral grinding. This face also shows corpses as carrion pitilessly scattered about a battlefield, amid scavenging vultures and crows. The carnage is being wrought by the lion, seen savaging a broken carcass. In front of him a naked, bound prisoner walks before a cloaked official, while above him two more naked prisoners are tied to standards, recalling the standards parading past the decapitated ranks on Narmer's

84 Obverse of the Battlefield Palette. Probably from Abydos. Mudstone. 33 cm (1 ft 1 in.) high (preserved fragments). 1st Dynasty or earlier.

85 Reverse of the Battlefield Palette.

palette. The prisoners are as trapped and helpless as the birds in Nebamun's hands (see p. 125).

The reverse is a more cryptic composition and the total loss of the top of the palette hampers our understanding [85]. A pair of giraffes or antelopes (gerenuks?) graze on a date palm, while a fancy bird (a guineafowl?) looks on. Neither kind of animal is prominent in later art, so how should we interpret the scene? Is it, at face value, a bucolic alternative to war, a far-off exotic land like Punt (see p. 207) or, more topically, the view of a conquered land? Are there themes here about kingship that we fail to recognize because, unlike the bull and lion, these animals did not survive into later imagery? If we apply the 'hieroglyphic' interpretation and 'read' the scene (see pp. 98–101), we must take our readings from hieroglyphs otherwise known only centuries later to suggest a text about 'foreseeing sweetness', which would certainly be a telling counterpoint to the battlefield but nevertheless seems like interpretation as special pleading. No doubt, without later variations on a scene or its main elements to guide our comprehension, any interpretation of its meaning this early in Egyptian history is speculative at best.

86 Palette in the shape of a river-going boat with central cabin or shrine. Unknown provenance. Schist. 25 cm (10 in.) long. Pre-dynastic, 4th millennium BC.

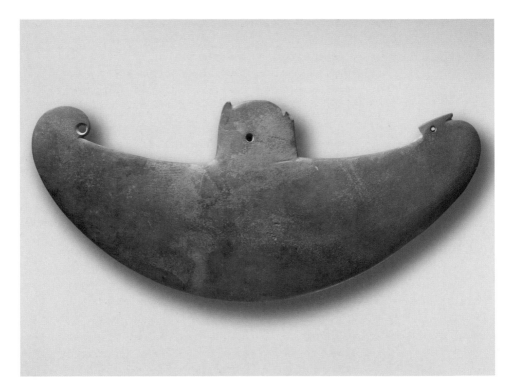

87 Palette in the shape of a river-going boat decorated with animals. Unknown provenance. Schist. Pre-dynastic, 4th millennium BC.

Boats 'like a burnish'd throne'

Insofar as the miscellany of animal images is characteristic of pharaonic art, this was already the case at the dawn of the 3rd millennium BC, including artworks that may pre-date the first pharaoh, Narmer. This is not only the case with animals. For example, the pairing of animals with boats, another staple of pharaonic art, elicits a theme we can follow from the ages of the pharaohs back to an earlier flowering of art in pre-dynastic Egypt.

Because pre-dynastic homes, workplaces and temples were built using perishable materials, few traces survive even in the rare instances where the archaeology is not entirely lost beneath later settlements. Consequently, most of our information about Egyptian art during the 4th millennium BC derives from cemeteries, in which the most obvious archaeological phenomenon is the emergence and spread of a burial tradition often termed 'Naqada culture'. In fact, Naqada – the site of ancient Ombos, midway between Hieraconpolis and Abydos – is simply where this burial tradition was first identified by archaeologists, and by no means the presumed origin of 'Naqada culture'. More to the point, within this 'Naqada' burial tradition – among the grave goods placed with the dead – various characteristic objects, forms and images become common all over Egypt, and parts of Nubia, at some distance in time before the first kings. The numbers of cemeteries and burials involved are significant so, though we cannot be certain exactly how a common burial tradition relates to widely held beliefs or patterns of life shared by different communities, we may presume that there is some sort of relationship. In 'Naqada culture' graves, animal imagery is prominent in various features, such as the painted decoration of ceramic jars or forms sculpted in schist, ivory and so on, including palettes, game pieces and decorated knives. Such items often seem too large, too small or too elaborate to have had an obvious practical use, whereas a straightforward comparison to animal imagery in pharaonic times suggests that the objects are associated somehow with gods and religion. For example, a boat-shaped palette may be incised with animal images or its curved prow and stern may take the forms of animals [86, 87]. If this were an appropriately decorated festival boat, or an abstract image combining a god and his boat in procession, then we discern clear connection to pharaonic art, and indeed pharaonic religious practice.

88 Rock-drawing showing processional boats and animals, the top boat carrying a central figure with raised arms and a plumed headdress. Wadi Barramiya, in the desert east of Edfu. Presumably pre-dynastic, 4th millennium BC.

89 Rock-drawing showing a processional boat with several cabins or shrines and animals. Wadi Hellal, in the desert near el-Kab. Presumably pre-dynastic, 4th millennium BC.

Moreover, images of boats with high prows and decorated cabins, accompanied by tall, elegant figures with crowns and sceptres, appear away from cemeteries in rock-drawings conventionally dated to the late 4th and early 3rd millennium BC [88, 89]. These drawings are not uncommon on promontories and steep rock-faces throughout the principal *wadis* (seasonally dry river valleys), which cut through the deserts to create highways into the Nile Valley. Some boats have dozens of rowers, while others are pulled by ropes. In their own context, we may think the meaning of these boats uncertain, but once again the art of later times simply suggests they are festival boats of gods in procession before priests and other worshippers (see pp. 194–201). If so, the decorated 'cabins' would actually be the shrines from temples and occasionally, in fact, other evocative images, such as a bull or a crescent, sit on board in place of a 'cabin'. Figures with regalia may be gods or priests or perhaps the nascent images of proto-kings, while more slender figures with upraised arms may be their female equivalents. We may imagine an ancient vision akin to 'the barge she sat in, like a burnish'd throne, / burn'd on the water: the poop was beaten gold / purple the sails' (*Antony and Cleopatra II*, Act 2: 2). If so, art in 'Naqada culture' was religious in character, tied to festivals, and this flowering in late pre-dynastic times had the same basic inspiration as monumental art in the pharaonic era.

90 The 'Gebel el-Arak' knife handle, showing fighting in the vicinity of processional boats. Probably from Naqada. 26 cm (10½ in.) high. Ivory. Pre-dynastic, late 4th millennium BC.

91 The other side of the 'Gebel el-Arak' knife, showing the 'lion-strangler' at top, plus the flint blade. Pre-dynastic, late 4th millennium BC.

On the other hand, could we not postulate that 'Naqada culture' boats meant something completely different in their own time? For example, perhaps the spread of 'Naqada culture' in cemeteries is evidence of the immigration of a 'boat-people' into Egypt – the record of a singular prehistoric event. To play Devil's advocate, a magnificently carved pre-dynastic knife handle among the treasures of the Louvre is said to have come from Gebel el-Arak, in the general vicinity of Naqada [90, 91]. In the exquisite decoration, among familiar images of violence, animals and so on, the dramatic intrusion of a so-called 'lion-strangler' – an artistic motif well known in contemporary Mesopotamia – may be interpreted as the mark of foreigners in Egypt around the time of the first pharaohs. In other words, could this be evidence not just of the influence of foreign crafts and foreign ideas but of foreign invaders? In which case, perhaps even the origin of pharaonic art is to be found outside Egypt. Of course, here is the nub: questions of origins are a notorious problem in prehistory, generally because there is little unequivocal, objective information. Modern scholarship tends to maintain that people arrived in Egypt to take up farming when the Nile floodplains became significantly drier, probably some time between 6,500 and 9,000 years ago. Without overstating the evidence, presumably people had been living on higher ground round the fringes of the Nile for such a long time before farming was adopted – perhaps even tens of thousands of years – that the only meaningful explanation of where Egyptians originally came from may well be … elsewhere in Egypt. In other words, there is no compelling reason to suppose that the people who populated or eventually ruled the Nile floodplains came from one place, at one time, nor indeed for one reason. On the other hand, many scholars in the 20th century – when speculation on the formative role of race, immigration and miscegenation in human origins was rife – did reach that very conclusion, which serves to demonstrate how tentative any conclusions about prehistory must be. In the 21st century, how we discuss the first inklings of pharaonic art in prehistory, and its connections with art elsewhere in the world, is essentially still going to be determined not by the nature of the evidence but by our own expectations of early human activity, and that discussion lies beyond the scope of this book.

Masterpiece
'Tomb 100', or the 'Painted Tomb', Hieraconpolis

92 Copy of the wall decoration, now lost, from 'Tomb 100' (the 'Painted Tomb'), Hieraconpolis. Plastered and painted limestone. 1st Dynasty or earlier.

At Hieraconpolis, an entire city dating back to the late pre-dynastic and early pharaonic era has been the subject of archaeological excavations since the 1890s. At the heart of the early city was the huge mud-brick enclosure of a temple, later certainly the temple of Horus (see p. 23). In contemporary cemeteries nearby the emergence of elite burials, distinguished by their size and their wealth of grave goods, is quite clear, though what explains their pre-eminence is less obvious. Among them 'Tomb 100' or the 'Painted Tomb', discovered by F. W. Green in 1899, is perhaps the oldest known example of an Egyptian tomb whose rock-cut burial chamber was lined with brick, then plastered and painted. Both the form and content of the wall-paintings bear close comparison to what we may expect during the pharaonic period, aside from the fact that there is no writing of any kind.

The paintings include familiar images rendered crudely with 'stick men': a veritable flotilla of boats with fancy cabins, processions of wild animals and hunting dogs, and several 'smiting scenes'. Even the enigmatic 'lion-strangler' puts in an appearance. At top, a plumed priestess (?) seems to be wailing over the unfolding violence. (Unless she is singing its praises?) Flotillas, men fighting, hunting with dogs – these are all motifs known in later tombs. Do they suggest a military subject, perhaps – celebrate a

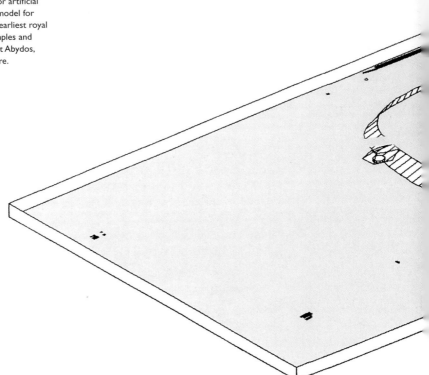

93 Reconstruction of the early dynastic enclosure at Hieraconpolis, which certainly later was a principal temple of Horus. The rectangular enclosure with central mound or artificial tumulus may be the model for (or a parallel of) the earliest royal tombs, mortuary temples and pyramid complexes at Abydos, Saqqara and elsewhere.

proto-king or an elite warrior? How else would we explain such a confluence of riverine activity and violence? Actually, a scene of several boats carrying the images of gods while surrounded by fighting corresponds exactly to the fullest descriptions of the festivals of Osiris at Abydos, though the written accounts were not set down until centuries later. Thus, '*I beat the rebels away from the sacred-boat, and overthrew the enemies of Osiris,*' claims Ikhernofret, an organizer of the festivals in the reign of Senwosret III (c. 1840–c. 1805 BC). What may seem a blatant statement of military might in an anonymous prehistoric context, in an Egyptian funerary context may well turn out to be a representation of one of the primeval festivals of kingship.

'Tomb 100' originally had a simple superstructure, using timber and reeds to create a rectangular wall round a tent or

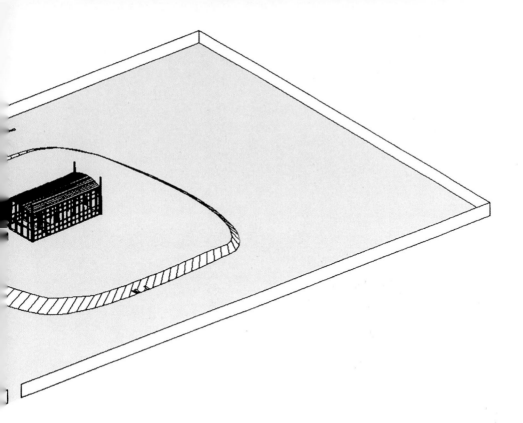

canopy (a 'proto-mastaba'?) covering the actual interment. Quite
possibly the superstructure emulated the form of the temple of
Horus [93], and accordingly may be understood as an ancestor
of the kings' tombs at Abydos and Saqqara. On the other hand,
we must avoid the temptation to assume that crude pictorial
forms and smaller size in relation to other tombs indicate greater
antiquity, or that a tomb without writing has to be prehistoric.
In other words, 'Tomb 100' may not be older than the much
larger and more sophisticated tombs of the kings at Abydos.
Perhaps 'Tomb 100' belonged to a distinguished *contemporary*
of the first kings, a member of the royal family or even a priest
of Horus?

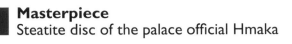

Masterpiece
Steatite disc of the palace official Hmaka

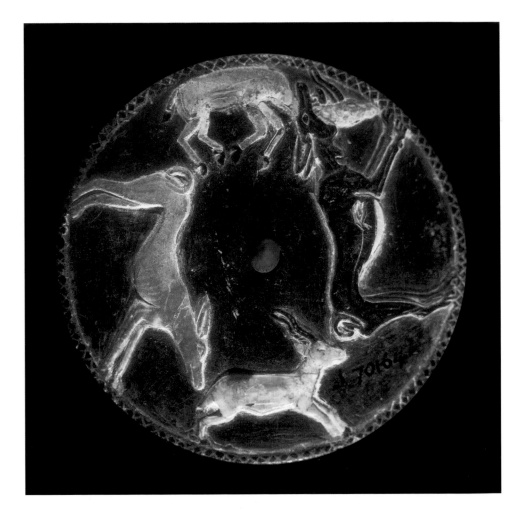

Hmaka was buried at Saqqara, the cemetery of Memphis. According to an ancient tradition, apparently confirmed by archaeology, Memphis was founded as Egypt's administrative capital at the beginning of the pharaonic period. Consequently, Saqqara came to prominence many decades before the Step Pyramid was built here (see p. 50). The earliest Saqqara tombs were constructed with a mastaba over a rock-cut burial chamber. Usually the mastabas had internal chambers, accessible only during construction, to allow for large quantities of offerings. Some at least had an enclosure wall and an offering chapel, while the largest were accompanied by boat burials.

Hmaka's tomb was among the most impressive, a mastaba nearly 60 metres (200 feet) in length. A huge collection found there included the oldest known papyrus writing scrolls, as well as this steatite disc, which is the best preserved of several. They might have been used as gaming pieces. The steatite bed has been carved in relief, with a cable pattern round the edge, to create a naturalistic scene of two dogs hunting gazelles. The black dog is mostly sculpted in the bed, but the highlight on his chest and the whole of his canine partner are inlaid calcite. Their quarry is also inlaid calcite apart from the horns and hooves, which are sculpted from the bed. The dynamic, sinewy dogs are shown in three dimensions, with a hint of perspective as the head of the pale dog closes in on his prey. In accordance with the standard principles of Egyptian art, the animals are arranged to fill the available space and do not hinder the view of one other. Indeed, the figures only touch at one point where, savagely and dramatically, the black dog crushes his victim's throat, courtesy of some precise cutting and inlay.

One great scholar of Egyptian art, Cyril Aldred, noted that the disc was 'an early example of the Egyptian predilection for squaring the circle and thus giving expression to the essential Egyptian feeling for space as rectilinear'. However, this does not mean the ancients could only understand the world in rectilinear terms or were insufficiently skilled to work otherwise. The mere fact of the disc itself is sufficient to demonstrate this and, while each animal is located upon a baseline as we would expect, the baseline is a circle and the dogs' bodies are appropriately curved. Rather, the point is that the ancient artists were able to deduce the meaning of the scene in a structured manner, and devise the most effective layout on that basis. The success of this scene in decorating the whole face of a disc is testament to how effective they were in their analysis, not how limited.

94 Decorated disc from the tomb of Hmaka. Saqqara. Steatite. 10 cm (4 in.) diameter. 1st Dynasty.

Chapter 9 'Stride Perfected on Perfect Paths': The Noble Offering Cult

Can a man or woman be worshipped after the manner of a god? In pharaonic Egypt the answer was yes, if he or she attained *duat* – literally, the state of 'Adoration' (see p. 38). Though some men, such as Amenhotep, son of Hapu (see Chapter 4), or the governor Pepynakht, whom we will meet later, were revered as exceptional even in life, the exceptional is not the issue here (see pp. 252–53). Rather, the Osiris myth allows that anyone may follow the mortal king into duat. Among Osiris' alternative names was Khentyimentu, meaning 'he who is ahead of the westerners': as the first to die he has gone to the sunset before us all to open the paths beyond death. Among the prayers for Ptahshepses we find '*an offering Khentyimentu, lord of Abydos, gives – bread and beer at the new month, the half-month, and every festival every day for all time that he [the deceased] may stride perfected on perfect paths, which revered ones stride before the great god, the lord of burial*' (see pp. 74–77). Consequently, 'Adoration' of the dead requires an appropriate space (the tomb chapel), appropriate acts (recitations and offerings), and a community of priests or officiants (the surviving family). Out of this requirement were born three of the characteristic media discussed in Part 2, namely the tomb statue, the offering stela and decorated tomb walls (the last of which we will return to in Chapter 11).

The statue of Meryrahashtef is most revealing: as a man of dignity and authority, wearing a fashionable wig and cosmetics, he hardly expected to be displayed naked [95]. Rather, his acacia-wood image was designed to be clothed in a manner that emulated a ritual for the gods entitled 'the business of the chapel of adoration'. An officiant entered the chapel speaking prescribed recitations, before introducing a light and kissing the ground. He or she purified the area with incense, then poured out a small mound of earth ('the Risen Earth'). The statue was placed on the mound and purified in turn with incense, unguents, water and natron (using vessels of prescribed shapes), wrapped in linen cloths of different styles, colours and sizes, then adorned with a collar. Lastly the statue was touched with various tools or sceptres and returned to its shrine or niche, after which the

95 Statue of the courtier and priest Meryrahashtef, one of a group of three showing him at different ages. Sidmant, near Heracleopolis. Painted ebony. 0.58 m (1 ft 9 in.) high with base. 6th Dynasty.

96 Statue representing the spirit of king Hor, with inlaid eyes and traces of a gilded collar, standing in its wooden shrine. Dahshur. Wood. 1.7 m (5 ft 7 in.) high. 13th Dynasty.

97 Statue of Ankhwa. Probably Saqqara. Granite. 0.66 m (2 ft 2 in.) high. 3rd Dynasty.

officiant withdrew from the chapel, brushing away any footprints [98]. The same purification was applied every day to the statue of every god or goddess in the principal shrine of every temple. Even the morning toilet of the king is presented as a version of the same 'business', and an analogous rite called 'opening the mouth' was used to consecrate every new statue and enable it to receive offerings [96].

Wooden tomb statues are relatively uncommon in the surviving record but stone images showing the official dressed and carrying symbols of authority are absolutely typical of non-royal tombs at every period. Usually they were enshrined in a rock-cut niche or a simple stone box, known as a *serdab* after a modern Egyptian word for a cellar. As was the case when representing kings, artists developed archetypes for representing officials early in history, then used them through three millennia with variations only in details of dress, hairstyles, specific placement of hands and so on. For example, the statue of Ankhwa, a carpenter and shipwright (perhaps of the boats of the gods' festivals) during the 3rd Dynasty, has been carved unfussily out of a granite block to form a cubic chair, whose shape is that of the hieroglyph for 'place' or 'position' [97]. Accordingly Ankhwa occupies an official 'position'. Working in hard stone, the sculptor keeps the details simple but clear: the neck is abbreviated but the face well modelled, as are the powerful legs. There is no clothing other than a kilt, but the definitive tool of his trade – an adze – is slung over his shoulder, and his wig's crimped pleats testify to elegance and grooming beyond that of a jobbing tradesman. A hieroglyphic inscription states his specific identity. Thus, Ankhwa awaits the *'requested offerings'* brought by his family or by priests during the gods' festivals.

The point is that an Egyptian tomb is not just a burial place – first and foremost it is a chapel for the adoration of an immortal presence. The officials' standard tomb has a form derived directly from that of the kings' tombs, based on three elements: (i) a stone-built offering chapel, which adjoins or penetrates (ii) a tumulus – usually a mastaba but, from the New Kingdom, sometimes a pyramid – raised over (iii) a burial chamber. Alternatively the offering chapel and burial chamber may be cut out of the living rock of the desert hills, especially in those areas where the hills sweep close to the Nile. In either case, the undecorated burial chamber sits at the bottom of a steep shaft, often 4 metres (13 feet) or more below the tomb floor, its mouth covered with a dressed slab or discreetly out of sight. On the

98 What purports to be an image of Ramose in his tomb chapel actually shows the purification of his offering-cult statue, dressed in linen with staff and sceptre, standing on a raised base. West Thebes. Limestone. 18th Dynasty.

99 Detail from an offering panel in the form of a niched wall from the tomb chapel of Metjen (cf. [43]). Saqqara. 4th Dynasty.

other hand, the offering chapel is a public area, often decorated throughout with colourful, traditional scenes. Inscriptions round the door ask passers-by (specifically officiants attending other chapels) to say a prayer on behalf of the deceased. The largest chapels have the standard elements of a temple – a straight axis leading through the gateway to a Sun-court, then to one or more hypostyle halls beyond, and finally the offering chapel. In the chapel there may be one or more niches with statues, stelae or false doors, as well as an altar marked for the offerings.

The tomb of Metjen, a royal-estate manager in the 4th Dynasty, may be the earliest extant example of this phenomenon, his tomb chapel having survived in sufficiently good condition to be removed from Saqqara and displayed in Berlin [99]. However, tombs of this kind developed no later than the 1st Dynasty in areas of royal patronage including Hieraconpolis, Giza and Saqqara, before spreading from the 5th Dynasty onwards to include the king's whole domain (see Chapter 10). They are distinct from the 'satellite burials' round the earliest kings' tombs insofar as they are not aspects of another edifice. Rather, each is a place of worship in its own right, whose location usually

100 Statue of Metjen, who rose from obscurity to become one of the king's companions and a member of his elite boat-crew. Like most of the earliest hard-stone statues, this example has no back pillar. Saqqara. Granite. 47 cm (1 ft 6½ in.) high. 4th Dynasty.

overlooks the route of a festival procession. (In fact, the word we translate as 'cemetery' or 'necropolis' is apparently the phrase 'horizon where the god is carried'.) Hence Metjen's statue [100] is not a memorial of the living person but a functional aspect of a cult, whose subject is the adoration of his immortal spirit.

The 5th Dynasty tomb of Rawer at Giza is one of the largest from any period in Egyptian history, royal or otherwise [101]. The entrance is through a Sun-court beside the causeway of Khafra's pyramid, and an exceptional complex of dark passages, hypostyle halls, further Sun-courts and offering chapels extends more than 100 metres (328 feet) to his burial shaft. There are some twenty-five serdabs, several of which have multiple statues or slots for viewing, cut from different angles. Until this time serdabs completely enclosed the offering statues, which could be seen but not reached; like false doors, they marked the line between the living and the dead (see p. 75). However, from this time on serdabs could be entered and some of Rawer's even incorporate steps. (Another innovation is the choice of limestone for his statues, the use of granite and other hard stones having become exceptional for non-royal statues by the 4th Dynasty.) The excavator, Selim Hassan, estimated that there were originally more than a hundred statues of Rawer in the tomb, at least

101 View of an open Sun-court in the offering complex of Rawer. The ramp leads to the shrine in which his biographical inscription appeared. Giza. 5th Dynasty.

103 Archive image of the triad of Rawer as discovered in its serdab.

two of which show him in triplicate and perhaps relate to the contemporary triads of kings (see pp. 58–60) [102, 103].

A sequence of biographical inscriptions also punctuated his tomb, though only one is sufficiently well preserved to be legible. This is a limestone block originally set high in a wall behind a chapel door, and facing a life-size statue of Rawer. Unusually the approach to this particular chapel doubles back on the main axis, almost forming a separate chapel with its own Sun-court, hypostyle hall and serdab. The inscription on it goes to the heart of the relationship between king and official, with a remarkable show of affection. It begins, '*The sovereign king Neferirkara made an appearance as sovereign on a day when the god's prow-rope gets taken.*' In other words, the king has arrived in procession at a sacred site – perhaps his own pyramid – by boat and must disembark. Of course, stepping off a boat is among the most awkward manoeuvres faced by any man, divine or otherwise. 'Consequently the priest Rawer was at the feet of his person in his eminence as priest in order to manage the robes, when the staff which was in the grasp of his person struck the foot of the priest Rawer. Whereupon his person said, "Are you all right?"' The crux of the incident was the king's concern for Rawer, and the inscription adds, 'So his person said, "O, beloved of my person, he is fine, one I have not hurt".' As a final note, the account of the incident 'was written beside the king himself at the palace's lake-pavilion'. However, though the king checked the inscription's accuracy at his leisure, and the block was positioned so Rawer's statue would face it in perpetuity, probably no other audience read this text until modern times.

Rawer's inscription is one of many emphasizing that the king was an active figure moving through his realm, while officials constantly attended him or travelled about on his business. To express the wide-ranging authority of these men, early artists developed the archetype of the official as a writer, emphasizing

104 Statue of an official shown as a scribe. Painted limestone with eyes of inlaid rock crystal. Saqqara. 0.54 m (1 ft 9 in.) high. 4th or 5th Dynasty.

how letters and documents keep them close to the king (and his literate culture), even when separated from him in space. The official in a celebrated statue in the Louvre – tentatively identified as a king's brother named Kai – is seated with extended knees stretching his kilt tight to support the scroll he is unrolling from his left hand [104]. The specific pose, showing the scribe as though his right hand were holding a brush, is typical of the 4th and 5th Dynasties, though the same 'writing' pose is used in a statue of Amenhotep, son of Hapu [39], a millennium later, and in one of Harwa 600 years after that (see p. 245).

Of course, the adoration of ancestors and the artistic paraphernalia of the offering cult remained fundamental to pharaonic religious belief until its demise (see Chapter 15). Thus, more than 2,000 years after Kai's passing, an inscription from

105 Statue of an anonymous priest with prominent ears, from the vicinity of the temple of Pnepheros and Petesouchos. Basalt. 1st century AD.

a statue of Senusheri, an artist and engineer, describes him as *'one skilled in writing, to whom understanding came quickly, of whom his lord thought much'* (see p. 66). Later still, from the town of Karanis thriving under Roman government, comes an anonymous, unfinished statue of an official, perhaps a priest to judge from his shaven head [105]. At first glance he still wears no more than a kilt, though the cursory line across his chest may evoke a toga or the leopard skin of a cult-priest. His hands, which in the 5th Dynasty might have held the suggestion of a staff or a brush, have become so stylized they only seem to hold *something*, but he is still seated on the official's cubic seat or 'position' to receive offerings. So much remains the same, it may be hard for us to fathom that the Karanis statue belongs far nearer in time to the reader of this book than to Ankhwa or Metjen.

Portraiture and the self

In a culture predisposed to celebrity, a modern reader may casually assume that any portrait is an attempt to record a physical identity forever or even conjure an imperishable form – 'self-preservation', to use one Egyptologist's phrase. Is this a straightforward assumption? After all, who are you really? What do you really look like? Ancient Egyptian texts rarely use the word 'to be' meaning 'exist' (as in 'to be or not to be – that is the question'), preferring the word 'becomings' (*kheperu*) in the sense that moments are constantly happening. This seems counter-intuitive because, in some sense, surely I am me, and you are you, from one moment to the next. However, look through photographs of yourself aged one, five, ten, twenty … thirty … sixty … and ask yourself what is there at every moment. Then ask which of your ideas, beliefs, values and expectations have remained constant. There are bound to be resemblances of course, but resemblances to what? Something permanent? In what sense are you a constant being, not a sequence of connected 'becomings', each of which immediately passes away? (To be sure, even a football season or a long, hot summer has its own biography.) More to the point, which moments or resemblances are 'the real you'? As ever, in ancient Egyptian art what matters is not the 'you' apparent to the eye at any one specific moment. In this sense, a sculpture of 'you' is an artistic exercise every bit as abstract as sculpting the gods.

On the other hand, in ancient Egyptian funerary texts the verb 'to be' (*wenen*) is often used (see p. 277). In other words, in death we do 'exist'. More than that, the dead are typically said to 'exist

106 Archive image of the statue of Hemiunu as discovered in its serdab.

107 Statue of the 'overseer of all the king's works' Hemiunu. Giza. Painted limestone. 1.55 m (5 ft 1 in.) high. 4th Dynasty.

perfected'; that is, in death we may become who we are meant to be or should be. As the philosopher Ptahhatp notes, '*the wise man is the one who nurtures his soul by realizing on earth the perfection within him*'. The Egyptian phrase 'he who is and perfect' (*wenen nefer*) happens to be another name of Osiris. So just as the shifting mortal frame becomes the true self only in death, following the lead of Osiris / Khentyimentu / Wenennefer, so too the archetype (the statue) represents the individual not in life but during the rituals of 'Adoration' and the mortuary offering cult. Much is made in Egyptology of the 'ideal' in art, which is to say that people may be shown ever young, ever beautiful, free from blemish or deformity, and so on. However, it is important to recognize that this is not the 'perfection' Ptahhatp is talking about. Today we may judge a photographic model or a film star against a phantasmic 'ideal' of beauty and even judge our own looks against an 'ideal' of youth, but Ptahhatp is talking about the relationship between any apple seed – and they all look more or less the same – and the mature, magnificent tree it may become to '*exist perfected*'.

108 Dyad of the courtiers Memi and Sabu. Giza. Painted limestone. 0.62 m (2 ft ½ in.) high. 4th Dynasty.

For example, Hemiunu, cousin or nephew of king Khufu, has been identified as the overseer of the project to construct the Great Pyramid. Certainly he was one of the most dignified people of his day, but in his tomb statue it is impossible to ignore the pendulous breasts of a corpulent, older man – nor those appearing centuries later on the statue from Karanis [105, 106, 107]. Hemiunu's rolls of abdominal flab and flaccid belly are as intrusive as Kai's [104]. Seemingly the grandest folk of Old Kingdom Egypt, in the hands of the most accomplished artists, have statues that highlight the morbidity of flesh because physical decay may be the sign of maturity and increasing wisdom. Ptahhatp prefaces his great philosophical teaching with a moving description of his own extreme old age, lamenting that '*what age does to people is unpleasant in every way*'. Far from eternal youth, this is the radical opposite – spiritual growth. Of course, a statue is a physical object because it cannot be otherwise, but sculpture in a tomb chapel illustrates the authority of the spirit. Hence these statues defy modern expectations of physical perfection and 'self-preservation', which may demand cosmetic surgery and denial of mortality. But then what do we know of the meaning of life, if our only purpose is just to stay alive?

Moreover, if we are moved to tears by something profound in art (or music or sport), we do not feel tied to that moment forever: rather we are moved by the momentary sense of something eternal – the sense of what 'really means something'. Although ancient Egyptian officials did not rally to a flag or anthem, they rallied to their spiritual king, the 'lord of Truth'. Ptahhatp had the following instruction for any official invited to the palace: 'If you get to the Audience-hall, stand and sit at every step. The first day has been ordered for you. ... The Audience-hall is set at the standard, all its conduct measured from plumb.' In the presence of the king, Ptahhatp is saying, we see not what is (now) but what has always been – the standard against which the framework of the present state of affairs may be measured. In the statue of Memi and Sabu [108], a sculptor – albeit one less accomplished than the sculptor available to Hemiunu – has devised contortions to make their embrace visible from the front. Memi's left arm reaches crudely over the shrunken Sabu, though typically their embrace need only be suggested – as it is where Sabu's hand presses against Memi's waist – or simply lost from sight at the back of the sculpture. Consequently their embrace is the most obvious feature of the statue, so what does this all-important gesture mean? A couple first in love may insist they will

109 Anonymous 'reserve head' with its ears knocked off and a rough groove cut from the crown through the back of the head. Giza. Limestone. 30 cm (1 ft) high. 4th Dynasty.

110 Undamaged 'reserve head' from the same tomb as [109]. Consequently this head has been described as the latter's 'wife', though there was only a single burial in the tomb and no specific indication that this head even represents a woman. An alternative suggestion is that one or other of the heads was displaced from another tomb by robbers. Giza. Painted limestone. 30 cm (1 ft) high. 4th Dynasty.

never be parted, while an old married couple might have grown accustomed to one another's face; but these are only episodes, and Memi and Sabu are shown neither ardent nor aged. However, love itself – another spiritual virtue – is the relationship most often specified in the inscriptions of the temples and tombs. So to return to the start of the chapter, Memi and Sabu are not shown falling in love, nor getting married, nor together in the autumn of their years (this is not photography). Rather the statue is a function of the offering cult in which the two *together* are the subject of 'Adoration'. If their statue refers to anything, it talks about who they are perfected in death and what 'really means something', not what they once were when alive. Who could

111 King Tutankhamun shown emerging from a lotus flower. The artwork, whose purpose in his tomb is unknown, may evoke both an act of purification and the god Nefertem, associated with the moment of creation. His youthful appearance is consistent with such iconography and not necessarily, as has been claimed, with a portrait taken from childhood. West Thebes. Plastered and painted wood. 31 cm (1 ft) high. 18th Dynasty.

extrapolate how they look now on the basis of their mortal forms, any more than we could extrapolate the form of the apple tree from the individual pip?

For the purpose of drafting such statues a simple canon of proportion may be sufficient to generate a standard human figure so, in fact, the only possibilities for personalizing or individualizing the figures may be the faces and the ubiquitous hieroglyphic inscriptions. There is obvious artistic utility in making Memi and Sabu's faces different, and an obvious basis for doing so would be their respective appearances in life, at least if these were known to the artist. Of course, there might well have been times when artists 'went through the motions', adding a generic face to an archetypical body, though the cult statue would still be as useful. On the other hand, there are instances when actual portraiture seems the likeliest explanation including, of course, images of kings, which, we may assume, are the work of the finest artists adhering to some official model of the royal face (see p. 221). Other instances also tend to involve the highest strata of society, including the enigmatic 'reserve heads' (a modern designation) found among the tombs of the royal family in the Old Kingdom cemeteries [109, 110]. The enigma is precisely that they are only heads, shown with close-cropped hair or skullcaps and no body. Each has been modelled – from the same brilliant white limestone used to case the Giza pyramids – so precisely that George Reisner, who found most of the known examples, claimed he could identify family relationships among the subjects. Typically the heads have distinctive deep-cut eyes and nostrils, though even more characteristically the ears are often chipped away or carefully chiselled off, and at least half have grooves gouged more or less crudely down the back. All the known 'reserve heads' were found in obviously disturbed contexts or in the subterranean burial – in some instances on the floor beside the coffin – but never in a tomb chapel, so they were not the subjects of offerings like the statues discussed earlier. Indeed, any conclusions about portraiture drawn from 'reserve heads' must be qualified by the fact that their original use is entirely unknown. They are an exceptional phenomenon: only thirty-one have ever been discovered, all dating to the end of the 4th Dynasty. More than half come from a single cemetery at Giza, the rest from the immediate vicinity. Undoubtedly the actual faces of these royal individuals were relevant for some unknown purpose but there is no indication the sculptures had an intended audience following the interment – any more than, say, the astonishing mask of king Tutankhamun (c. 1332–c. 1323 BC) (see pp. 212–15).

Analogous examples of isolated human heads modelled above the miniature scale are likewise hard to come by. A wooden model of Tutankhamun's head emerging out of a lotus [111] may be an artistic interpretation of a purification ritual, and as such offer a clue to interpreting the use of 'reserve heads'. However, Tutankhamun is so far removed in time from the 4th Dynasty that the examples seem disconnected, or at best tenuously connected by some unsubstantiated factor. Other apparent analogies are the so-called 'ancestor busts' (another modern designation) known from the 18th and 19th Dynasties. These derive from slightly less elevated social circumstances than 'reserve heads', and most are no more than 25 centimetres (10 inches) tall, though a handful are near life-size. Formally 'ancestor busts' are individual heads modelled on top of a shapeless, vaguely anthropoid base, the latter occasionally decorated with a collar or a lotus flower. Each has a distinct face, but none is modelled so clearly and attractively as the 'reserve heads'. Are their less specific faces the product of less able artists or a different intention? A handful of offering scenes show these 'busts' as the subject of a purification ritual, though several examples were found in houses and others might

112 False door in the tomb chapel of the high priest Idu. Giza. Painted limestone. 6th Dynasty.

have come from temples rather than tombs. So they may have some uncertain association with the offering cult but, other than their form, they have no obvious connection to the much more ancient 'reserve heads'. Moreover, 'ancestor busts' are a specific phenomenon: no more than 150 are known, half of them from the village at Deir el-Medina and, according to one interpretation, they represent only women. Are they intended as portraits? In fact some scholars suggest they are intentionally generic, intended for use when offering to any ancestor.

A great deal of ink was spilled during the 19th and 20th centuries regarding the first appearance of 'portraiture', 'naturalism' and 'the individual' in the art of the * (here insert your own preferred choice of Old Kingdom / Middle Kingdom / Amarna Period / Late Period / Greco-Roman Period). None the less, such discussions usually overlooked the fact that in pharaonic belief the true self – the real subject of the offering cult – is spiritual, not physical. Moreover, in discussing specific differences from one sculpted face to another, without careful study we can rarely be sure how far they are affected by matters such as the choice of material, or the work of a single workshop, or an artist of exceptional skill (or the reverse). In truth, even the specific lighting of a museum display or an influential photograph of a single statue may become part of telling the story of an artwork. Sad to say, on

113 Statue of the high priest Setkai. Abu Roash. Granite statue with painted limestone base. 30 cm (1 ft) high (without base). 4th Dynasty.

114 'Block statue' of Senwosretsenebefni, shown as though with knees drawn up to create rectangular planes for inscription and a background to display the image of his wife. The composition may perhaps merge the image of the official with his seat of office (cf. [107]), or the disproportionately large head may emerge in analogous fashion to [111]. Unknown provenance. Quartzite. 0.68 m (2 ft 3 in.) high. 12th Dynasty.

more than one occasion heads have been deliberately removed from statues in modern times, partly because they are then easier to transport but also because pharaonic torsos tend to make them look less modern – too 'ancient Egyptian' – and the modern eye can more easily see whichever 'face' it wishes to see without such inconvenience (see p. 288). After all, perhaps nothing is more credulous than the eye of the beholder.

Offering stelae
Returning to the functional character of a tomb statue, Idu's false door [112] is a useful visual summary of the funerary context: the blatant request for offerings; the physical form of the offering shrine enclosing the image of the deceased; and the inscriptions, which specify the identity of the deceased and

115 Offering stela for the chamberlain Amenemhat. Unknown provenance. Painted limestone. 0.56 m (1 ft 10 in.) wide. 12th Dynasty.

116 Offering stela for the king's daughter Nefertiabet, who makes a gesture of greeting, wearing a 'dress' incorporating or suggesting a feline pelt. Giza. Painted limestone. 0.52 m (1 ft 8½ in.) wide. 4th Dynasty.

restate the required offerings. From the 5th Dynasty on, such inscriptions may develop into a specific biography, such as those of Ptahshepses or Rawer, but detailed accounts are few and far between at any era. Instead, most tomb inscriptions also adopt the 'archetypal' character of the statues. At the heart of the offering cult are the crucial relationships between the king and the tomb-owner, and the tomb-owner and his son or daughter, which expresses the integrity of the family and seeks to ensure the transmission of values across the generations, so these are the principal subjects of most inscriptions. The setting of the statue of Setkai, son of the 4th Dynasty king Radjedef, epitomizes the conjunction of the statue, inscription and offering slab [113]. The composition has been individualized only by stating his name and the offices he held in service of the king. Together these constitute his 'spirit' (ka) – the face of service he turned towards the world, embodied in the archetypes of the statue and inscription (see pp. 74–77). This archetypal aspect contrasts with his 'soul' (ba), the sense of self known only to Setkai and his Creator, which is rarely talked about in art and even then shown with wings, as though free of the earth.

The monuments of Idu and Setkai are suitably elaborate for the highest officials, but simpler forms were developed. For example, the inscriptions may appear on the statue itself. Before the end of the Old Kingdom, forms showing the deceased wrapped in a heavy cloak [126] or with the knees pulled under the chin ('block statue') become increasingly common, offering simple sculptural forms as well as large areas for inscribing [114]. Of course, once these new forms were established as archetypes themselves, they could be developed in more or less elaborate ways or used in specific contexts. The most straightforward reduction in the paraphernalia of the tomb chapel is the offering stela, where effectively the statue, offering slab and inscriptions are combined into a single two-dimensional relief [115]. Such stelae may stand as the centrepiece of an elaborate decorative scheme, as the lone decorated element in a humbler chapel, or occasionally be used to cover the mouth of a tomb shaft. The standard elements of the offering stela form a balanced composition, showing the tomb-owner seated to receive offerings presented in front of him, while the offerings are both illustrated and stated as hieroglyphs. For the offering scene of Nefertiabet, the statement of offerings is clearly itemized pictorially and linguistically [116]. She herself was the daughter of an unidentified 4th Dynasty king and is shown wearing the leopard skin of a cult-priest, so her stela is one of the earliest statements of the authority of a woman in her own right. The quality of the relief work is exquisite; an offering stela may be economical in form, yet of the highest-quality craftsmanship.

In fact, two-dimensional decoration was a feature of the finest decoration in tomb chapels from earliest history. The painted 'Tomb 100' at Hieraconpolis was discussed in Chapter 6 and relief work also appears in the earliest surviving tomb chapels, including that of Metjen. The beautiful wooden panels from the chapel of Hezyra [117] have become emblematic of the pyramid age and the artist has simply adapted the form of a tomb statue into two

117 One of a group of wooden panels, each placed in one of eleven separate niches (cf. [43]) along a wall of the tomb chapel of the high priest and high official Hezyra. Saqqara. Wood, probably acacia. 1.14 m (3 ft 8 in.) high. 3rd Dynasty.

dimensions, following the usual principles for representing a two-dimensional human figure (see Chapter 7). The staff and sceptres in Hezyra's hands clearly illustrate what is *apparently* grasped by a three-dimensional statue, which typically strides forward as though to balance its staff, though the actual staff and sceptre have been reduced to a mere 'nub' grasped in the hands [95, 96, 105, 107]. Likewise, the priest Ty's stela [60] simply elaborates in painted low relief the two basic forms of tomb statues. In two dimensions, the cubic seat is more obviously a chair, and once again the standing figure is clearly holding a staff and sceptre. In a sense both images signify earthly authority but in a more authentic sense they are the functional equivalents of statues in a chapel.

As an artistic medium the offering stela potentially makes the paraphernalia of the offering cult accessible beyond the confines of the royal family, and the growth of the cult through many centuries is part of our topic in the next chapter. In our own culture, where sacrifice and loyalty are liable to be explained as reproductive strategies, it may seem suspect to read about lives devoted to the service of a spiritual leader. Cynical minds may assume slavery or, worse still, servile submission on the part of the 'ruled' – though we may wonder what even a pharaonic farmer would make of the lifelong indebtedness, indentured employment and civil supervision that characterize ordinary life in the modern world. We should also recall that the tombs of officials emulate those of kings, which are likewise decorated using archetypes essentially devoid of specific personal information. Above all, tomb chapels are not records of the living but places of worship, where gifts of love and adoration are gathered in by the spirits. As the tomb inscription of Ineni, the overseer of works, tells us, *'may you make the perfection that I have made, may you make the same'*.

Masterpiece
Bust of the vizier Ankhhaf

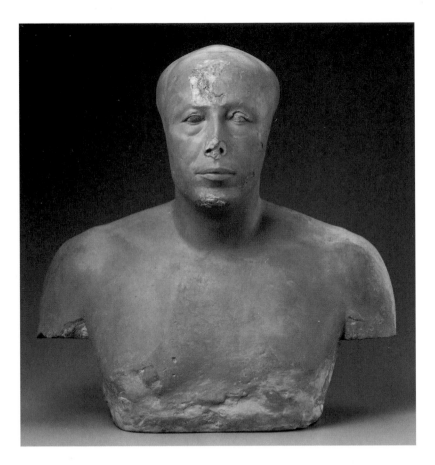

118 'Bust' of the vizier Ankhhaf
(cf. [112]). Giza. Plastered and
painted limestone. 0.51 m (1 ft
8 in.) high. 4th Dynasty.

Ankhhaf was a vizier for Khafra, and probably the person responsible for overseeing the creation of the Great Sphinx. His celebrated limestone 'bust' from Giza is the most accomplished and affecting example of sculpture illustrating the morbidity of flesh. The pronounced bone structure of his face contrasts with the flaccidity round his eyes and cheeks, or the lines round his nose and lips, to create a harsh account of ageing as well as a poignantly credible human face. As an isolated upper torso, the sculpture seems unique in ancient Egyptian art, though we may be inclined to compare it with the contemporary 'reserve heads'. However, Ankhhaf's statue, unlike any of the 'reserve heads', is from his tomb chapel. The flattened head may be designed to wear a wig or headdress, so perhaps the bust was made to be dressed after the manner of Meryrahashtef's wooden statue. However, plastered and painted stone may well be too delicate a vehicle for such activity. More likely, perhaps, the 'bust' was originally provided with separate arms and posed on an offering altar, like the image of Idu [112].

119 Offering stela for Inyotef, son
of Ka, and three wives. Thebes.
Painted limestone. 1.02 m (3 ft
4 in.) wide. 11th Dynasty.

Chapter 10 'I Was The One Who Opened Up This Area': A Study in Change: The First Intermediate Period

Despite the unflinching confidence manifest in the art of the Old Kingdom, words such as 'anarchy' and 'disorder' have regularly been used to characterize the ensuing era, the First Intermediate Period. This tradition was already known to the Classical authors. The Church historian Eusebius (c. AD 260–c. 340) quotes Manetho's comment on the 9th Dynasty: '*The first of these, Achthôes, harsher than the generations before him, brought corruption to the people of all of Egypt*'. Manetho wrote 2,000 years after the First Intermediate Period but a Middle Kingdom teaching offering a notably pessimistic vision of Egypt is ascribed to a king Khety, who is conceivably the 'Achthôes' of Manetho. This Khety does claim to have provoked 'a shameful event' – an assault on Thinis, the very district of Abydos. Though we may be wary that incriminating words have been put in his mouth by later generations, in the manner of Shakespeare's Richard III, there is further evidence from texts of the First Intermediate Period itself. For example, the stela of Inyotef, son of Ka [119], carries blunt corroboration: '*Year 14. That destruction occurred in the year of the rebellion of Thinis*.' In texts of all periods, the word 'rebels' (Ancient Egyptian *sbiu*) denotes those who oppose the king – but to do so here in Egypt, still less at ancient Abydos? How did things come to such a pass? More to the point, our eyes are drawn to the clumsy figures on Inyotef's stela, which may lead us to speculate whether disorder and 'corruption' are embodied in a rough-and-ready art style.

Indeed, awkward, clumsy figures are almost characteristic of Egyptian art immediately after the end of the Old Kingdom when, according to a noted early Egyptologist, Francis Ll. Griffith, 'barbaric stelae present many extraordinary attempts to render the half-forgotten signs'. On Inyotef's stela the canonical image of the Egyptian official has been distorted by a clumsy, disproportionate 'egg-head', while the braids of his wig are no more than pocks in the stone. The figures of the three wives '*whom he loves*' are cut square from the stone more crudely than those found in earlier tombs at Saqqara and Giza, as well as being awkward and inconsistent in form, with heads of different sizes and legs of varying lengths. Oddly,

120 Offering stela for Semin. Presumably from Thebes. Painted limestone. 41 cm (1 ft 4 in.) high. First Intermediate Period.

the minor figure making the offerings seems better proportioned, and actually most of the artistic conventions have been respected in representing the bodies, their dress, and their relative sizes and arrangements within registers. Could there even be a suggestion that the artist, though clumsy, is trying more or less successfully to improvise on the conventions? Certainly the accompanying text supplements traditional phrases about the king and the offering cult by adding original (but not 'half-forgotten') phrases about his service, apparently as a scout. However, the most telling aspect of his stela is that Inyotef has no formal title. He is not even a palace official, let alone a member of the royal family. Likewise, though a less 'peculiar' figure has been carved to depict Semin on his stela, he is apparently just an archer or hunter to judge from the tool of his trade in his hand [120]. Neither stela is the work of a first-rate artist, but as such are they evidence of artistic decline, or something more positive and dynamic? Apparently the crude forms testify to the use of funerary paraphernalia at a lower, more diverse social level than we met in Chapter 9, and whatever may (or may not) be happening politically the people of Egypt increasingly seem to be embracing the art of the offering cult and the concept of 'Adoration'. The clumsy-looking stela of Nun [121] illustrates another aspect of this phenomenon: he has no formal title either but is described as 'the Nubian', while the non-Egyptian name of his wife also suggests they are immigrants or from immigrant stock. Do the stelae of Inyotef, Semin and Nun illustrate the 'corruption' of Old Kingdom skills and values, or the common aspiration of people from diverse backgrounds? As the Egyptologist Ludwig Morenz has noted, in this era 'people from social groups that are nameless to us in the Old Kingdom emerge from the shadows'.

A final aspect of this phenomenon is geographical. Take the scene of the harvest being transported to granaries in the tomb of Ity [122], which shows human figures with slender, angular bodies and shrunken heads – in fact, the opposite distortion to the figures on Inyotef's stela. Nonetheless, the scene reproduces themes known from the finest tombs at Saqqara, though here worked in paint and plaster rather than first-rate relief. More to the

121 Offering stela for Nun and his family. Reportedly from El-Rizeiqat, near Armant. Painted limestone. 45 cm (1 ft 5½ in.) high. First Intermediate Period.

122 Scene of storehouses in the tomb chapel of the courtier Ity. Gebelein. Plastered and painted limestone. First Intermediate Period.

point, Ity's tomb is at Gebelein, some 700 kilometres (435 miles) upstream from Saqqara, so this may well be the work of a regional artist or workshop seeking to learn and interpret traditional themes for traditional purposes (see p. 184). By contrast the stelae of Inyotef and Semin, quite different in their appearance, are from Thebes. In other words, do the awkwardness and inconsistencies of First Intermediate Period art illustrate the failure of central government or the devolution of knowledge, skill, confidence – and even success – to the Egyptian regions?

The end of the Old Kingdom

Of course, the reality of political upheaval and social turmoil during the First Intermediate Period is properly a question for the history books, but the mere suggestion is bound to affect our understanding of the art of the era. If we suppose the time from the end of the 6th Dynasty until the Middle Kingdom to be an era of turmoil and failure, it becomes straightforward to explain relatively crude artwork as evidence of cultural decline. If we see the era as one of greater inclusion and social aspiration, then the material evidence takes on a different tenor, even on the massive scale. For example, the pyramid of Pepy II, last king of the 6th Dynasty, looks starkly unimpressive between Snofru's two pyramids at Dahshur. The scant remains of a handful of royal pyramids from the First Intermediate Period seem even more reduced, though what can still be deduced of their form and decoration is otherwise the same as those of the 6th Dynasty.

All this is true, but the size of the actual tumulus in royal pyramid complexes had already peaked – by far – during the 4th Dynasty; indeed, king Snofru has been credited as the greatest 'pound-for-pound' builder in the history of humanity.

In other words, the 'decline' in pyramid size is not a phenomenon associated with the end of the Old Kingdom at all. In fact, after the 4th Dynasty the most massive royal pyramids ever built were not those of the late Old Kingdom but those of the 12th Dynasty, so in a broader historical perspective pyramid building is a practice that connects the Old Kingdom to the Middle Kingdom. Nonetheless, perhaps the declining scale of pyramids hints at gradually dwindling royal authority? After all, during the 5th Dynasty non-royal cemeteries began to multiply away from the traditional royal burial grounds. One authority lists at least 150 cemeteries by the end of the Old Kingdom, stretching from Aswan in the south of the Nile valley to Abu Roash in the north, from Kom Ausim to Mersa Matruh across the Nile Delta. On his tomb doorway at Meir [123] the priest of Hathor, Pepyankh, claims, *'Certainly I have had an official's reward made in the west, in the area of the lady of Truth, in a pure place, in a perfect place, where nothing had been made, where no-one had ever done anything. I was the one who opened up this area'* [124]. Djau, governor of the 12th district of the Nile valley, explains in his tomb that he preferred to be buried beside his father rather than in a new tomb but, he insists, *'not because there was no written authority for making a second tomb'*. So, did the kings of the Old Kingdom gradually lose their grip on their officials or did they encourage or endorse the proliferation of tombs and cemeteries, knowing that each new burial embodied the pharaoh's authority and values? If the latter, it would no longer have been feasible for each and every inscription to have been carved by the finest artists of the palace to the standard required by the king (see p. 155).

This was also the moment when tomb biographies, however brief, became typical of tomb chapels – once again identifying

123 General view of the Old Kingdom and Middle Kingdom governors' cemetery in the western desert at Meir.

124 Scene of offerings from the tomb of the high priest Pepyankh. Meir. Plastered and painted limestone. 6th Dynasty.

owners with the king, the offering cult and Osiris. Not every official involved in this development was born to greatness: some attained greatness precisely through the king's recognition. For instance, the lengthiest surviving Old Kingdom biography has come to us from the tomb of Weni (see p. 82), the first non-royal tomb to overlook the processional route of Osiris at Abydos. At the door to the tomb chapel, the man himself is shown speaking his own account of a career that began with him supervising the palace cloakrooms. This task he did well enough to become 'elder of the robing-room' for the king's son, Pepy, and when the latter succeeded as king Pepy I, '*his person put me in the position of companion and manager of his pyramid-town*'. Weni remained the king's confidant, and in six promotions moved from the fringes of the palace community to become the most powerful official in Upper Egypt. The first reward Weni asked of the king was a sarcophagus so '*his person made a royal seal-bearer cross over with a troop of workmen under his command to fetch me the very sarcophagus from Tura, and it came with him on a great palace-barge, along with its lid, a false door, a lintel, two jambs and an offering-table*'. Of course, this is just the paraphernalia of 'Adoration' that is likely to have made its way into a modern museum display.

Late in the Old Kingdom, Weni owed his whole career to the king who, far from losing authority, seems to draw worthy people into the royal sphere. In archaeological terms this results in adding more and more of the deserts to the royal funerary domain [125]. Weni's near contemporary, Harkhuf, was born at Aswan, where he succeeded his father as governor of the far south. Consequently

Harkhuf's tomb lies some 850 kilometres (525 miles) from Memphis, and his biography recounts three trips into Nubia and the surrounding deserts on behalf of his kings, Nemtyemzaf I and Pepy II. Alongside the door of his tomb chapel, Harkhuf has also had copied the complete text of a letter from Pepy II, in which the king makes a breathtaking promise:

> Truly you do spend day and night arranging to do all your lord wishes and praises and commands. His person is going to reciprocate and establish your offerings so greatly and so excellently as to enspirit the son of your son through all time, so that all men, when they hear what my person has done for you, may say, 'Is there anything such as was done for the sole companion Harkhuf, returning from Yam because of the vigilance he demonstrated in doing all that his lord wishes and praises?'

Once upon a time, the Step Pyramid of Djoser conveniently marked the beginning of the Old Kingdom, whereas now we understand that iconic monument in the context of ongoing developments in art, architecture and kingship that reach further back in history (see p. 49). Likewise the (relatively) puny pyramid of Pepy II once seemed to underline the final failure of the Old Kingdom, whereas now we may understand it too in the context of developments spanning the 5th Dynasty right through to the First Intermediate Period. The pyramids of this era are all much reduced compared with those of the 3rd and 4th Dynasties by one measurement (the mass of the tumulus) but greatly increased by another (the geographical and demographic scope

125 General view of the Old Kingdom and Middle Kingdom governors' cemetery in the western desert at Qubbet el-Hawa, near Aswan.

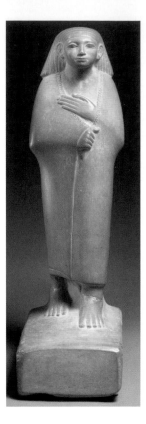

126 Statue of an anonymous Middle Kingdom official. After the end of the Old Kingdom, new forms in art often employ new contexts to develop ancient themes, such as wrapping the figure in a cloak (cf. [79]). Provenance unknown. Limestone. 27 cm (10½ in.) high. 12th Dynasty.

of pharaonic funerary practice). This expansion of the offering cult is the appropriate context in which to understand the cruder, aspirational art of minor officials and local artists during the First Intermediate Period, or even during the late Old Kingdom for that matter. Initially the offering cult incorporated regional priests and officials such as Meryrahashtef (see p. 148) and Ty (see p. 109), then people of less or even no official distinction, such as Inyotef, Semin and Nun. In modern parlance, we are seeing the emergence of an aspirational middle class but, like Weni, they do not aspire to a worldly lifestyle so much as the earthly paraphernalia of 'Adoration'. Such inclusivity expands from the heart of Egypt to its edges, and also from the Old Kingdom into the First Intermediate Period and beyond [126].

Heracleopolis and Thebes

None of the above is meant to suggest that there was no political difficulty during the First Intermediate Period. The later traditions – like Shakespeare's History of Richard III – were well founded in facts. While the kings of the 9th and 10th Dynasties still reigned, a rival dynasty set itself up in Thebes. For the first time since kingship had come to Egypt there was more than one king, and civil war ensued. Eventually, around 2000 BC, Montuhotep II (c. 2020–c. 1970), having been first 'a' king at Thebes, became 'the' king of all Egypt. Therefore, the conundrum for the history books is not only to explain how Egypt reached such political division but also to determine whether this situation characterized the First Intermediate Period as a whole. Most modern authorities assume the period between Pepy II, last king of the Old Kingdom, and Montuhotep II, all-conquering founder of the Middle Kingdom, was at least 150 years, and it would be unwise to assume that such a long time entailed unremitting strife and disorder.

The historical reality of kings from Heracleopolis is not in doubt. In terms of art and archaeology, an impressive cemetery of high officials of the era has been excavated at the city, taking the form of traditional stone-built mastabas in an area which is generally a low-lying plain [127]. The reliefs and paintings from the tombs are of a high quality and entirely traditional, as can be seen from examples now in the National Archaeological Museum in Madrid. Likewise, there is no doubting the reality of the 'second' kingdom at Thebes, least of all because of the magnificent tomb of Montuhotep II himself. His tomb is one of the most distinctive architectural creations of ancient Egypt, though its distinctive

127 Photo showing tomb chapels during excavations in the First Intermediate Period cemetery at Heracleopolis.

128 Reconstructed statue of Montuhotep II from a group that lined the processional route to his tomb complex at Deir el-Bahri (see [24]). West Thebes. Painted sandstone. 2.53 m (8 ft 3½ in.) high. 11th Dynasty.

129 Statue of Montuhotep II from an offering shrine in his tomb complex. Note the shift in skin colour compared to [128] and the powerful legs, characteristic of the earliest seated statues (cf. [97, 100, 107]). West Thebes. Painted sandstone. 1.38 m (4 ft 6 in.) high. 11st Dynasty.

form has simply been caused by the ingenious device of piling the traditional elements of an Old Kingdom pyramid complex one on top of the other in order to accommodate the structure within a restricted bay in the Theban cliffs (see p. 44). Again the sculpture and decoration is of a high standard, not at all inconsistent with Old Kingdom models [128, 129]. In time, Montuhotep's tomb would become a touchstone for the great monuments of the New Kingdom pharaohs – a model of royal architecture rooted in the past, in which later generations would find inspiration (see p. 206). So whatever might have been in dispute during Montuhotep's lifetime, the basic tenets of Egyptian kingship, religious belief, art and architecture were not. Likewise, on the Theban stelae of Inyotef and Semin both are represented as loyal officials according to the conventions of the offering cult. The only question arising is, to which king were they loyal? At Thebes and at Heracleopolis traditional art and architecture persisted, adapting readily to local factors, and there is no indication that anybody renounced the artistic practices of the Old Kingdom at either royal city or anywhere else in Egypt.

The civil war, when it came, lasted at least two generations and a scene of Montuhotep II from a temple of Hathor at Gebelein may be the only example known from any era of a 'smiting scene' in which the king's victim is another Egyptian [130]. However, this is still first and foremost an example of the 'smiting scene' – the most ancient depiction of the king, updated to the moment. Plausibly the war arose amid dynastic uncertainty following the ninety-four-year reign of Pepy II, who presumably outlived all his children, most of his grandchildren and no doubt a goodly portion of a third generation. Later in Egyptian history, uncertainty about the royal succession provoked political violence at the end of the 19th Dynasty and the end of the 20th Dynasty, and in both instances the problem can be traced back to the long reign of Ramesses II, who outlived his first twelve sons. The same uncertainty may explain the aftermath of the much longer reign of Pepy II and in such circumstances, whatever the politics may be, the cultural life of the nation is not likely to be at stake.

The point is that historical change is another of the topics that actually betrays the anxieties of the historian. Thus in the early 20th century Flinders Petrie, under the influence of Darwinism, explained the deterioration of the Old Kingdom by reference to racial miscegenation, while during the 1960s and 1970s explanations relied more on social tension and excessive government – then contemporary anxieties in Western politics. More recent explanations have tended towards climate change, or even ecological catastrophe caused by the Nile itself. In our new 'lifestyle-centred' century we may just as well question whether there was an end to the Old Kingdom at all, but rather an extended period of aspiration, wealth and increasing cultural homogeneity before a vicious war initiated the Middle Kingdom.

In terms of art history, this raises interesting puzzles. For example, today in the West we have more centralized government and immeasurably more wealth than ever before so will future archaeologists assess the success/failure of our times by emphasizing the proliferation in this century of new and bigger houses, or by emphasizing the sudden decline in building standards through reliance on cheap materials and slavish imitation of outmoded architectural forms? In the same vein, how should we understand the stela of a powerful and successful individual such as Indi, governor of Thinis [131]? There is the usual rough-and-ready art style and unusual phraseology characteristic of the First Intermediate Period, which describes him as 'one who rose from the bottom of his father's house through the strength of [the god] Onuris, ruler of Thinis, through desiring integrity and through

130 Archive photo of a scene showing Montuhotep II 'smiting' a line of foreign enemies, though it has been suggested that the victim whose hair he is pulling may be Egyptian on the basis of appearance. Gebelein. Limestone. 11th Dynasty.

131 Offering stela for the governor Indi and his wife Mutmuti. Nag el-Deir, near Thinis. Painted limestone. 0.71 cm (1 ft 4 in.) high. First Intermediate Period.

desiring most perfect action'. Does this novel characterization and clumsy provincial artwork indicate an era of declining standards or does it illustrate the very social success he claims for himself? Or both?

The tomb of Ankhtyfy at Mo'alla

A compelling parallel for Indi's success may be the most talked about – and ostensibly the grimmest – source of information we have for the First Intermediate Period. This is the tomb biography of Ankhtyfy, governor of Edfu and Hieraconpolis, who rose from origins so obscure he uses the word 'darkness' to describe them [133]. The tomb at Mo'alla is securely dated before the victory of Montuhotep II. Indeed, the tomb biography apparently mentions the advent of the civil war, and in another passage incorporates an infamous quote about '*dying because of hunger, everyone eating their children*' – surely an appalling indictment of the times? His king was the Heracleopolitan candidate, though Mo'alla is south of Thebes, and Ankhtyfy claims to have assembled a council of the leaders '*of the South from Thinis*', after which he led attacks on Thebes and nearby Armant. Was this the moment Thebes was condemned for disloyalty? Was this the event later characterized as '*the rebellion of Thinis*' by Inyotef, son of Ka? Be that as it may, Ankhtyfy's biography recounts a career characterized at times by violence – but then as a young man he was a career soldier. Moreover, Ankhtyfy affirms a commitment above all to establish peace wherever it may be threatened, espouses loyalty to his people, and claims that, '*I made a man embrace the killer of his father and the killer of his brother in order to stabilize the district of Edfu*'. Characterizing himself as a person of faith, service, decisive action and conviction, he backs this characterization repeatedly with the phrases '*I am the beginning of men and the end of men*' and '*what I am is a man, for whom there can be no substitute*'. (No doubt just this phraseology ruffles feathers in the modern world because we may prefer humility of the kind whereby a man's stated opinion of himself is much less than his actual opinion of himself.)

What of the tomb itself, the centrepiece of a cemetery on a pyramid-shaped hill in front of an amphitheatre of cliffs? Outside, its appearance is consistent with the success Ankhtyfy claims for himself. A mud-brick wall, plastered and painted white, once created an impressive façade, and columns cut in the living rock were apparently the base of a monumental gate. Through the gate was a colonnaded Sun-court, its floor levelled out of the rock. Beyond, the hypostyle hall excavated from the hill itself is a forest of columns [132], decorated throughout with conventional images of the offering cult, including a splendid fishing and fowling scene and a boat-filled festival on the Nile, at which the king is named. The columns seem an odd mix of shapes, precariously twisted and broken, but this is largely because of the poor quality of the stone. In fact, the roof has collapsed on various occasions, sometimes shearing through columns. The mere fact that a tomb exists in this unpromising place at all is evidence of skill and commitment, not viciously straitened circumstances. Eventually, however, the artists were able to employ a mix of sunk relief and painted plaster decoration, and among their vivid paintings are oddly proportioned figures recognizably similar to those in the nearby tomb of Ity (see p. 176). Quite possibly they were painted by artists from the same local workshop [134].

132 General view of the hypostyle hall in the tomb of Ankhtyfy. Mo'alla. First Intermediate Period.

133 Stela in the chapel of Ankhtyfy presumably showing the governor and his anonymous wife, though there is no accompanying text. He carries the traditional staff and sceptre of an Old Kingdom official, while beneath her chair is a bag with a mirror (see p. 262).

134 Wall painting in the chapel of Ankhtyfy showing the transport of offerings from storehouses (cf. [122]).

In any event, Ankhtyfy's tomb certainly fits the bill for his *'gateway to the far side of the sky'* (see p. 100). In this context, we must understand that his reference to famine is rhetorical: what he actually says is, *'All of the South may die of hunger, with people eating their own children, but death from hunger will never happen in this district.'* In other words, famine may happen – but not in his time. In fact, his was an era of surplus when, he claims, *'It is my grain that has gone upstream and reached Wawat and gone downstream and reached Abydos.'* Ankhtyfy's biography is a statement of unequivocal success, despite the localized political troubles that brought him to prominence – and, for that matter, the political misfortune about to befall his nation. He even employs an image of national unity amid regional diversity – he and the people of his southern hometown, Hefat, are the tail of a crocodile. *'Therefore, if this band of Hefat is content, likewise this land is content; but, if it is trodden on, like the tail of a crocodile, then the North and South of this entire land will tremble.'* Of course, the head of a crocodile, when provoked, bites its opponent not its own tail. The tomb is a notable feat of engineering, beautifully decorated in a style that follows the conventions of the Old Kingdom and exemplifies the dynamism of regional art at this time. Either the success Ankhtyfy claims for himself as a leader and peacemaker during the First Intermediate Period is ably demonstrated by his tomb or, in the worst of times for his fellow Egyptians, he was the cruellest of tyrants and liars.

185

Masterpiece
Tomb of Sarenput II

135 General view of the hypostyle hall and shrine beyond in the tomb chapel of the governor Sarenput II. Qubbet el-Hawa, near Aswan. 12th Dynasty.

136 Closer view of the shrine of Sarenput II, including sunk statues of the tomb owner as Osiris.

Following the events of the First Intermediate Period, the Middle Kingdom saw a straightforward continuation of the artistic traditions of the previous millennium. While there was renewed emphasis on the size of the royal pyramid complex, cemeteries distributed widely throughout the regions also continued in use. Accordingly, the rock-cut tombs of the governors of Elephantine, far from the areas of the civil war, are among the finest surviving from the Middle Kingdom – alongside those of Sabni and Pepynakht and some of the most important and impressive tombs from the end of the Old Kingdom (see pp. 101, 252). Their large-scale and splendid decoration reflects the ongoing importance of the officials who controlled the southern border, where the Nile emerges out of an almost intractable granite cataract to become Egypt's free-flowing highway. Beyond Aswan lay hostile deserts and barely civilized (as the Egyptians understood it) peoples in the oases and Nubia, while the importance of the region for the ivory trade is reflected in the Greek name Elephantine, whose Egyptian precursor likewise was Abu, 'Ivory-town'. All in all, no other governors were more valued by the pharaohs nor more distant from Memphis.

The tombs are cut from a dense red, black and honey-coloured sandstone in the cliffs at Qubbet el-Hawa, whose aesthetic characteristics are shown to finest effect in the hypostyle hall of the tomb of Sarenput II, from the middle of the 19th century BC. Six columns cut directly out of the striated stone, smoothed and left undecorated, frame an elegant, austere axis approaching the offering chapel [135]. Accordingly the chapel immediately appears in front of an officiant entering the tomb, approached up steps after the manner of the chapel in any god's temple. Three pairs of statues of Sarenput in the form of Osiris flank the narrow corridor connecting the hypostyle hall to the chapel, though they have been sunk into the living rock in relief so as not to obscure the view of the chapel [136]. Consequently, the chapel, painted so colourfully, is beautiful and utterly engaging when seen from the entrance, even in just the natural light. Moreover, the paintings in the corridor and the chapel are not only handsome but technically almost perfect, and in Chapter 7 furnished examples of the finest artists at work.

137 Intricate detail showing Egyptian officials in the presence of the pharaoh, from the tomb chapel of the vizier Horemheb. Saqqara. Painted limestone. 18th Dynasty.

138 Dyad of the king's treasurer Maya and his wife Meryt, from a shrine in their tomb chapel. Saqqara. Limestone. 1.58 m (5 ft 2 in.) high. 18th Dynasty.

Chapter 11 'She Who is Facing Her Lord': The Tombs and Temples of Thebes

Tombs decorated according to archetypes from the Old Kingdom continued to proliferate throughout the 2nd millennium BC. At Saqqara in particular, officials' tombs along the desert edge from Meidum to Giza, among the pyramids and causeways of their kings, developed as a hive of extraordinary complexity and artistic elaboration for century upon century. In the northern and central reaches of the Nile Valley, using the superior local limestone, the tradition of decorating tomb chapels with low relief and fine sculpture often still attained the marvellous artistic success of the 3rd millennium [137]. Certainly no art from Egypt at any time is more elegant and refined than reliefs in the finest tombs at Saqqara dating to the late 18th and early 19th Dynasties – in general terms, from the late reign of Amenhotep III until the early decades of Ramesses II, c. 1350 to c. 1250 BC. At this time, the soft plastic forms of human bodies and the intricate details of their elegant clothes and extravagant wigs bear witness to Egypt's confidence as a cultural and economic authority [138]. Elsewhere, art of the highest quality graces contemporary foundations from Egyptian Nubia to Abydos (see p. 17).

Sadly the intervening millennia and the sprawl of Cairo have all but obliterated the temples, palaces and settlements corresponding to Saqqara and Memphis so, in order to appreciate how officials' tombs were arranged in relation to the entirety of a great city, we must turn to the example of New Kingdom Thebes. Here in the south, the poor-quality local limestone – friable and flinty, prone to fracturing, and punctuated by bands of unstable 'Esna shale' – mitigates against relief work, though tombs such as that of Ramose vividly demonstrate the artists' ability to overcome such difficulties when tasked to do so [72]. Typically, however, Theban artists preferred painting on a dry plaster base and so created masterpieces of the ancient world, such as the exemplary tombs of Sennefer, Nebamun and Sennedjem. Of course, fine painting may be seen throughout Egypt during the 2nd millennium, including well-known cemeteries from Aswan to Meir, Beni Hassan and Meidum, but the profusion and elegance of the New Kingdom

139 Scene from the burial chamber of Irynefer, showing the deceased embarking on the Sun's procession through the world (cf. [57]). Deir el-Medina, West Thebes. Plastered and painted limestone. 19th Dynasty.

140 Scene from the tomb chapel of Irynefer, showing the deceased drinking from a pool of water beneath the shade of a burgeoning palm tree. Note how the tree grows from the bottom of the composition, whereas the man is located on the parallel edge of the pool as a baseline so as not to appear in the water.

tombs at Thebes reflect the city's importance after the reign of Montuhotep II. During this age, literate and theologically astute artists and their patrons developed specific interpretations of ancient themes, and the ruling men and women of Thebes were literally drawn into the age-old beliefs.

First, the ancient spiritual order is proclaimed repeatedly in scenes showing the world laid out before the king. In this life, officials kiss the ground where he walks in procession, and the different peoples of the earth pay homage and make offerings, while the tomb-owner stands beside him. Meanwhile, on nearby walls Osiris receives the deceased into the next life – sometimes literally, sometimes through the symbolism of sailing to Abydos or more obscure mythological imagery. Next, as we have seen, the world is also laid out before the tomb-owner, who gathers in the harvest of an abundant estate along with the acclamation of his peers and the king's praise. The tomb-owner makes offerings out of his bounty to deceased relatives, who in turn greet him on his arrival in Osiris' kingdom. Ubiquitous boat scenes relate the gods' festivals to the funerals of mortals and the Sun's procession and, of course, the Elysian fowling goes on forever (see p. 124). Irynefer, a man from Deir el-Medina, standing in the Sun's boat beside a heron (which represents the soul of the Sun, and whose name sounds similar to benben) proclaims the twin miracles of Creation – that anything exists at all, and that what exists is ordered and comprehensible [139].

In this spiritual context, Irynefer's garden pool [140] is a paradise of rest and refreshment, thankfulness and relief, a theme picked up in an older poem:

Today death seems to me like a whiff of myrrh;
like sitting beneath the sail on a windy day.
Today death seems to me like a whiff of lotus;
like sitting on the shore of intoxication.
Today death seems to me like a trodden-down path;
like when the man returns from a journey to their home.
Today death seems to me like a clearing sky;
like when a man grasps what he did not know.

Sennefer and his wife [141], standing under a canopy of grapevines painted across the undulating ceiling of their rock-cut chapel, also look forward to a shady eternal summer from 'the shore of intoxication' but they are being purified with water, like the statues of gods in their shrines [98]. Sennefer's bulbous ceiling is bursting with charm as well as meaning – and it is such a distinctive artistic achievement that aficionados still travel the world to see the so-called 'Grapes Tomb' in Thebes.

On the other hand, amid this fruitful vision of eternity the songs of the 'unseeing harper' are a familiar counterpoint in New Kingdom tombs [142]. As though singing in Sinatra's 'wee small hours', he laments the fleeting moments of life because 'no-one remains in the land of Egypt'. The haunts of Imhotep and Ptahhatp, he sings, have gone forever, so place your trust not in men's words but in your heart.

141 Scene from the burial chamber of Sennefer, showing the purification of offering-cult statues for the deceased and his wife Meryt (cf. [98]). Plastered and painted limestone. 18th Dynasty.

The West of Thebes

Throughout the New Kingdom, Thebes was also being developed as the principal royal cemetery, utilizing the desert wadi we call the Valley of the Kings, where the Sun sets behind the Theban hills. Working drawings indicate that each royal tomb was intended as a monumental sketch of the descent of the Sun (Ra) into the earth (Geb), and successive chambers mark the hours of the night, adapting themes already developed in Old Kingdom pyramids [144]. The earliest tombs here date from the reign of Thutmose III, unless a tomb winding through the cliffs between the Valley and Deir el-Medina, in its original form, might have been the tomb of his grandfather, Thutmose I. The younger Thutmose's tomb stands at the end of a rock-cut staircase, high in cliffs beneath a natural pyramid at the head of the Valley. From this moment on, the traditional use of pyramids for royal burials is to be replaced by a huge, integrated project to construct a single royal burial complex behind the hills, with a mortuary temple for nearly every king at the edge of the floodplain in front (see [150]).

142 Detail showing the unseeing harper, from the tomb chapel of Nakht. West Thebes. Plastered and painted limestone. 18th Dynasty.

143 General view of the burial chamber in the tomb of king Thutmose III, with the king's sarcophagus in the foreground and scenes of the Sun's circuit of the night on the walls. Valley of the Kings, West Thebes. 18th Dynasty.

144 Detail from a wall in the burial chamber of Thutmose III, showing the goddess Isis in the form of a sycamore-fig tree suckling the king (cf. [165]). The king's late father stands behind him. Plastered and painted limestone.

Thutmose III's tomb descends steeply from a discreet entrance in a natural rock-chimney until it reaches a rock-cut vertical 'well' – perhaps simply a safeguard against flash flooding – beyond which stairs enter a chamber painted with the personifications of more than 700 words for gods and shrines, towns and roads, fields and crops, the essential fabric of human communities. Immediately below here is the burial chamber, painted with the unfolding narrative of the Sun's journey through night – his allies battling every malevolent agent who tries to interrupt the rhythm of the universe and provoke not death, but Nothing [143]. A pivotal moment in this tableau is the fifth hour of the night when 'Creation' in the form of a scarab beetle erupts through the artists' registers and emerges as the Risen Earth at the grave of Osiris. The ancient name for all the decoration in the Valley is Amduat, 'where there is adoration', and in this chamber the physical remains of Thutmose III lay in a nest of coffins inscribed with his name and a speech by Geb, who says '*this son of mine is the king, whom I have given purity in the earth and transfiguration in the sky*' (see p. 37).

Later in its history, tombs in the Valley doubled in size in terms of the number of chambers and grew ever larger in terms of dimensions, but the essential character of the decoration did not change [145]. Simple painting was often replaced with vividly painted reliefs and, though the number of masons and artists also doubled, by now they were so painstaking and ambitious – and work had to be fudged with plaster in the poor stone – that the decoration was rarely complete at the time of the king's death, which is why the Valley provides some of the best evidence for ancient working techniques.

145 Graphic presentation of decoration in the descending corridors and chambers of the tomb of king Sety I in the Valley of the Kings, from the original account of its discovery in 1817 by Giovanni Battista Belzoni.

Temples and festivals

As in the earliest times, the New Kingdom pharaoh was the focus of social organization and religious observance as much as he was the centre of government. His procession from temple to temple to celebrate festivals remained the basis for structuring the calendar, and ongoing belief in his supernatural nature is illustrated by a larger than life-size stela erected for Thutmose III in the temple of the god Montu at Armant. Here a narrator offers '*a collection of instances of might and success performed by this very god ... over and above the instances of action his person has made at any moment because, if they were related individually, they would be too numerous to put in writing*'. First, we are told the king overpowers the mineral world because '*he shoots at bars of copper, all wood having split like papyrus. Afterwards his person placed an example of that in the estate of Amun, a target of wrought copper three-fingers thick with his arrow in it*'. Next he slays the mightiest of animals – lions, elephants, even a rhinoceros. After shooting wild bulls at dawn, '*breakfast-time came and their tails were at his backside*'. Finally we learn how Thutmose set out from Memphis to defeat a coalition of every human opponent at the Battle of Megiddo in Palestine about 1458 BC. Whichever audience the stela and the copper target were intended for, the narrator adds,

'*I tell you what he does without lying, without exaggerating*'. Such continuity in religious belief and practice, harnessed to renovation or rebuilding, is exemplified by the way the White Chapel was moved round and reused at Karnak more than once before it was deemed redundant and broken up to become a rubble in-fill (see p. 27). However, as was the case with burial in the Valley of the Kings, the temples of the gods took on a new scale from the reign of Thutmose III, who began to fashion Thebes as the 'Heliopolis of Upper Egypt'. A granite stela from a temple of Ptah at Karnak gives an insight into Thutmose's intentions:

> Now, my person found this very chapel built of bricks,
> and the poles and its wooden doors fallen to decay. My
> person commanded stretching the string once again
> on this very chapel, which is now built in perfect, hard
> limestone with the walls round it in brick, worked
> sufficiently hardwearing for all time. My person has put
> doors in place for it in the finest, straightest cedar, plated
> with Asian copper. In effect a brand new chapel for Ptah
> in the name of my person.

Such new foundations grew bigger through time because the mathematics they embody required them to grow exponentially along the main axis, or be demolished and built from 'square one' when the scale of development became impractical (see pp. 45–46). So for the architectural landscape of ancient Egypt as we see it today, the reign of Thutmose III was a watershed, though a distinctive new feature of these massive temples, the twin-towered pylon gateway, is first recorded even earlier in the reign of his grandfather, Thutmose I. The difference between the massive New Kingdom temples and those of earlier periods has been characterized as a shift from a natural, accretive development at

146 Standing behind the mud-brick ruins of a later town, the temple of the goddess Renenutet at Medinet Maadi is probably the best-preserved stone-built temple from the Middle Kingdom.

each site to a consistent, formal plan. Undoubtedly New Kingdom pharaohs often cleared away existing structures – even those of their immediate predecessors – to allow for new building, but for that very reason we have limited information about the forms of most temples before then, apart from the pyramids themselves.

In some instances, as described by Thutmose III above, the king is not reinventing a temple so much as switching perishable materials for stone. No doubt, in some temples the original 'nucleus' might have been preserved in perishable materials and only subsequent buildings removed to accommodate new development. However, stone temples conforming to New Kingdom architectural practice have survived from earlier periods at places such as Medinet Maadi [146]. None the less, most of the pharaonic temples as they appear today have their origins in the reign of Thutmose III, at least insofar as he established a formal template that was embodied in later temples, whether by extending or replacing the New Kingdom foundations.

At Thebes the whole city was shaped by the festival routes along which statues of Amun-Ra would process. Hence Thebes 'proper' is bounded north and south by his great temples at Karnak and Luxor, and its central stone avenue is a causeway between them, running parallel to the river. Of course, the architectural form of both temples – and any others directly associated with them – is dictated by the requirements of processions: each has a central axis formed with gateways and ramps, which lead straight into the offering chapel, as discussed

147 The first entrance pylon beside the principal quay of the great temple of Amun-Ra at Karnak, which stands on the sphinx-lined route of the Perfect Festival of the Valley. The pylon and modern crane in the background mark the route of the Harim-festival procession to Luxor Temple.

148 Decoration on the wall of a Sun-court showing a Harim-festival scene, with priests collecting and distributing offerings. Luxor Temple. Limestone. 19th Dynasty.

in Part 1 [147]. In fact, Karnak as laid out by Thutmose III has a second axis because two principal festival routes meet here.

The first route is that of the Harim (Opet) festival, lasting a week or more during *akhet,* the Inundation season, when brightly painted statues of Amun-Ra, Ptah and the other gods of Karnak 'sailed upstream' (by river or being carried along the causeway) to 'greet' the statue of Amun-Ra of Luxor [148]. There, the king kept a night of vigil beside the shrine, where Amun-Ra spoke to him '*in the way a father talks to his son*'. Indeed, most of what we know about this divine relationship is based on relief scenes in and around the central shrine, which illustrate the king's life from conception (arising in sex between Amun-Ra and the queen) to enthronement. Next day the king returned to his officials, who acclaimed his physical union with Amun-Ra, and during the subsequent festivities cakes and alcoholic drinks were distributed to crowds, while folk vied to set a question before the gods' statues in the hope of an oracular response. Accordingly the essential theme of the decoration of Luxor Temple away from the shrine is the sequence of episodes in the festival itself.

Back at his Karnak shrine, Amun-Ra looked directly west across the Nile to Kheftethirnebes, 'she who is facing her Lord' – the name of a distinctive natural eruption of hills along the western horizon. At the heart of these hills the tombs of ancient kings were clustered round Deir el-Bahri, and in the desert behind Kheftethirnebes lay the new royal cemetery in the Valley of the Kings. The counterpoint to the Harim-festival was the Perfect Festival of the Valley: once a year, during *shemu,* the dry season, processional statues left Karnak and 'sailed' west to Deir el-Bahri and the mortuary temples of New Kingdom pharaohs, to spend dark nights in the shrines of kings who had gone before and celebrate the incarnation of Amun-Ra in his son's mortal body. Accordingly the ramps of the temples at Deir el-Bahri align with the east–west axis of Karnak, and the route was furnished on both sides of the river with a sphinx-lined causeway as well as processional shrines in the manner of the White Chapel. However, over the centuries many of these chapels became temples in their own right. For example, one in the floodplain in front of Deir el-Bahri became the mortuary temple of Sety I [149]. The pioneering Egyptologist Amelia Edwards visited this temple in 1874 and found that 'it is, at least in part, distinctly a memorable edifice as the Medici Chapel at Florence or the Superga at Turin'. Sety began this temple in tandem with the extraordinary hypostyle hall at Karnak – furnished with 134 columns, those flanking the main axis reaching 21 metres (69 feet) high – as well as the masterpiece of a temple at Abydos. To take another example, at the southern end of the procession, at modern Medinet Habu, Thutmose III and his co-regent, Hatshepsut, developed new temples in place of a Middle Kingdom chapel upon 'the mound of Djeme', which the statue of Amun-Ra from Luxor Temple otherwise visited weekly. Several mortuary temples were subsequently developed alongside this site until eventually Ramesses III (c. 1187–c. 1156 BC) incorporated the whole area into his own mortuary temple [150]. A network of canals connected all these west-bank temples and chapels together, just as the Old Kingdom royal pyramids had once been mooring points for boats. An inscription of Amenhotep III explains how his mortuary temple 'takes the bow-rope of the Valley and the stern-rope of the Delta' as 'a resting place for the lord of the gods in his Valley-festival'.

149 General view across the ruinous Sun-court in the temple of Sety I, built on the site of a processional shrine along the route of the Valley-festival. Gurna, West Thebes. 19th Dynasty.

150 Aerial view of the complex surrounding the central stone-built mortuary temple of king Ramesses III, which incorporates earlier temples as well as a palace, administrative offices, housing and storehouses. Medinet Habu, West Thebes. 20th Dynasty.

151 Scene of Sety I going to war in his chariot, from the exterior decoration of the great temple of Amun-Ra (cf. [213]). Karnak, near Thebes. Limestone. 19th Dynasty.

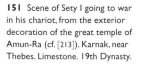

Whereas the Harim-festival celebrates the king's divine conception and descent, the Valley-festival highlights each king's mortality, so specific events from his life may exemplify his vocation and his intimacy with the Creator, including inscriptions concerning an expedition to the exotic land of Punt as we shall see below (see p. 207). Most famously, at the start of the 19th Dynasty Sety I and then Ramesses II led Egypt against the empire of Hatti. The war was conducted far from Egypt, mostly in the area round Qadesh in modern Syria, but is memorialized in the kings' mortuary temples as well as temples at Karnak, Luxor, Abydos and other places, where scenes of ancient, contemplative rituals complement scenes of conflict and brutality we can but wish had been confined to the first age of history [151].

At Karnak a stela of Thutmose III talks about the relationship without which none of this monumental festivity would happen [152]. The scene at the top shows the king offering to Amun-Ra, supported by Kheftethirnebes depicted as a goddess. The god states what he intends shall be the outcome of Thutmose's reign: '*I will perform a miracle for you,*' he says, '*I will put your power and*

152 Top of the so-called 'Poetical Stela' of Thutmose III, from the great temple of Amun-Ra. On either side, offering to the plumed figure of Amun-Ra, the king is shown with Kheftethirnebes behind him. Karnak, near Thebes. Granite. 1.7 m (5 ft 7 in.) high. 18th Dynasty.

might over every highland, put your power and fear of you in every lowland, and dread of you at the corners of the sky.' In the present context, the most telling remark is his final one:

> You have erected my sanctuary in the work of eternity, made longer and broader than anything which existed before. The gate named 'Menkheperra is very, very great' – its perfection graces the estate of Amun. Your legacy is greater than that of any king who has come into being and, though I commanded that it be done, still I am satisfied because of it.

Immediately behind this stela was the chapel where offerings were placed before the principal statue of the god, while the other end of the processional route facing the statue is Kheftethirnebes – the Theban hills – where offerings were

153 Scene with preserved colour from a chapel at Karnak, showing multiple images of Alexander the Great in the presence of Amun-Ra. Painted limestone. 18th Dynasty, reworked in the 4th century BC.

laid before the stelae and statues of the innumerable dead. Accordingly, officials vied to build tombs overlooking the Valley-festival route: the oldest overlook Deir el-Bahri itself, the most impressive look down from the slopes of Khokha and Asasif, while others spread along the hillsides, northeast along Dra Abu el-Naga or south along Sheikh Abd el-Qurneh.

The decoration of temples

By comparison with the pyramid complexes of earlier kings (see Chapter 3), a different kind of temple is associated with the New Kingdom. At the heart of the temples of gods and of mortuary temples alike is not a pyramid or an obelisk, but a small, dark offering chapel and shrine. The surviving foundations may seem as bleak and austere as they are overwhelmingly massive, but in places the decoration is still sufficiently well preserved to indicate that almost every detail might have been coloured originally [153]. Indeed, reconstructions suggest the temples would have had a garish impact on the surrounding landscape. In addition to brightly coloured reliefs, gold and inlays highlighted scenes that would have been almost painful to look at under the daytime Sun. Pairs of stone obelisks typically flanked the pylon gateway, each made from a single piece of stone stretching to the sky to catch the Sun-rays in a gold-covered pyramidion (or *benbent*) [154]. In archetypal scenes on the exterior walls, the temple is characterized as a dynamic place because of the king's activities – above all the king leading the festival processions and overthrowing enemies in the wider world beyond.

Through the main gate of the mud-brick enclosure wall a pavement leads to the stone temple itself, entered through the twin-towered pylon [155], behind which one or more enclosed courtyards stand open to the Sun but for a colonnade round the perimeter. Monumental statues of the king may flank the doorways, sometimes with their eyes fixed as though on the horizon, sometimes angled down awaiting a visitor's approach. Consequently, entering these temples even today you are immediately conscious of the massive presence ahead. Passing through the courtyards and entering the hypostyle hall, you experience the phased shift from intense sunlight to darkness: the hall is roofed so light can only enter through the door or through a clerestory – more than 20 metres (66 feet) above visitors at

154 The well-preserved pylon of Luxor Temple, showing the original locations of colossal statues of the pharaoh and one of a pair of obelisks, with four niches for wooden flag-poles apparent in the façade. Limestone. About 65 m (215 ft) wide, which is the same size as the nearest pylon at Karnak. 19th Dynasty.

155 Reconstruction of the pylon entrance to the mortuary temple of Ramesses III at Medinet Habu (see [150]). 20th Dynasty.

156 The ceiling of an offering shrine decorated with a vivid blue sky and a sequence of crowned, flying vultures denoting the goddess Nekhbet, carrying fans as symbols of a festival procession and cartouches as symbols of the Sun's circuit. Medinet Habu, West Thebes. Painted limestone. 20th Dynasty.

Karnak – while the columns create a massive stone 'marsh'. Indeed, the column-capitals are formed as the flowers or umbels of marsh plants, and the bottoms of both columns and walls are typically decorated in relief with marsh plants or scenes of the districts of Egypt offering their agricultural bounty (see p. 222). The roof, the rising floor and encroaching walls are entirely intrusive so walking through the temple from the pylon to the chapel you must climb the Risen Earth, passing through a monumental 'marsh' to ascend the mound where the god's image stands hidden in a bolted shrine.

Unsurprisingly, the principal decoration of the columns and walls occupies a central band, neither high nor low, and is divided into horizontal registers of information, usually showing scenes of the rituals that take place in the darkened areas, though the king may be the only priest visible. Hieroglyphic texts reproduce the gods' words to the king as they hand him the symbols of authority. A ceiling of stars seems endless except where the procession of the Sun marks the axis to the shrine as a sequence of winged discs or as a golden disc moving through the body of the sky goddess, Nut [156]. Following this axis with the help of a lamp, the visitor arrives at the chapel of the god's shrine or nearby discovers other chapels, perhaps housing the processional boat of the god or a life-size statue of the king and god [157], such as Sobk-Ra and Amenhotep III at the beginning of this book. Paradoxically, therefore, the entrance of the temple is its most massive aspect, whereas the extraordinary heart of darkness is

157 Statue of Horemheb kneeling to make offerings before Atum. From a cache of statues beneath Luxor Temple. Diorite. 1.91 m (6 ft 3 in.) high. 18th Dynasty.

small, still and confined. On the other hand, viewed from within, the movement away from the god's shrine is an atomic eruption out of singularity, silence and darkness, which expands to form the world outside.

The arrangements of scenes in temple decoration also reveal areas of specific activity in ways scholars are becoming increasingly aware of. For example, columns displaying different titles and regalia for the king may mark his actual progress in procession through different episodes of a ritual. To take another example, a frieze showing lapwings with human arms nesting in bowls may be read by rebus as the phrase 'all the people are adoring', and columns marked with this group perhaps indicate areas of access during festivals for persons other than priests. Such 'hieroglyphic' meanings may occur even where they are not conspicuous: as we have seen, the stars on the ceilings effectively repeat the word for 'adoration'. To take another example, almost without exception the ancient 'smiting scene' [155, 158] decorates the twin towers of the pylon gateway, behind which the Sun may rise (or set, if the pylon is on the west of the Nile) so the temple '*resembles the horizon formed from the sky when the Sun is rising there*', in the words of an inscription of Amenhotep III. The Egyptologist José-Ramón Pérez-Accino has suggested that the smiting scene here sets up a pun based on the homophony (common sound) of two Egyptian phrases – for 'punishing the earth' and for 'dawn'. Of course, the significance of the Sun rising between the towers of a temple is perfectly comprehensible, as is royal authority expressed in the utter overthrow of enemies. However, the 'hieroglyphic' identification of the images together in the most massive decorative space on the outside of the

158 Scene of Sety I being handed enemies to 'smite' by Amun-Ra, from the exterior decoration of the great temple of Amun-Ra. Karnak, near Thebes. Limestone. 19th Dynasty.

159 Archive photo displaying the astonishingly large coffin of Ahmose-Nefertiry, Great Wife of king Ahmose II. West Thebes. Plastered and painted cedar wood and cartonnage. 3.78 m (12 ft 5 in.) high. 18th Dynasty.

160 Aerial view of the reconstructed temples of Ramesses II at Abu Simbel in Wawat, Nubia. 19th Dynasty.

temple adds layers of possible interpretation, whereby the king's authority becomes part of the created order – his temporal authority re-created in the fabric of each day, his activities unbounded and defining like the Sun's, and so on.

King and queen

As a final note, a significant aspect of monumental art at Thebes during the New Kingdom, especially during the 18th Dynasty, is that the king is often accompanied on his throne. In an offering chapel he may be enthroned with a god, of course, but elsewhere in the statues or reliefs of temples he will often have a mortal companion, and this earthly peer is usually one of the royal women [163]. Typically she is the King's Great Wife [159] but not unusually may be his mother or a daughter. By contrast, men – royal or otherwise – are mostly absent from his company until the 19th Dynasty (see p. 229). The relevance of royal women is apparent in other ways, as at Abu Simbel [160] where there are temples dedicated to the worship of Ra-Horakhty in the form of Ramesses II and the goddess Hathor in the form of the King's Great Wife, Nefertiry.

Of course, royal women had been prominent in the pyramid complexes of Old and Middle Kingdom pharaohs and, during the Middle Kingdom, Sobknefru became king alongside her father, though for reasons unknown to us. Nonetheless, the queens'

status at the beginning of the New Kingdom is exceptional [161], and reached its apogee in the career of Hatshepsut (c. 1475–c. 1458 BC), the daughter of Thutmose I, who then became King's Great Wife of her half-brother, Thutmose II. However, after the latter died and was succeeded by his son, Thutmose III, Hatshepsut did not step aside and instead became co-regent as 'king' in her own right. We do not know specifically why she became king, though we can understand her accession in the context of the exceptional significance of queens at this time, and appreciate that she did not simply steal the throne – in fact, she had no independent reign at all. More to the point for present purposes, Hatshepsut essentially acted as would be expected of any king, not least in being a prodigious builder of temples [162].

The temple most often associated with her, though completed by Thutmose III after she died, literally took the place of earlier structures at Deir el-Bahri. Its 'stacked' terraces rising

164 Detail from a wall in the mortuary temple of Hatshepsut, showing houses raised on stilts along the shore of the Red Sea or a river in Punt. Deir el-Bahri, West Thebes. Painted limestone. 18th Dynasty.

under the hills emulate the tomb of Montuhotep II alongside, though Hatshepsut's own burial lay behind the hills in the Valley of the Kings. A pair of chapels, one for the goddess Hathor nursing the infant king, another for Anubis and other gods of burial, flanks the principal Sun-court of the temple, while at the top of the temple the central shrine for Amun-Ra is flanked by a pair of chapels for the dead king and the risen Sun. The most famous scenes in the temple – showing a celebrated expedition to the mystical land of Punt [164] – are the decorative counterpart of scenes in which Hatshepsut is fathered by Amun-Ra and guided by him to her enthronement (see p. 197). Subsequently, an oracle of Amun-Ra obliges his royal child in the presence of the entire palace to '*seek out the paths to Punt*' and '*guide an expedition on water and on land to bring wonders from God's Land to the very god who created its perfection*'. In other words, Hatshepsut is seen to be born to commission a voyage of discovery to the end of the earth. The inscriptions disclose that the expedition was also a survey, which recorded specimens of the different species of fish it encountered at sea. After the ships returned, the records were set in stone, just as later Thutmose III had botanical specimens his army encountered on military expeditions inscribed on the walls of a chapel at Karnak. One scene shows the Egyptian captain camped on a beach, where he is greeted by Parohu, the chief of Punt. Although Parohu demands to know how Egyptians could have reached such far distant shores, the exchanges are friendly and the Puntites first '*give praise for the lord of the gods, Amun-Ra*' before loading the Egyptian ships with tribute to the brim. Evidently a pharaoh's god-given authority did reach the ends of the earth.

Masterpiece
Limestone chapel, Deir el-Bahri

165 Detail from the statue of king Amenhotep II, showing the king suckling from the goddess Hathor in the form of a cow. Deir el-Bahri, West Thebes. Painted sandstone. 18th Dynasty.

This limestone chapel, decorated with brightly painted low relief, is the stone cladding from a rock-cut chapel in the hills at Deir el-Bahri – part of a temple built by Thutmose III above the better-known temples of Montuhotep II and Hatshepsut. The sandstone statue of Hathor in the form of a cow – as long as the chapel is tall (2.2 metres or 7 feet) – was added by his son and successor, Amenhotep II (c. 1426–c. 1400 BC). (When discovered in 1905 the statue filled the middle of the chapel and it has been shifted forward only for museum display purposes, as the slot in the pavement indicates.) The cow's horns seem to frame an elaborate headdress made up of the king's uraeus-cobra, the Sun-disc and the twin plumes of Amun-Ra. In front of her, Amenhotep is shown in the gesture of greeting, so in a sense this is a double statue of both king and god awaiting offerings, though the adult king is also shown as a diminutive figure under the god's care. Then on the left side, where the statue could hardly be viewed originally, the king is also shown as an infant, naked and suckling at the udder [165].

The decoration of the walls is equally as abstract and wonderfully illuminating. The tops of the walls are decorated with a stylized frieze of knotted plants, known by its Egyptian name as a kheker-frieze, which represents the marshy columns of a temple and is commonly used to indicate a sacred location in two-dimensional art. The starry ceiling is also that of a temple, shaped here as the vault of the sky. On the side walls, the king (Thutmose, in this case) is seen entering with his Great Wife, Merytra (on one wall) or his daughters (on the other). In front of them, beside the statue on each side, is an illustration of the chapel itself, including the cow and the twin figures of the king. At the far end, beyond where the statue stood, the king is shown on both walls adoring Hathor 'five times', and she is described on either side as patron of Thebes (city of Amun) and of Heliopolis (city of Ra). Finally, on the back wall the king is seen offering incense and water to Amun-Ra, seated in his shrine at Karnak.

In other words, the decoration of the chapel exhibits layers of meaning, or – if we prefer – illustrates a sequence of transitions during the ritual that took place here. First, the king and royal women enter the chapel, where they make offerings before a statue of the king as a divine child with a divine mother. Hence the king is both the officiant and the subject of the ritual, and so indeed are his female relatives – whether or not we understand the mortal women to be identified with Hathor. Literally beyond this simple illustration of what we could have seen had we been

here for the ritual, another scene summarizes the meaning of what is taking place: the king adoring the goddess. However, the whole scene is then presented as a reflection – or another aspect – of the king's offering to Amun-Ra, on the opposite bank of the River Nile.

Although comparable statues of Hathor and the king have been discovered at Saqqara and elsewhere, the goddess was specially venerated at Deir el-Bahri, and there were various other chapels for her in the immediate vicinity, including the one in Hatshepsut's temple. Interestingly, in illustrations in Theban tombs, even on coffins, the image of a cow emerging between marsh plants, just as this statue shows, seems to be a motif representing Deir el-Bahri itself or more generally the view of the Theban hills – Kheftethirnebes, 'she who is facing her Lord'. On a stela in Karnak directly facing this chapel, Thutmose III again stated his intentions: *My person desired to make a commitment for my father Amun-Ra in Karnak, erecting a sanctuary and consecrating the horizon, renovating for him [the view of] Kheftethirnebes, which since the first age has been the intention of my father, Amun-Ra, lord of the thrones of the Twin Lands.* The 'Twin Lands', of course, are the banks of the Nile, east and west, the rising and setting Sun, life and afterlife (see pp. 214–15).

166 Offering shrine of king Thutmose III from his mortuary temple at Deir el-Bahri. Painted limestone. 2.2 m (7 ft 2½ in.) high. 18th Dynasty.

Masterpiece
Gold mask of Tutankhamun

167 Gold funerary mask from the burial of king Tutankhamun. Valley of the Kings, West Thebes. 0.54 m (1 ft 3 in.) high. 18th Dynasty.

The tomb of Tutankhamun (c. 1332–c. 1323 BC) is the most famous
discovery in Egyptian archaeology, and the only intact burial
so far recovered from the Valley of the Kings. His iconic gold
mask was found where it had last been placed on his embalmed
face – the last layer of a cocoon wrapping his mortal remains.
Indeed, the king's subterranean burial chamber as found was filled
by four gilded wooden shrines, one inside another, enclosing a
granite sarcophagus and three nested coffins within – the last
coffin and lid made of inlaid 22-carat gold [168]. Gold strips, inlaid
with hieroglyphs of coloured glass and semi-precious stones, laid
on the king's mummy identify him with Osiris, while a pair of
burnished gold hands clasp the dead king's crook and flail.

The face is a single sheet of gold, burnished to a remarkably
uniform consistency, with chasing for details such as the
headband, eyes, neck and especially the precisely defined lips,
characteristic of the late 18th Dynasty. The headdress was
possibly hammered on a mould, with pleats added to retain a
blue glass inlay and create the characteristic stripes of a *nemes*
headcloth and its knotted tail. The collar consists of at least two
soldered sheets of burnished gold inlaid with blue glass, carnelian,
feldspar and lapis lazuli. These three principal elements of the
mask were joined with tiny gold rivets, while the king's ears, the
inlaid cobra and vulture on his brow and his false beard were
cast separately in gold and attached with either solder or rivets.
The combination of the vulture and cobra on the king's brow
in place of the single uraeus-cobra seems to be a specifically
funerary image. The fine collar beneath the beard is a separate
gold sheet inlaid with carnelian, lapis lazuli and faience. The
beard itself is inlaid with blue faience, lapis lazuli is used for
the brows and eyeliner, and the eyes have been formed from
quartz with obsidian pupils. Red paint laid behind the king's eyes
adds a texture of life. The whole is so expertly made that the
mask measures 54 by 39 centimetres (21 by 15 inches), and 49
centimetres (19 inches) from front to back, but weighs little more
than 10 kilograms (22½ pounds).

Of course, the most startling aspect of the mask is its
flawless beauty, which is consistent with the meaning of the
mask according to the text pressed into the collar. This is a
speech often used on funerary masks and coffins, taken from the
so-called Egyptian Book of the Dead (see p. 262):

Greetings, O, perfect of sight, possessor of light-rays,
whom Ptah-Sokar has completed, whom Anubis has

exalted, to whom Thoth has given the distinctions of one perfect of sight, which are as the gods, and your western eye is the evening-boat and your eastern eye the morning-boat. Your eyebrows are as the Nine. Your forehead is as Anubis. The back of your head is as Horus. Your braiding is as Ptah-Sokar.

Here the deceased's face is a microcosm, whose featured pairs embody the balance of sunrise and sunset, life and death. Ptah-Sokar is a god of Creation and death, Anubis of burial, while Thoth signifies esoteric wisdom and the moon – the light in the darkness. The eyebrows arch over the eyes just as the Nine – the first gods – preside over a Creation in which time passes, and birth and death are the lot of everyone. The face is turned

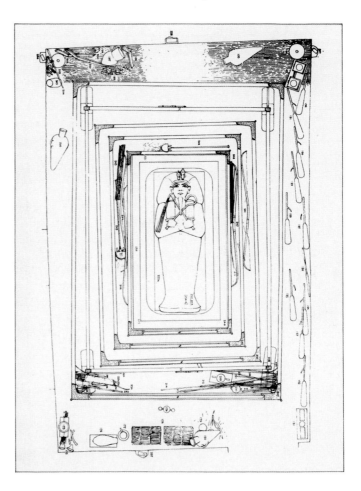

168 Sketch of the nest of shrines that surrounded the king's sarcophagus and coffins, made by the tomb's discoverer, Howard Carter. Note the oars laid along one edge of the burial chamber.

towards death but the risen king, Horus, follows just as surely as the back of the head follows the front of the head under the coiffed hair. Most strikingly, the Egyptian phrase 'perfect of sight' introduces the deliberate ambiguity of a face that is physically perfect (to behold) and spiritually perfect (of vision), thereby evoking the enlightened condition of the afterlife. Once again, the ancient Egyptian portrait of the deceased is not an idealized portrait of the person but an evocation of their spiritual eminence in death. The phrase 'possessor of light-rays' – meaning, of course, the Sun – is embodied in the unchanging gold of the mask, latent within the eternal darkness of earthly burial.

Outside the nest of shrines that finally enclosed his interment, the departing priests laid a row of oars to signify the spiritual journeys awaiting the dead and new-born king [cf. 19, 139].

Chapter 12 'You Create the World as You Will in Your Uniqueness': Two More Studies in Change

1: The Amarna Period

No other chapter in the story of Egyptian art has been discussed as much as the Amarna Period (c. 1360–c. 1330 BC), at the end of the 18th Dynasty; and towering over any discussion is this startling, sinister image of king Akhenaten – looking as if it had been carved by Jacob Epstein for some Modernist reimagining of pharaonic Egypt [170]. Rather, we should say this image of the Creator because the statue is explicitly named as Ra-Horakhty, the ancient god of Heliopolis, or more specifically 'Ra-Horakhty exalted in the horizon in his identity as the energy (Shu) which is from the Sun'. However, as is typical of the period, the god's name has been written in pairs of name rings or cartouches, ordinarily used for kings' names. So this image of divinity takes as its starting point the mortal form of Akhenaten and the physical characteristics of a woman who has given birth (prominent breasts, engorged thighs, flaccid belly and distended navel), along with exaggerated sense-organs. Not least, there is also a pair of hands grasping the king's crook and flail in the emphatic manner of Osiris to complement the crown that once stood on the statue's head. In other words, the composition begins in the realm of the mortal and royal but reaches to the unworldly and supernatural, becoming reminiscent of Hermann Hesse's description of the mystical Max Demian:

> In fact I saw – I thought I saw or felt – that it was not even a man's face, but something rather different. There was almost something there of a woman's face, and in particular this face seemed to me, for an instant, neither adult nor childlike, neither old nor young, but somehow a thousand years old, somehow timeless, marked by spans of time unlike those we live. Animals could look like this, or trees or stars ... I do not know what he was like, but he was different – unimaginably different – from all of us.

170 Statue of the Sun-god based on the form of king Amenhotep IV (Akhenaten), from the great temple of Amun-Ra at Karnak. Sandstone. 4 m (13 ft) high. 18th Dynasty.

In fact, the sandstone colossus was one of a series erected in a new Sun-court on the east side of Karnak, whereas a more traditional image of the king employed in a Theban colonnade would have taken the form of Osiris, king of the west. The hermaphrodite character of this statue may well reference the prominence of the King's Great Wife at this time, and in a chapel of the new Sun-court Akhenaten's Great Wife, Nefertiti, was shown as the officiant instead of the king, while the Harim-festival avenue was provided with sphinxes alternately wearing the faces of Akhenaten and Nefertiti. Indeed, according to a fragment of a festival scene now in the Metropolitan Museum of Art, one of the gods' statues was carried in procession in a wooden shrine decorated with a scene of Nefertiti smiting enemies [171] – the definitive image of a king.

The so-called Amarna Period centres on Amenhotep IV, who early in his reign changed his name to Akhenaten, which means 'enlightened spirit of the Sun'. During the 20th century his reign was often presented as a singular event – a turning point not just in Egypt's history but in human history – by interpreters as diverse as Thomas Mann, Sigmund Freud, Philip Glass and Naguib Mahfouz. In art, his reign might have begun 'a quest for naturalism and realism', in the words of the Swiss Egyptologist, Robert Hari. Doubtless, the distinctive art of the period has helped characterize both king and reign as peculiar, and Akhenaten's bizarre reputation may well be overstated as a result. A discussion of the history of the period – still more its modern reverberations – lies beyond the scope of this book, but for present purposes we have to recognize that the Amarna Period is first and foremost a matter of art history. Questions, such as whether Akhenaten was physically deformed, or a heretic, or whether his Great Wife became king after him, are much debated but, in the end, depend upon close interpretations of sacred art,

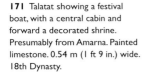

171 Talatat showing a festival boat, with a central cabin and forward a decorated shrine. Presumably from Amarna. Painted limestone. 0.54 m (1 ft 9 in.) wide. 18th Dynasty.

172 View across an open Sun-court towards the hypostyle hall and shrine area of the smaller temple at Akhetaten, showing in the foreground the reconstructed platform of an open-air altar surrounded by bases for smaller offering tables.

taken from the temples and tombs of the ruling group after the usual pharaonic fashion.

Nonetheless, from the perspective of art history there is much that is new. First is the fact that Amenhotep IV founded a new city at Akhetaten ('the Sun's horizon') – including temples and palaces, festival avenues, highways, government offices, farms and factories, and sprawling suburbs – in the middle of the country, near the modern town of el-Amarna from which the era takes its name [172]. In itself establishing a city was nothing new – the history of Egypt is punctuated with new royal cities from Memphis in the earliest days, through such foundations as Itjtawy, Per-Ramesses, Tanis and eventually Alexandria. Akhenaten himself founded another city at Sesebi in Nubia. Rather, the unusual aspect of Akhetaten is that the place was soon abandoned, probably within a decade of Akhenaten's death, and since the 1880s has offered a unique opportunity to deconstruct an entire ancient city consigned to the sands almost in its original form.

Then there is a subtle but crucial difference – the use of smaller stone blocks. Much of the art that survives from Akhenaten's reign, whether at Thebes or Amarna, is associated specifically with his 'tail festivals'. Often the extent of a pharaoh's monumental building does not correlate simply with the length of his reign, but with the number of 'tail festivals' he celebrated. Of course, there may well be a direct correlation between the number of 'tail festivals' and the reign length but most pharaohs only celebrated the first festival after three decades on the throne, whereas Akhenaten began to do so in a three-year cycle from his accession. Moreover, kings who were building or adding to temples for such festivals typically made liberal use of monuments from earlier kings and other places, whereas Akhenaten's artists, as we shall see, were more or less obliged to craft their monuments from scratch. Hence, in order to work sufficiently quickly, his builders employed smaller-than-usual stone blocks known to Egyptology as *talatat* [171] – a word whose origin is uncertain but has become assimilated to the modern Arabic word for 'three', as though perhaps each block measured just three palm-widths. In any event, Akhenaten's monuments take on a distinctive appearance because of this reduced medium. In turn, talatat-buildings were ideal to demolish and use as in-fill for the monuments of later kings, so individual talatat have been recovered in large quantities as rubble, especially at Karnak, thereby providing an exceptional number of examples of art from the Amarna Period to add to the remains of Akhetaten.

Exaggerated claims about the novelty of the Amarna Period abound. For example, the standard assumption that 'a revision of the written script to more closely reflect the spoken language of the time' is unfounded because, apart from a small handful of new writing conventions, there is nothing in the language of Akhenaten's monuments that cannot be found in the monuments of Thutmose III or even earlier kings. The distinguished curator W. Stevenson Smith noted that '[even] at the most revolutionary point in the early part of the reign of Akhenaten the instinct to formalize kept naturalistic impulses within bounds which are basically Egyptian'. Inevitably there is a degree of continuity between art in the Amarna Period and those periods that preceded and followed, including aspects that seem to be innovations simply because they pass from the subtle to the flagrant at this time. For example, the apparent 'feminization' of images of kings throughout the whole of the 18th Dynasty – developments such as increasingly slender limbs, raised buttocks and long legs – is a subjective topic long debated among scholars. Even the startling, almost bestial style of the colossi is prefigured in earlier work especially by Akhenaten's father, Amenhotep III [173], while some of the novel conventions of 'Amarna' art, such as allowing an area of colour to flow into another using fine overlapping lines, appear in the tombs of Amenhotep III's officials. In the Theban tomb of Ramose [174] we can almost discern the moment of the 'shift', when the exemplary, traditional decoration of its magnificent hypostyle hall was eventually completed in the new 'Amarna style'. Indeed (as described in Chapter 4), the sculptor Bak, who served Akhenaten, was the son of Men, who served Amenhotep III, so we need not suppose that we are suddenly looking at a new breed of artists (see pp. 65–66). In an area of Akhetaten populated mainly by the king's artists, at the house of a sculptor named Thutmose, the famous painted 'bust'

173 Head of a colossal statue from a series in a Sun-court of the mortuary temple of king Amenhotep III. The pronounced stylization of eyes, nose and mouth prefigure the surrealism of pharaonic iconography early in the reign of his son. West Thebes. Quartzite. 1.17 m (3 ft 10 in.) high. 18th Dynasty.

174 The artists' draft of a single scene in the tomb of Ramose in the so-called 'Amarna style', showing Egyptian officials and foreign dignitaries gathered in the presence of the royal family. West Thebes. Painted limestone. 18th Dynasty.

175 The celebrated 'bust' of Akhenaten's principal wife, Nefertiti, discovered in an artists' workshop at Akhetaten. Plastered and painted limestone, with inlaid rock crystal. 0.5 m (1 ft 7½ in.) high. 18th Dynasty.

of Nefertiti came to light – a form so determinedly figurative and human it is still hailed today as a model of female beauty [175].

Revolution or reformation?

To judge from the cursory treatment of its other features, the head of Nefertiti was actually a model for copying her face during the production of other artworks. Its elegance indicates that the most excessive abstractions in Amarna art were not universally applied in the period but were reserved for specific contexts, especially temples. In fact, Akhenaten's inscriptions reveal his commitment to discerning the most appropriate ways of acknowledging and representing the Creator, in words as well as plastic arts. Among versions of a famous Hymn to the Sun inscribed in the tombs of his ruling officials, the key sentiment may be the line, 'for you are my desire, and there is no other who comprehends you apart from your son'. Only the king can truly make sense of his divine father, the Creator. Accordingly, in the iconography of household shrines as well as in tombs, the king and the royal women take the place of traditional images of the 'many' gods. This is the real discrepancy between art of the Amarna Period and what came before and after: that traditional images of gods and kings together have been rejected in favour of images based on the royal family alone. Perhaps there is an analogy here with the effect of the Protestant Reformation on European art. Akhenaten's commitment involved eliminating whatever was perceived (by him?) as specious, deceptive or redundant in traditional art. Two traditional images of divinity seem to have been especially decried: first, Amun, a name meaning 'the hidden one', whose name and image were often removed from existing monuments; secondly, the image of the dead king, Osiris, and the iconography of death and the afterlife. Instead Akhenaten's artists preferred the manifest brilliance of the sunshine as the embodiment of Ra-Horakhty, his rays reaching down to press life on the king and his female family, with no other gods appearing as intermediaries either in worship or in iconography.

Scenes from the Amarna Period also adopt a distinctive, distorted form for the human body, analogous to the hermaphrodite body-shape of the colossi. This form was not drawn using a traditional eighteen-row grid but using a twenty-row grid, with two rows apparently simply inserted above the waistline to provide for the elongation of the upper torso and (often) the face, while the legs become proportionately shorter though drawn the same length as previously. In addition, the small of the back was raised with the upper torso, and accordingly moved up from the tops of the legs to generate a distended backside. With engorged buttocks, thighs and bellies, these canonical human figures have straightforward similarities with more traditional figures personifying the fecundity of the Nile, typically used to decorate the lower reaches of 'marshy' temple walls and columns [176]. In such fecundity figures too, broad hips and flabby stomachs foster the impression of squat legs, and there

176 Personifications of the Nile Valley (left) and a temple estate presenting their produce as offerings at the 'Red Chapel' of the female king Hatshepsut. From the temple of Amun-Ra at Karnak, near Thebes. 18th Dynasty.

177 The lunette of a boundary stela at Amarna, showing the royal family standing alone at an offering table beneath the Sun's rays. This stela stood at the southern edge of the city, so the family face north. Limestone. 2.0 m (6 ft 6½ in.) wide. 18th Dynasty.

is exaggerated emphasis on the pendulous bellies and breasts of ostensibly male figures. The abundance of Creation, not to mention the singularity of the Creator, is the principal topic in Akhenaten's Hymn to the Sun, summarized in this verse: 'How numerous are your achievements, which are hidden from sight, O, sole god, there being no other of the same form, for you create the World as you will in your uniqueness.'

The Amarna boundary stelae

An instructive instance of the new conventions may be found on the fifteen boundary stelae known to delimit the site at el-Amarna [177]. Since the earliest kings, the stela had been a standard vehicle for presenting monumental royal inscriptions. The developed form typically in use during the New Kingdom is exemplified here by a limestone stela of Amenhotep III, originally from his mortuary temple at Thebes and carved with a detailed low relief, standing more than 2 metres (6½ feet) high [178]. At the top centre, the Sun describes an arc from horizon to horizon, identified by the hieroglyph ▭ 'sky' arched over as a canopy. Of course, the Sun is provided with wings partly to illustrate his motion but also because he is explicitly identified as the falcon, Horus. Textbooks call the area defined by the Sun's arc 'the lunette'; this is the area where the king stands offering to the gods as a link between heaven and earth (see p. 17). Beneath the lunette, a rectangle represents the earth itself, where the king's temporal activities are usually described in words (cf. [152]). In this example, there is a balanced pictorial scene instead, showing the king twice in his chariot, with Nubian captives and a statement of the subjugation of Kush at right, then beaten Syrians and a statement of the subjugation of Naharin (the lands of the kingdom of Mitanni) at left. At the base of everything is the lapwing-frieze for the phrase 'all the people are adoring' (see p. 204), and the stark summary that '*every lowland, every highland, all the people, all the aristocracy,*

178 Stela of king Amenhotep III shown offering to Amun-Ra, originally from his mortuary temple but reused by king Merenptah of the next dynasty. West Thebes. Limestone. 2.07 m (6 ft 9½ in.) high. 18th Dynasty.

179 *El Entierro del Conde de Orgaz* by El Greco, painted from 1586 to 1588. Toledo, Spain. Oil on canvas. 4.8 m (15 ft 9 in.) high.

and Naharin, impotent Kush, the Palestine hills and the Palestine plains are beneath the steps of this perfect god, like the Sun, for all time'. The layout of a standard royal stela may be compared, for instance, to El Greco's wall-painting *The Burial of the Count of Orgaz* [179] in the Church of Santo Tomé in Toledo: at top centre, Christ presides over the heavens above and the mortal community of Toledo below, while the intercession of the Virgin, John the Baptist and the blessed dead within a 'lunette' connects the two realms.

However, compared to Amenhotep's stela, a (literally) different perspective may be found on the Amarna boundary stelae. In the lunettes of stelae at the northern and southern corners the royal family is turned to face into the city, while on those stelae along the edges of the city they are shown twice in a mirror image. In keeping with the 'fecund' characteristics of the Amarna human form, there is obvious transparency in the king's kilt so the fold following the line of his 'near' leg is extended to define his genital area, while the queen's gown simply gapes to expose her genitals and a fold under her belly indicative of childbirth. Beside the stelae were statues of the king and queen and two daughters, who are offering either a miniature obelisk or a stela inscribed with the names of Ra-Horakhty, Akhenaten and Nefertiti. On traditional royal stelae the winged Sun is shown as though in profile, with the uraeus curled down one side or down both sides when there are balanced scenes, as in the stela of Amenhotep III. Hence the Sun is above, the earth below, and the king and gods are between them. Here, however, the Sun has no wings and its uraeus is turned towards anyone approaching the stela, as though the Sun were facing them in the distance, and the royal family were preceding them. Since ancient times, of course, the dead king had been Khentyimentu 'he who is ahead of the westerners' (see p. 149), whereas here the living king is shown ahead of those facing the *rising* Sun. In a context where once kings offered to gods or family members offered to the deceased, instead the royal family stands alone before the altar as creatures of the earth, weighed down by the gravity of flesh, their faces caressed by the invisible fingers of the Creator. Indeed, sometimes, instead of the traditional altar piled with offerings, we find only words – the first few words of the boundary inscription, naming the Creator.

While the image of the royal family standing alone in front of the altar may be an innovation in art, in reality it was a most ancient ceremony, enacted every day in the presence of the Sun. At Akhetaten the principal temples fused the formality of New Kingdom temple architecture with the architectural pattern of the Old Kingdom pyramid complexes and Sun-temples, in which the heart of the temple was not a hidden chapel but a single, massive obelisk (see p. 55). Rather than innovation, this may seem a conservative – even reactionary – development compared with the temples at Thebes, for example, where obelisks were typically erected in pairs on either side of the pylon gateway (see p. 202). However, there are no surviving remains of the New Kingdom temple of Ra-Horakhty at Heliopolis, which undoubtedly still existed on the site of its Old Kingdom forebear and might well have provided the model for the temples at Akhetaten (see p. 53). Moreover, at Karnak, Akhenaten's grandfather Thutmose IV (c. 1400–c. 1390 BC) erected an obelisk originally prepared by Thutmose III, and its inscription states that he was erecting 'a single obelisk', as though perhaps introducing an aspect of the traditional Sun-temple to the fabric of Amun-Ra's principal temple. In other words, the novelty of religious practice at Amarna may be more apparent than real – a misapprehension arising from the assumption that Thebes presents the preferred model for temples in the New Kingdom, compounded by the novelty of seeing the royal family at the altar, free for once from any artistic interpretation of the scene in terms of 'other' gods.

The tombs at Akhetaten

The genuine innovation of Akhetaten as a royal city lies in the removal of the royal tomb from the Valley of the Kings to a site nearby, where the Sun rises out of a wadi in the eastern cliffs. The prospect here is fascinating, analogous to the site of the oldest royal cemetery at Abydos – an utterly barren desert where a southern stretch of the cliffs runs down to cross a northern stretch, and the wadi concealed behind them twists eastwards towards the horizon. At the end of this wadi is the tomb of the royal family all together, decorated in relief with more effort and across more surfaces than had previously been attempted within a royal burial. Here, instead of scenes taken from traditional mythologies, the royal family is presented as the embodiment of the gods and their own lives become the organic mythology. Accordingly the artists are tasked to introduce a temporal aspect and, most evocatively, emotions run high at the death of a beloved daughter, Meketaten. For once, an Egyptian artist is required to bring 'the moment' into the formality of a tomb, and is heart-wrenchingly up to the task.

Here too, in the desert, away from the wadi but overlooking the plain of the city, are the cemeteries of the ruling group, some of whom had already prepared tombs at Saqqara or Thebes. The tomb of the high priest of the Sun, Meryra, has a traditional layout: a four-columned hall carved from the cliffs as though it were the hypostyle hall of a temple, with a massive statue of the tomb-owner in the chapel beyond. So too the tomb of the vizier Ay (who later became king himself) has a hypostyle hall designed with no less than twenty-four papyrus-shaped columns, though few have been completed. In each instance, the tomb-owner is shown in the doorway praising the morning Sun, while inside are analogous scenes of children capering at the morning appearance of the king. All the tombs are decorated with scenes of other formal appearances, when people gather in the presence of the king and queen or run beside them in procession. Where once the Sun's boat was seen to journey through the heavens, now the king and queen ride in chariots along festival avenues. Where once Osiris welcomed the deceased into adoration, now king and queen dispense collars of threaded gold out of their own beneficence.

Like the artists of the Reformation, the artists of the Amarna Period wrestled with 'more authentic' ways of revealing Truth in art. Their inspiration was the supposed past but the resultant imagery might have distanced the pharaoh from the expectations of his followers (it is hard to say 'his people' in a context where so much of the evidence is restricted to the 'few'). Perhaps the familiar, evocative and accessible in sacred art were abandoned in favour of the distant, precise and intellectual. In such an exercise, the risk of throwing the baby out with the bathwater is too real. Traditionally Egyptians had turned for spiritual comfort and inspiration to age-old images from mythology and now they were offered only the present – the royal family – as their inspiration in this life and the next.

So it was that the specific style associated with Akhenaten was abandoned shortly into the reign of his son and successor, Tutankhamun. In fact, images late in Akhenaten's own reign seem less extreme in their abstraction than the colossi from Karnak, perhaps in part because later examples are mostly from domestic shrines rather than the now-completed temples. Further variations on human figures and the artists' grid were devised in the latter part of his reign, and emphasis on 'supernatural' aspects gradually reduced. As Stevenson Smith noted, because 'the innovators of the Amarna Period had left intact the foundations of Egyptian art' an immediate return to former conventions was straightforward. For example, if we analyse the statue of Ay – its traditional block form, the finely braided wig – there is little to distinguish the details in the art of high officials of Amenhotep III or Ramesses II, on either side of the Amarna Period [181]. Traditional funerary gods have returned to the inscriptions.

180 Men and horses fallen along a stretch of the River Orontes during the Battle of Qadesh, shown on a wall of the northern temple of Ramesses II at Abydos. 19th Dynasty.

181 Statue of the high priest Ay. West Thebes. Limestone. 47 cm (1 ft 6½ in.) high. 18th Dynasty.

However, the use of specific moments in formal art continued so, whereas Thutmose III offered written accounts of the Battle of Megiddo, Ramesses II uses images of the Battle of Qadesh in his temples as 'real' instances of the archetypal smiting scene [180]. Suddenly the graphic slaughter is as brutal and frightening as Picasso's *Guernica*. However, it is Ramesses' sons, as the generals on the battlefield, who now come to the fore in such scenes, not his daughters, though the latter still appear in certain ritual scenes. Without doubt, discussions about Akhenaten will go on for many years but, to return to the beginning, we must never forget that the images on which we base historical conclusions are first and foremost sacred art, and what has ever challenged the human intellect so much as the correct expression of the ineffable and transcendent?

Masterpiece
Gold throne of Tutankhamun

182 Gold seat or throne of king Tutankhamun. 1.04 m (3 ft 5 in.) high. 18th Dynasty.

The gold throne of Tutankhamun is one of a half-dozen chairs found in his burial, in this case made of wood overlaid with gold and silver, and inlaid with the same materials as his funerary mask (see pp. 212–15). The heads of lions at the arms descend to clawed feet, while the side panels are decorated with winged uraeus-cobras gesturing protection over the king's names. On the sloping back of his throne, the king is reclining beneath the Sun – whose rays reach out in the 'Amarna style' – on a chair with a footstool, and, indeed, a stool was found on the seat of this throne. On either side of this scene are the stylized columns of a temple or a palace, with a frieze of uraeus-cobras, such as would be found above a shrine (see p. 16). Though the setting is entirely formal and abstract, the King's Great Wife, Ankhesenamun, is anointing him with oil, and we find here perhaps the most tender example of the apparent informality of the royal family characteristic of art during the Amarna Period.

Such informality may seem novel, though such tenderness is implied more formally in the scenes of many couples (see [71, 108]). More to the point, informality may well appear in earlier times, if only in different artistic media. For example, a limestone stela in the Cairo Museum shows king Ahmose II (c. 1539–c. 1514 BC), founder of Tutankhamun's dynasty, offering to his deceased grandmother, Tetishery. This much is entirely conventional, but the text is less so, and begins with the king relaxing, painting in words the scene on Tutankhamun's throne: 'Now his person happened to be relaxing in the throne-room ... The one speaks before his partner, asking what is best for those who have passed on.' His wife responds with all the seeming concern of a loving partner: 'To what purpose are you bringing this up? Why has this matter been spoken? What has come to your mind?'

This is as close as we may find to a written description of the domestic circumstances of a pharaoh and his wife, as they consider what is appropriate for the offering cult of a distinguished family member. In this case, the outcome would be the pyramid built for Tetishery at Abydos, along with the tomb chapel in which the stela itself was found in 1903. So, in a formal, pharaonic context, this is hardly a glimpse of an unguarded moment but rather a scene presented with considerable artifice as a statement of something sacred. Likewise, the scene of Tutankhamun and his young queen is novel only insofar as it is a new way of saying old and very important things.

2: An imperial legacy

The only populous nation that shared a land border with ancient Egypt was the land we call Nubia. From the earliest historic times, the peoples of Nubia had various indigenous languages, systems of government, and religious practices distinct from those of Egypt, and we can probably identify the same clear distinction in pre-dynastic burial practices. On the other hand, Egyptians and Nubians were already travelling across the border at Aswan or through the deserts in pre-dynastic times, so rock art and monuments found in Wawat – the area of Nubia adjoining Egypt – carry familiar images from early Egyptian royal art, including kings, boats and bound enemies [183]. Egyptians remained active in Nubia throughout the dynastic period, not least quarrying local stone such as diorite for monuments. However, from the beginning of the New Kingdom in the late 1500s BC, the Nubian lands of Wawat and populous Kush were systematically brought under Egyptian control during a century-long military campaign, which ended in the reign of Thutmose III. An official titled the 'King's Son of Kush' was created with equivalent authority to the twin viziers of the Nile Valley and the Delta – second in authority only to the pharaoh. Any analysis of New Kingdom government must recognize the temples as a principal tool of administration (see p. 72), and this fact must also be considered when we appraise the magnificent New Kingdom temples in Nubia, at places such as Abu Simbel, Sulb, Sesebi and Gebel Barkal. They represent more than the imposition of Egyptian values and religious practices – they are a statement of Nubian lands assimilated to Egypt. By the end of the New Kingdom the paraphernalia of pharaonic rule was long established in Wawat and Kush, and all the evidence we have about government, religion and even burial practice at this time is effectively Egyptian.

Conversely, the decisive moment marking the end of the New Kingdom was the loss of control of Nubia at the end of the

183 Decoration on the outside of an incense burner, showing an Egyptian pharaoh in one boat, flanked by a boat with an animal image and a temple banner and another with a bound prisoner. From a cemetery in Qustul, Wawat. Limestone. 9 cm (3½ in.) high. Presumably 1st or 2nd Dynasty.

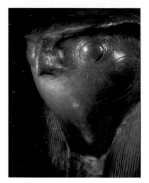

184 Detail showing the falcon-headed face and chased decoration of the inner coffin of a king identified as Shoshenq II. Tanis. Beaten silver. 1.9 m (6 ft 3 in.) long. 22nd Dynasty.

185 Finely detailed pendant representing king Osorkon II as the newborn Osiris, protected on either side by Isis and Horus. Tanis. Gold and lapis lazuli. 9 cm (3½ in.) high. 22nd Dynasty.

20th Dynasty, and this was the result of a civil war. The trigger might have been no more than rivalry and uncertainty at the very top, perhaps because two competing lines during the 21st Dynasty were descended from two daughters of Ramesses XI (c. 1099–c. 1069 BC). Also at this time the royal cemetery was moved from Thebes to Tanis, a splendid new city in the far north – though, like Thebes, a site devoted to Amun-Ra. Since 1940 Pierre Montet and others have uncovered at Tanis a sequence of intact royal tombs where the magnificence of the burial goods is the equal of the Valley of the Kings [184, 185], and the city's monuments illustrate something other than decline, at least in this part of Egypt, amid whatever change and uncertainty affected the nation.

Whatever the situation in Egypt, the Nubian lands of Wawat and Kush were certainly lost from Egyptian rule by this time and, as summarized by John Taylor of the British Museum, the 'three centuries which followed the collapse of Egyptian authority constitute one of the most obscure phases of Nubian history. Written sources are non-existent and the attribution of archaeological material to this period is a matter for debate'. In other words, explanations for the loss of Egyptian control in Nubia based on, for example, nationalism are speculation, and a simpler alternative may be the same dynastic dispute that ended the 20th Dynasty and divided the 21st Dynasty. Be that as it may, during the 8th century BC, as kingship in Egypt grew ever more divided between competing lines of the ruling family, a single, powerful line of kings emerged from Kush to dominate Egypt so effectively that they are conventionally listed as the 25th Dynasty of Egyptian kings. Although they did not rule Egypt as such, in c. 728 BC one of their line, Piye, launched a military invasion to force Egypt's leaders to concede Kushite supremacy.

Understanding the emergence of the 25th Dynasty is not easy, but the principal archaeological sites and the handful of inscribed texts that survive are associated both with traditional pharaonic art and with sites founded under Egyptian rule, such as Semna in Wawat and especially Napata in Kush. Historically, Napata was an Egyptian fortress, founded together with its sacred precinct at Gebel Barkal during the original New Kingdom military occupation. The ongoing association between the Kushite kings and all things pharaonic is no coincidence, and the resemblances are not simply

186 Pyramid I at Kurru, conventionally dated to the 4th century BC, illustrates the ongoing use of pharaonic models in the royal cemeteries of Kush for centuries after the passing of the 25th Dynasty.

187 Scene above a doorway in the tomb of the steward of the God's Wife of Amun Pabasa, identifying the traditional festivals of Thebes with the Sun's journey through the night sky. Asasif, West Thebes. Painted limestone. 26th Dynasty.

apparent. For example, Piye (*c.* 747–*c.* 715 BC) was buried at Kurru in Kush beneath a pyramid, embalmed in Egyptian fashion, though his burial chamber was also furnished with a rock-cut bench to support a wooden bed, following indigenous burial practice. The pyramid of the mighty Taharqa (*c.* 690–664 BC) at Nuri included many traditional Egyptian burial features, such as a splendid collection of more than one thousand *shabty* figures (see pp. 270–71). The pyramids themselves are relatively small and consequently steep-sided, less like the royal pyramids of earlier ages and more like those of private tombs during the New Kingdom [186]. Nonetheless, Taharqa's ruinous sandstone tumulus measures 52 metres (170 feet) along the base of each side, with a projected original height of at least 39.5 metres (130 feet), and consists of a true pyramid enclosed within a later pyramid, recalling the oldest tombs at Abydos and Saqqara. In fact, the design of Taharqa's descending staircase and columned subterranean burial chamber has been compared to both the tombs of the 1st Dynasty kings and a New Kingdom subterranean temple at Abydos, known today as the Osireion. Interestingly, several members of the 25th Dynasty royal family were actually buried at Abydos, and provided with a standard Egyptian offering cult.

Masterpiece
Sphinx of Amenhotep III from Sulb, Nubia

188 Statue of king Amenhotep III shown as a lion. Probably from Sulb in Nubia, but later reused at Gebel Barkal. Granite. 2.16 m (7 ft 3 in.) long. 18th Dynasty.

This is one of a pair of red granite statues of Amenhotep III, originally named in the brief text on the breast, but shown as a life-size recumbent lion. As a lion the statue is perfectly naturalistic, lying with his paws crossed, his huge rump reclining so far that the rear paw emerges beneath him, the tail curling round his rump along the statue base. The mass of the beast is worked with a mix of deft, uncomplicated modelling in the musculature and fine details in the fur of the chest, shoulders and back. The ribs raised along his neck and flank are full of potential and power, and compellingly tactile. His raised head has powerful jaws and a solid muzzle, with eyes hollowed for inlay so they would have seemed especially alert. Presumably these statues, from the king's temple at Sulb in Nubia, were designed to flank a doorway, which is why the head is turned towards the approach, whereas a traditional sphinx would be posed frontally to oversee a processional pavement. Like the royal falcon, the recumbent lion embodies the king's immense power and lethal intent, even in repose (see pp. 34–35).

In contrast to the naturalism of the modelling, the abstraction of the composition arises in the statue's identification with a king, and perhaps the stylization of the mane as a circle with radiating striations, as though it were the disc of the Sun. An inscription near Aswan describes the same king's attack on a Nubian enemy, 'Ikhny, the boaster, in the midst of his army, but he did not recognize the lion in front of him.' The lion, of course, was king Amenhotep. The statue might have been subsequently adapted for Akhenaten, but Tutankhamun rededicated it for his grandfather by adding the inscription on the base. Eventually the statue, along with several sphinxes and other monuments from Sulb, seems to have been removed by the 25th Dynasty king Piye (c. 747–c. 715 BC) to the precinct of Amun-Ra at Gebel Barkal in Kush, which was a pharaonic foundation dating back to the reign of Thutmose III. During the 3rd century BC the names of yet another king, Amanislo of Meroë (who appears as the king of Ethiopia in Verdi's opera *Aida*), were added to the base inscription and the forepaws. In modern times, the lions seem to have been discovered still flanking the processional gateway into Piye's palace beside the great temple at Gebel Barkal, from where they were removed by Lord Prudhoe in 1835.

Masterpiece
Statues of Taharqa at Kawa, Nubia

189 Sphinx of king Taharqa from the temple of Amun-Ra at Kawa. Granite. 0.73 m (2 ft 5 in.) long. 25th Dynasty.

190 Statue of Amun-Ra in the form of a ram protecting king Taharqa, from a processional colonnade. Kawa. Granite. 1.63 m (5 ft 4 in.) long. 25th Dynasty.

191 One of a group of sphinxes representing king Amenemhat III, then inscribed by several later kings. Discovered at Tanis but originally from elsewhere. Granite. 2.36 m (7 ft 9 in.) long. 12th Dynasty.

Taharqa 'king of Cush' is mentioned as such in the Bible (2 Kings 19:9), but here is shown as a traditional Egyptian sphinx. His human face wears the traditional *nemes* headcloth of a pharaoh and twin uraeus-cobras, perhaps to symbolize his kingship in two nations. Taharqa constructed several processional colonnades and courts for Amun-Ra at Karnak and at Gebel Barkal, but this sphinx is from a temple he dedicated to Amun-Ra at Kawa in Kush. His temple replaced an earlier 25th Dynasty temple, which in turn stood beside an even earlier temple built by Tutankhamun. Taharqa also furnished it with a processional pavement from the Nile flanked by statues of Amun-Ra as a massive ram tending the king, emulating the processional approach to Karnak. Inside the temple, however, his sculptors – like those of Akhenaten in an earlier age – found their inspiration and their models in the decoration of Old Kingdom pyramids at Abusir and Saqqara. Not least, a scene on the pylon at Kawa showing Taharqa as a sphinx trampling Libyans was first used in a Sun-court in the mortuary temple of Sahura in the 5th Dynasty, then copied in the pyramid complex of Pepy II in the 6th Dynasty, and finally copied for Taharqa, still retaining the names of a Libyan king's wife and sons – Khuwetyotes, Weni and Wesa – more than 1,700 years after they lived. Likewise, on the sphinx shown here, the shape of the mane may be compared to the 'Prudhoe lions' [188], which were visible at Gebel Barkal in Taharqa's time, while the pattern of the mane clearly imitates the much larger 12th Dynasty sphinx of Amenemhat III, then standing at Tanis in the Nile Delta [191].

So, the kings from Kush, a land assimilated for centuries to pharaonic ways, maintained pharaonic rule and pharaonic religious beliefs, and in architecture and art drew inspiration from every era that had gone before in Egypt. A deep 'fleshy' furrow from the nose to the side of the mouth – often termed 'the Kushite fold' – and prominent lips are among specific features often considered to be a naturalistic aspect of 25th Dynasty art, arguably based on a distinct physiognomy discernible in the Nubian ruling group. Maybe so, but the preponderance of evidence indicates that the Kushite kings were looking to traditional art – even the primeval past, discernible at Abydos and Saqqara – to pinpoint the correct expression of their authority, and the face they chose to show was 'pharaonic'.

The kings' men and women

For sixty years, Piye and his successors remained more powerful within Egypt than any of Egypt's own rulers. They added to the great temples of Egypt, and their officials were buried there in traditional fashion. Statues of the officials, many of them from an ancient cache unearthed at Karnak in 1904, have characteristically heavy bodies with short, stout legs, perhaps deliberately rejecting the more slender forms of the late New Kingdom and harking back to the pronounced authority of canonical forms from the early Old Kingdom [192]. It was at this time that artists adapted the grid system to use twenty-one lines to the top of the eye (see p. 114), and adjusted the placement of specific anatomical features, such as buttocks and nipples, slightly downwards to enhance this 'stockiness'. However, the artists may recall specific details from any and every period in history, for example copying heavily

192 Statue of an anonymous official, originally shown offering to a god, exemplifying the almond-shaped eyes and 'fold' along the nose and mouth characteristic of the Third Intermediate Period. Karnak, near Thebes. Greywacke. 37 cm (2 ft 2½ in.) high.

193 Sphinx showing the God's Wife Shepenwepet II making an offering to Amun-Ra (see [190]). Karnak, near Thebes. Granite. 0.83 m (2 ft 8½ in.) long. 25th Dynasty.

194 Statue of Iriketakana. Karnak, near Thebes. Granite. 45 cm (1 ft 6 in.) high. 25th Dynasty.

braided wigs from the late Old Kingdom or the post-Amarna period, or the almond-shaped eyes of the anonymous official above, which are reminiscent of the Amarna Period itself. The officials' tombs at Saqqara freely adapt Old Kingdom scenes and texts from the ancient cemeteries round and about, while tombs at Thebes for obvious reasons copy scenes from local tombs and temples, mostly dating to the Middle Kingdom and New Kingdom [187]. Even in the subterranean chambers of the venerable Step Pyramid, there are stelae with twenty-one-line grids traced on them, presumably by artists of this period who were studying them. Nonetheless, far from derivative or reactionary, sculpture of the period is 'technically superb', to quote the Egyptologist Jaromír Málek, producing works in which 'qualities of maturity and experience are valued more highly than youth and promise'.

For the kings, sustaining their pharaonic heritage was not a matter to pursue far from Egypt. For example, they vied with the other rulers of Egypt to have their daughters adopted into the entourage of the God's Wife of Amun, a priestess of utmost authority. Such authority is obvious in the statue of Taharqa's sister, the God's Wife Shepenwepet II, represented both as a priestess offering a ram-headed jar and as a royal sphinx [193]. Indeed, Shepenwepet, like other God's Wives, was eventually buried in the grand old pharaonic complex at Medinet Habu. Probably from the entourage of one of the God's Wives comes the statue of Iriketakana [194], which, according to Cyril Aldred, 'is in the more realistic and even brutal style of the dynasty'. More recently Robert Morkot, a historian of both Egypt and Nubia, has

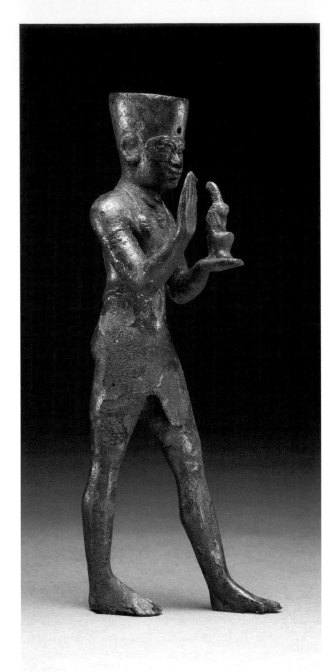

195 Statue of the God's Wife Karomama, originally shaking a pair of sistra (rattles), presumably in front of the image of a god now lost. Probably Karnak, near Thebes. Bronze, inlaid with gold and silver. 0.59 m (1 ft 11 in.) high. 22nd Dynasty.

196 Bronze figure of an anonymous pharaoh offering Truth to the image of a god now lost (cf. [6]). Kawa. 16 cm (6 in.) high. 25th Dynasty.

suggested Iriketakana's corpulent form may rather be a means to express his status as a royal eunuch, an observation that may temper the word 'realistic' as well as 'brutal'.

Bronze-working, working either from sheet metal or by casting, was a medium employed with increased frequency and delicacy in the early 1st millennium BC. An exceptionally fine example is the bronze statue of Karomama, God's Wife of Amun and daughter of Osorkon II (c. 875–c. 835 BC), which was once entirely covered with gold leaf and exhibits the slender human form characteristic of the late New Kingdom, though this is now the 22nd Dynasty [195]. The treatment of her dress is especially effective, adding the fine details of birds' wings, symbolizing a goddess, to what would appear to be the sheer fabric on her lower torso. However, the dress at her shoulders is heavily pleated and billows about her arms, constrained only by the weight of her collar inlaid with silver and electrum. From Kawa a collection of bronze figures of 25th Dynasty kings, probably originally elements fitted to processional boats or religious standards, also conforms to traditional archetypes. For example, the king is shown kneeling before a shrine or offering the figure of Truth, in the manner of Sety I at Abydos (see p. 17) [196]. On the other hand, these particular bronzes exhibit features distinctive of Kushite kings, such as the twin uraeus-cobras or the ram's-head collar worn as an emblem of Amun-Ra.

Historically Taharqa's reign was entirely overshadowed by the aggressive expansion of Assyria into Levantine coastal areas once dominated by Egypt, until a devastating invasion of Egypt herself in 664 BC drove Taharqa into Nubia, where he was to die. Nonetheless, Assyrian domination of Egypt was short-lived, and a sequence of massive tombs at Thebes for officials in the next generation belies any suggestion that Egypt was left in dire straits (see p. 235). Moreover, Taharqa's descendants also kept the traditions of pharaonic rule alive in Kush and, further south, Meroë for another 1,000 years. The tomb decoration of his successor, Tanwetamani (664–657 BC), and the kings who followed remained traditionally Egyptian, even drawing on the Old Kingdom Pyramid Texts, though kings at Kush no longer had obvious access to the monuments of Egypt. Pyramid burials were still used by this royal line until the middle of the 4th century AD, so just as the twin cobras of Taharqa had once stood for two nations under a single pharaoh, now the two kingdoms of Egypt and Kush flourished with distinct but essentially pharaonic identities [197].

197 Stela presumably from a cemetery in the kingdom of Meroë. The figure conforms to a later Meroitic archetype but ultimately his staff, hand-held strap, Sun disc and two-dimensional pose derive from Egyptian funerary stelae. Sandstone. 0.55 m (1 ft 9½ in.) high. Perhaps 2nd or 1st century BC.

Masterpiece
Seated statue of the chief steward Harwa

198 Statue of the chief steward Harwa (cf. [38]). Karnak, near Thebes. Schist. 25th Dynasty.

Harwa was chief steward for Amenirdis I, God's Wife of Amun and daughter of the early Kushite king Kashta. His tomb at Thebes is the first in the sequence of massive tombs of the 25th and 26th Dynasties – perhaps the largest non-royal tombs ever built in Egypt – at Asasif, a prime location adjoining the Valley-festival route where it reaches Deir el-Bahri. However, the granite statue shown here is from Karnak, one of a group showing Harwa in various poses at various ages, after the fashion of the statues of Amenhotep, son of Hapu (see pp. 64–65). This is the most conspicuously corpulent of the group, with huge sagging breasts and flesh as soft and ill defined in the hard stone as we saw in the limestone bust of Ankhhaf (see pp. 170–71). Harwa's pose is ostensibly relaxed, though the arrangement of his knees, held apart, recalls the ancient scribal pose of an official, and is consistent with the written scroll obviously stretched across his kilt (cf. [104]). His shaved head is indicative of a priest, while its disproportionate size adds the suggestion that he is not simply older but wiser as a result. So, though the composition may not be so obviously intimidating as a king represented as a lion, nonetheless in Harwa we see a quiet, contemplative man who is now at rest precisely because he brings to bear a massive presence and enormous authority.

199 Detail of mourners from the
funeral scene in [200].

Chapter 13 'I Drove Away the Killers': Service to Others

As we near the end of a study of art focused by its very nature on the temples of kings and tombs of individuals, the question undoubtedly arises whether pharaonic art is founded not so much in the meaning of things as in the determination of a few successful men and women to refuse to pass away. In other words, are the artworks of ancient Egypt no more than a magnificent vanity – the comments about portraiture in Chapter 9 notwithstanding? Of course, a fair-minded democrat ought not to begrudge the dead their place in this world, and Chapter 10 discussed how ancient people even from outside Egypt sought to become part of the funerary cult centred on the pharaoh. More than that, however, surely there is no pride in death, which is the commonest gift to mortal folk. As Shakespeare's King Richard II notes, 'whate'er I am, / nor I, nor any man that but man is, / with nothing shall be pleas'd till he be eas'd / with being nothing' (*Richard II*, Act 5: 5). The mourners in the tomb of Ramose openly profess what we know to be true anyway: that the Egyptians were not fond of the prospect of dying, whatever beauty their artists may bring to bear in the tomb [199]. The Middle Kingdom poem quoted in Chapter 11 also includes this lament: '*If you think about burial, it is ripping out the heart. It means squeezing tears out of the reduction of a man. It means taking a man out of his house and casting him on the hills.*'

On the other hand, if anything of an individual's presence in this world may be rescued beyond death – in the tomb, in art, in the offering cult, in the afterlife – perhaps the same may be transmitted as a gift to others. We have seen many times how traditional scenes allow a king or a tomb-owner to invoke or represent his family and friends. In fact, the patterns of decoration in a given pharaonic foundation usually provide for more than a simple representation of others: the artists can literally draw others into temple worship or the offering cult – virtually bring them into the afterlife or 'adoration'. For example, consider the scene of Ramose and his party guests discussed in Chapter 7: where the scene sits within his tomb is part of its meaning. Ramose's tomb is divided in half by the east–west axis of the doorways, which lead visitors straight through the hypostyle hall to the chapel where offerings

200 Funeral scenes covering the south wall of the tomb chapel of the vizier Ramose. West Thebes. Plastered and painted limestone. 18th Dynasty.

are to be laid before his statue. To get there the visitors must pass through two doorways, in both of which Ramose is shown facing east and praising the Sun, with the words of a hymn accompanying him. To the left or south of this central axis – orientated with the passage of the Sun – the party guests are shown on the east wall. Consequently they are looking ahead to the scenes of Ramose's funeral, which cover the south wall [200]. To put this another way, according to the relative arrangements of the scenes, the party guests are inexorably facing the funeral. Of course, the funeral procession itself is a grim, emotional affair, leading Ramose away from the joy of the east and the mortal gathering to the west. In the top register the funeral is a simple procession, but below is shown for what it really is – heartbreak and casting Ramose on the hills. Look more closely at the procession; what is the odd black form, called *teknu*, dragged on the leading sledge? Is it a religious totem? A symbol of the embalmed corpse? Something obscure sewn in a bull's skin? Is it a stylized womb? More to the point, where is the procession heading? Unsurprisingly, in the corner adjoining the west wall Ramose appears in his tomb, received into the presence of Osiris, king of the dead. However, in the next step – that is to say, in the same corner but on the west wall – Ramose now offers bouquets of flowers to the living king.

If we turn to the scenes on the west wall but north of the central axis, we find Ramose is the one receiving bouquets of flowers, and not only that, he is also receiving praise from prostrate courtiers, Egyptian and foreign. Here too, beside the shrine door, he is shown receiving gifts from Akhenaten and Nefertiti in the 'Amarna style', though, whatever we make of the new style, the meaning of the scene seems entirely appropriate here (see p. 116).

In a sense, receiving such praise was part of Ramose's job – he was a vizier. However, in a funerary context, and on the west wall, it is clear that Ramose's condition in death and in duat (the state of 'Adoration') is assimilated to that of the king. More generally, his journey to the west also leads his family and friends from a mortal gathering to his offering chapel. Following the layout of scenes round this hall, we are on the road together – king, courtier and all who follow. To complete the decorative circuit, on the east wall but north of the central axis, the living Ramose makes his daily ablutions in one scene, while in the adjoining scene priests purify the statue prepared for his offering shrine. Hence the adoration of the deceased has been laid out within an artistic circuit, bisected, or overarched, by the course of the Sun. As a final note, in the far northeast corner, Ramose, with his wife and brother, stands once again in the company of his late father and mother – a scene placed diagonally across the hall from the scenes of his reception by the king of the dead, Osiris, and the living king.

The decorative scheme of almost any Egyptian tomb chapel, if sufficiently well preserved, from the Old Kingdom to the end of pharaonic rule, may be deconstructed in similar fashion. On a more massive scale, the decoration of every room and hall in a temple may be broken down into areas of activity, and scenes of specific rituals presented, like Ramose's funeral, both in terms of what those physically present might have seen and of what the rituals meant to those who performed them (see pp. 208–11). Still, Ramose's tomb alone assures us that we do not live or die on our own; so part of the meaning of life is the influence each of us has on other people.

A 12th Dynasty stela from Abydos offers an interesting alternative demonstration of how an artwork prepared for the death of one individual may encompass several shared lives [201]. There are two registers with scenes of offerings for two couples, but the name of the woman is the same in each register, Khu. Bigamy was socially unacceptable, so if this woman is the same person, we may assume she outlived or divorced at least one of her husbands. At top, a son named Samenkhet approaches Khu and his father, Sahathor, but Samenkhet himself has already died, according to the inscription, and merely gestures a greeting. With him to make the actual offerings are two 'lesser' characters, a house manager Inyotef and a servant Emsaf. In the lower scene, there is no son at all, so a servant Sehetepib makes the offerings to Khu and her husband Saamun, while under the table appears 'his beloved friend, Inyotef'. In the register below this are three sons – two with their wives, and another named Amenemhat, who is with

201 Funerary stela for the household of the lady Khu. Abydos. Painted limestone. 1.25 m (4 ft 1 in.) high. 12th Dynasty.

his mother, Beta. In other words, Amenemhat is not Khu's son by either husband. In the bottom register are three men and three women, who work on the estate: a handyman, a housekeeper, a butcher, a servant and two cleaners.

In the upper register, perhaps the lines in Khu's face and her heavier breasts are an indication that here is the older, remarried Khu. Perhaps no son is offering to Saamun in the lower scene because none came to the couple before Saamun died or left the home, in which case all four sons in the stela would be from Khu's second marriage. Khu then marries Sahathor, who brings with him two sons by the other woman, Beta – though one of these, Samenkhet, predeceased his father. Alternatively, Samenkhet is Khu's son too, and the unmarried Amenemhat is the youngest of all, born to Sahathor and Beta after Khu's death. In either scenario, the composition of the stela has used Khu as a fixed point around which to arrange a complicated domestic history as though it were a straightforward family. In this sense, Khu is the pre-eminent character in the stela, though she is not the principal subject in either scene – the principal position in the offering cult belongs to her husband in each case. Complicated family stories like this must have been commonplace in a nation afflicted by both premature death and divorce leading to remarriage.

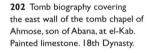

202 Tomb biography covering the east wall of the tomb chapel of Ahmose, son of Abana, at el-Kab. Painted limestone. 18th Dynasty.

Notice also how 'Khu's stela' commemorates other members of the household within the presentation of the family – even a 'beloved friend' who, with no other distinguishing title, might otherwise have had no opportunity to participate in an offering cult. In a straightforward representational sense he is only serving others, but as an actor he has become part of the offering cult, which is why we still know Inyotef's name today. José-Ramón Pérez-Accino has suggested that this 'friend' Inyotef may be the same as the house manager in the upper scene, in which case the unfolding lives of both Inyotef and Khu are revealed to us as part of the family's story.

An exceptional example of how people who would otherwise be forgotten may be adopted into another's funerary cult occurs at the very beginning of the 18th Dynasty, in the tomb of Ahmose, son of Abana, at el-Kab [202]. The wall facing a visitor entering the rock-cut tomb chapel includes the half-finished scenes from Chapter 7. These offering scenes are arranged round the central offering statue of the tomb-owner, and the remaining images in the chapel show his children and grandchildren. However, Ahmose was a distinguished marine commander, and the decoration is actually dominated by a monumental written account of his life in service to the king, which covers more than one wall of the chapel. At the start Ahmose tells us, 'Seven times before the sight of the entire land have I been rewarded with the Gold and male-creatures and female-creatures too, and endowed with fields in great numbers. The name of a Brave is what he has done, and cannot perish in this land for all time.' He ends with the comment, 'I have grown old, reached old age, favoured as before and loved by my lord [and] rest in a shrine I made myself.' We may be instinctively repelled to read, in an account of a self-made man's success, a statement of 'male-creatures and female-creatures' handed over as rewards – a statement of slavery, in other words, as though Ahmose's success were predicated on the bondage of others. On the other hand, we must be careful not to presume we know what unfamiliar words mean in another culture, nor what these people meant to Ahmose as a man. Elsewhere Ahmose's biography states clearly that the people concerned are prisoners-of-war, and where his tale ends, beside the entrance to his chapel, he has listed their names. Whatever the modern reader's instincts may suggest, the names of these 'creatures' are known to us only because Ahmose listed them in his tomb, alongside those of his family. They were the men Pamedjay, Payiabu, Senbef, Pahuq, Senbu, Sobkmose, Hadjroy and Aamu, and the women Taa, Sadjmesni, Satsobk, Taa'amitju, Wabnitasakhmet, Astolimi, Yotefnafer and Hatkush, plus another

203 Sun-court and colonnade at the entrance of the tombs of Mekhu, Sabni and Pepynakht. Qubbet el-Hawa, near Aswan (see p. 101). Sandstone. 6th Dynasty.

204 Detail showing the overseer of spirit priests Nesima (?), in the tomb chapel of Sabni. 6th Dynasty.

man and woman whose names have not survived. For all the millions of folk who died anonymously in pharaonic Egypt, they are among the relative handful whose names have passed down to us in modern times. They died after lifetimes of service – consensual or otherwise, who can say? – which is actually all the mighty Ahmose claims for himself.

Similarly, inside the enormous tomb chapel at Aswan of the governor Sabni [203], the tiny figure of a cup-bearer may seem insignificant but illustrates the very man who managed the priests of Sabni's offering cult [204]. Of course, this is no more than a picture and the man himself has been dead for forty-two centuries, but through the picture he too has become an actor in Sabni's cult. Sabni's tomb tells another, more unusual story about someone else. Sabni is buried alongside his father, Mekhu, so intimately that the chapels of their tombs have merged into one. However, a biography at the entrance reveals that Mekhu was only buried here after Sabni travelled with a caravan of 100 donkeys deep into Nubia in order to retrieve his corpse; Mekhu's life had been lost on a foreign expedition. In Chapter 10 we noted the moment when the great Weni initiated his offering cult, and here we see how Sabni, as it were, tied up the loose ends of his own cult.

Of course, Mekhu, a great official himself, presumably had prepared a tomb before his fate overtook him, and would have been known to posterity in any event. Nearby, however, the tomb of another 6th Dynasty governor, Pepynakht, recounts a similar, but potentially more critical, incident. Pepynakht had been a priest in the Sun-temples of his kings before becoming governor, whereupon he revealed his competence in a series of military strikes on Nubian lands. Eventually Pepy II 'sent me to the highland of the Asiatics to bring him [the courtier] 'Anankht, who had been building a ship there for Punt. Now, Asiatic nomads had slain him along with the troop of the expedition which was with him'. Accordingly Pepynakht sailed to the Sinai desert and fell on 'those Asiatics so that I drove away the killers among them'. We know little else about Pepynakht and nothing more about this incident, but he retrieved not only 'Anankht's body but also his name and his place in posterity. Intriguingly, a cult developed among travellers leaving Egypt that they would pray for a safe return to Pepynakht, using his second name, Heqaib. In time, his successors as governors developed on the nearby island of Elephantine a temple for the cult of Heqaib, which still flourished 500 years after his death [205]. It is as though Pepynakht's conduct became the archetype of what one person can do to secure another's uncertain future.

Art from abroad

Of course, most exchanges between Egypt and foreign nations were not so hostile as Pepynakht's. Constructive exchanges at every level of human activity had taken place with peoples near and far since pre-dynastic times (see pp. 141, 232). At one level, the nature and extent of foreign contact was determined by material needs. In theory, pharaonic Egypt was self-sufficient in most aspects of the economy, especially food, but Egyptians still lacked crucial resources, such as strong, straight timber, and others that were desirable, such as silver, incense and decorative semi-precious stones. The demand for such resources created overlapping networks of trade stretching deep into Asia, Europe and, of course, other African lands. In turn, these networks fostered long-lasting and defining contacts between Egypt and major centres of regional government and commerce, such as Punt, Kerma in Kush, Gaza in Palestine and Byblos in Lebanon. Here the Egyptians found the confluences of major trade routes and sea routes, as well as travellers from far distant lands.

205 The Middle Kingdom complex of shrines dedicated to Heqaib. Elephantine island, near Aswan.

207 The 'treasure hoard' from the foundation of the temple at el-Tod. 12th Dynasty.

In 1936, in the temple of Montu at el-Tod [206], the French archaeologist Fernand Bisson de la Roque unearthed four copper chests inscribed for Amenemhat II (*c.* 1875–*c.* 1845 BC). The chests, laid in the foundations as part of a consecration ceremony, included cylinder seals, beads and amulets made of semi-precious stones from Mesopotamia, Iran and Afghanistan, which probably pre-date the ceremony by decades or even centuries. The chests contained raw lapis lazuli – presumably from Afghanistan – and silver and gold as ingots and chains, but especially in the form of 153 cups and dishes, folded over and flattened to fit in the chests [207]. Various aspects of the decoration of the silverware compare closely to contemporary objects (albeit mostly ceramics) from Crete, the Aegean and Anatolia. As the silverware is thin and easily distorted, the likelihood is that the 'Tod Treasure' comprises of essentially decorative items sent to the Egyptian palace over the years as gifts, before being collected together for the consecration ceremony.

The god Montu is associated with war, so perhaps there was some hostile intent lurking behind the choice to commit these foreign objects to the foundation of his temple. On the other hand, discoveries at Avaris of plastered wall-paintings showing bull-leapers illustrate a cosmopolitan Egyptian city situated comfortably within both the Nile Delta and the broader culture of the Mediterranean Sea [208]. The paintings have appeared in a group of palaces alongside what was a sea-port at the beginning of the 18th Dynasty. Not only the bull scenes but also the colour schemes and decorative motifs are familiar from contemporary palaces as far afield as Crete, Cyprus and Syria. Of course, the imagery of sports involving bulls is still familiar today in parts of Spain and France, though we should not forget that the imagery of bulls also ran deep in Egyptian art. Nonetheless, the archaeology of Avaris has also turned up, for example, gold jewelry with designs influenced by styles from Crete and the Aegean islands [209].

The tombs of officials in the city at this time are essentially Egyptian and designed to accommodate the traditional offering cult, but in a few cases the burials of horses or donkeys alongside the principal grave may allude to the local importance of caravans. Such equid burials are known in contemporary Palestine and Syria, and evidence of a multi-cultural environment seems consistent with Avaris' location as a terminus for caravan roads through Sinai, as well as a sea-port. Historically, it had also been the city of the 'Hyksos' kings (the 15th Dynasty), who were represented in later Egyptian tradition as savage invaders. Whatever truth there may be in that tradition, the monuments of the Hyksos kings at Avaris and elsewhere present them as traditional pharaohs. As would be the case with the 25th Dynasty, the Hyksos kings, despite their reputed foreign origins, embraced traditional pharaonic forms of art. To put this another way, discoveries at Avaris underline the fact that even along the cosmopolitan borders of Egypt, the significance of the presence of foreign art is how exceptional it may be.

208 Reconstructed frieze from a palace wall at Avaris, showing young men leaping over bulls set against a labyrinthine background. Fresco painting on plastered mud-brick. 18th Dynasty.

209 Minoan-style pendant showing a pair of dogs, from the late Middle Kingdom palace cemetery at Avaris and illustrating the long-standing connections between Aegean culture and the Nile Delta. Gold. Probably 13th Dynasty.

Masterpiece
Ostracon of dancing girl

210 Ostracon showing a female
dancer or gymnast. Presumably
from Deir el-Medina. Plastered and
painted limestone. 17 cm (6½ in.)
wide. 19th Dynasty.

Do we ever come across an unguarded moment in pharaonic art – a moment when an artist sketched one of his companions simply for the sake of doing so? In fact, several such sketches have come down to us on palm-sized *ostraca*. In Egyptology 'ostracon' refers to limestone flakes or potsherds used typically as a writing medium, and most of the figured sketches are in black and red – the colours of a scribe's ink. Although they rarely have a provenance, there is little doubt many of the figured sketches come from the village at Deir el-Medina, and date to the 19th or 20th Dynasties. Some might have been used as stelae or devotional images in offering to ancestors or gods, but many seem relaxed in the treatment of the figures, and very few show signs of correction by an overseer or other such indications of 'formal' supervision. Among the subjects we do discover obvious trial pieces and students' practice in the usual scenes of gods and kings, but there are also unexpectedly intimate scenes, such as childbirth and sex, as well as animal stories, and other bemusing subjects. One sketch shows a dishevelled, stubbly king, perhaps in mourning. The ostracon of a bulky, unshaven stonemason at work, gasping for breath in the cloistered heat of a tomb, really does seem as though it may be a glimpse of a workmate – an artist or a scribe making an impromptu study of the toil and absurdity entailed in the sacred work in the Valley of the Kings (see p. 80).

This ostracon of a dancer or gymnast is an altogether more sophisticated piece of art, plastered and painted in full colour. At first sight, the composition seems to break the fundamental conventions of ancient Egyptian art, having been drawn freehand without a baseline, to create a lithe, skinny figure in true profile, and in dynamic, sensual movement. On the other hand, images of nearly naked young women posed informally in offering scenes are common enough in wall-paintings of tomb chapels of the New Kingdom, as we saw in Chapter 7, so the woman shown here may illustrate or rehearse a subject or theme intended for a more formal setting. In any event, such figured ostraca illustrate how ancient artists, though often bound by formal conventions in many professional contexts, were not otherwise limited in their thinking or ability. Scenes involving the moments within an action, such as movement, excitement and perspective, normally stand apart from the art of ancient Egypt but, as here, they do sometimes appear. In other words, they were known and understood by certain artists at least.

211 Wooden head-rest
decorated with an image of a
protective imp or *bes* (see p. 267).
Unknown provenance. 29 cm
(11½ in.) wide. 18th Dynasty.

Chapter 14 'A Perfect Joy to Look At': The Significance of the Minor Arts

By now, it will be clear that the wonderful artworks seen on a tour of the 'Ancient Egypt' galleries of distinguished museums come from tombs or temples. However, other ostensibly mundane artefacts – items of the everyday perhaps – such as furniture, toiletries or a young woman's jewelry, may also catch the visitor's eye. Part 1 discussed how little – not just relatively speaking, but in actual quantity – has survived from domestic contexts, so it is worth considering that even these 'everyday' items may, on closer inspection, also turn out to be funerary products. Of course, funerary objects were not produced in a cultural vacuum, and analogous or comparable items of furniture, jewelry and so on do occasionally come to us in urban archaeological contexts, at places such as Deir el-Medina, el-Amarna or Malqata. However, those artefacts we may classify as the 'minor' arts of ancient Egypt tend to be funerary objects not just by chance of survival but by intention – that is, they were often first manufactured for the tomb. Every one of these minor arts requires a study more detailed than is possible here, but a brief discussion may illustrate the point.

Furniture may be the most obvious example. The oldest surviving furniture dates from as far back as the 1st Dynasty and comes from burials in Tarkhan. From that moment on, certain technical features are common to furniture in any context. For example, Egypt's indigenous woods, such as tamarisk, acacia, persea, sidder (Christ's thorn) and sycamore fig, tend to produce timber that is restricted in size, and often twisted and knotty. Such timber may be suitable for smaller objects, such as head-rests [211], while superior foreign timbers, such as ash, beech, cedar and ebony could be imported by those with the wherewithal. However, more practical solutions were generally needed for much of the furniture in the tomb or home. So, for example, veneers and plywoods have been discovered in tombs as ancient as the Old Kingdom, and at all periods misshapen timbers were often pegged or bound together to create longer planks. Simple butt joints, box-and-frame joints or various types of mitres were developed for constructing the frames. Plaster and paint disguised the underlying inconsistency of the timber, while inlays or marquetry could create the impression of something more sophisticated, and inlays of luxury materials, such as ivory, provide decorative features. However, at the other end of the scale, in homes and workplaces doubtless plainer materials such as reeds and rushes were more typically used for simple pieces of furniture, such as boxes.

The furniture from Tarkhan includes bed frames, with details such as feet formed as bulls' hooves. Similarly, lions' feet characterize the magnificent 4th Dynasty furniture collection from the reburial of Khufu's mother Hetepheres. The collection was designed to sit under a gilded wooden canopy that had copper-reinforced joints so it could be taken apart for ease of carriage. The queen's wooden bed has a gilded head-rest and a wooden footboard inlaid with faience, and obviously is very far from being ordinary household furniture. Two gilded chairs have high, openwork sides formed as intertwined lotuses in one case and Horus-falcons in the other, while another chair has gilded carrying poles also shaped as lotus-flowers. A common feature of the bed and all the chairs is the use of low legs [212], which may suggest the high-sided chairs were designed for squatting or crouching, though this is far from certain, and such low chairs probably can be used comfortably in a sitting position. During the New Kingdom, the type of seat most typically deposited in burials was a latticework stool with three or four (longer) legs supporting a bowl-shaped seat, perhaps made of rushes or leather but often simply of wood. Nonetheless, the short legs serve to remind us that many depictions of people in domestic or professional environments show them squatting on the floor, while in art those who are seated typically have that position because they have superior status, whether in life or in terms of the composition (see p. 150). Hence we may question whether individual chairs – which we today take for granted – were truly everyday furniture.

The ubiquitous ancient Egyptian item of furniture is the simple chest or box, with a sliding lid or detachable leaf. Obviously storage boxes were likely to have been widely used by everyone, but doubtless many of those that have come down to us, in fine workmanship, were specifically prepared for burials, not least because their cubic form provides ideal decorative surfaces. Hetepheres' furniture included a gilded box for assorted draperies, and a chest with two boxes to hold ointments and a collection of bracelets. Tutankhamun's tomb contained almost fifty boxes and chests of different sizes, made of rushes, wood,

212 New Kingdom chair, constructed using mortise and tenon, dowels and glue, with a curved back, latticework seat (lost) and feet shaped as lions' legs. Probably from Thebes. Wood, inlaid with bone. 0.9 m (2 ft 11½ in.) high. 18th Dynasty.

213 Chest or box of king Tutankhamun with vaulted lid, decorated on all exterior faces. West Thebes. Plastered and painted wood. 0.6 m (2 ft) long. 18th Dynasty.

ivory or stone, which contained all manner of things from linen cloths to the poignant coffins and remains of his two stillborn children. His famous 'painted chest' [213] is a splendid example of a simple box plastered and painted to look more elegant, the work of an artist 'compared with whom the greatest artists among the Greeks and of the Italian Renaissance and of the Louis XIV period are mere hacks', according to the early American Egyptologist, James Henry Breasted. The image of the king in his chariot incorporates layers of symbolism linked to the decoration of temples, but the basic image of the king trampling the mass of his enemies clearly derives from the ancient smiting scene. The organized registers of Egyptian troops running behind his chariot contrast favourably with the disorganized enemy rabble he is running over. Likewise on the ends of the box Tutankhamun appears as a sphinx tearing his enemies apart, while on the lid he is hunting in the desert (cf. [9, 84]).

Small objects such as dishes, cups and spoons or toilet utensils may seem definitively utilitarian, but again are likely to be funerary, and not just in terms of their find-spot. Razors with decorated handles provide a case in point [214]. For most daily purposes people shaved with razors shaped like modern scalpels, the blade and handle formed from a single piece of metal with a projecting cutting edge. However, the style of razor most often discovered in New Kingdom tombs, for example, has a separate handle at a right angle to a large hatchet-shaped blade with a convex cutting edge. The handle's distinctive boss may help balance the razor,

214 Razor from the tomb of the lady Hatnefer. West Thebes. Copper alloy blade 1 cm (4 in.) long; boxwood handle 12 cm (5 in.) long. 18th Dynasty.

though some examples have a spur instead, which might have been used to agitate the blade. This is an altogether more sturdy depilatory tool than the everyday razor: the example shown here uses rivets to fix the bronze blade to a wooden handle decorated with spiralling striations, as though illustrating a grip. Of course, razors may be necessary for any adult but they were essential for an Egyptian priest (or priestess), who was required to undertake regular full-body depilation, so the appearance of these sturdy types in a burial may exemplify notions of purity and status as much as everyday toilet practice [215].

All sorts of combs, tweezers, pins and sticks offer the same conundrum as razors – how to distinguish essentially funerary displays from the ordinary toilet of living Egyptians. For example, mirrors whose handles are shaped as the face of Hathor are common in art, presumably 'marking' women for beauty (see p. 185) [216]. Accordingly, a form of polished metal mirror typically found in tombs, which has a handle with back-to-back faces of Hathor, may be a case of life imitating art or vice versa. However, a mirror's handle may be a blooming lotus flower instead, and the combination of the lotus flower handle and the owner's reflected face obviously compares to the carving of Tutankhamun's head flowering out of a lotus (see p. 162). Moreover, the image of the deceased's head in a blooming lotus appears in Spell 81A of the compilation of specifically funerary spells or speeches that we today call the Egyptian Book of the Dead, though their ancient name is 'Speeches for Coming Out in the Daylight'. These compilations, first set down on papyrus scrolls during the 16th century BC, were based on more ancient texts traceable directly from the Pyramid Texts (see p. 57). Typically the scrolls were placed in coffins or burial chambers. The finest were

215 Scene in the tomb chapel of the king's scribe Userhat, showing recruits for an expedition having their heads shaved. In fact, purification, being seated and the shade of sycomore trees have specific afterlife meanings in funerary art. West Thebes. Plastered and painted limestone. 18th Dynasty.

216 Mirror with a handle in the form of the goddess Hathor's face, reportedly from a tomb for several wives of king Thutmose III. West Thebes. Silver mirror, with gilded wooden handle. 33 cm (1 ft 1 in.) high. 18th Dynasty.

217 Mirror with a handle in the form of a young girl. Probably West Thebes. Bronze. 22 cm (8½ in.) high. 18th Dynasty.

illustrated, and extracts were also used as part of the decoration of coffins and other funerary artefacts from the New Kingdom and throughout the 1st millennium BC, as we shall see. Spell 81A begins, '*I am a pure lotus, which has come out in the daylight*', thereby locating this image – and presumably, therefore, certain mirrors – at the heart of the Book of the Dead.

Returning to mirrors, sometimes the handle may be a nude female, closely comparable to serving girls in art or the tomb models discussed below. For example, the handle from a bronze mirror now in the Brooklyn Museum shows a young girl, as indicated by her tied hair, who is completely naked except for crossties and a girdle [217]. Such an image on a mirror seems overtly sexual, which in turn probably refers to beauty, to Hathor and, of course, to new life in a place of death. She is also holding a bird, a reference to the marshes so characteristic of tomb art. Her well-defined, almond-shaped eyes are characteristic of the late 18th Dynasty, including the Amarna Period, though they have led to the suggestion that she represents a Nubian. Her hairstyle includes a quartet of 'buns', comparable to the serving-girl model below, though in this case one pair of 'buns' is formed by the ends of the rivet fixing the handle to the face.

The plain, unglazed ceramics of pharaonic Egypt typical in domestic use, even in palaces, usually carry little decoration other than a pottery slip or a pigment wash. The same plain vessels also appear in great quantities in tombs, where they will have been used for bringing offerings from the living. On the other hand, brightly glazed stones were used in pre-dynastic graves to imitate turquoise and lapis lazuli in beads and suchlike, and the glazed composite faience was used to create small decorative objects, amulets and tiles, whether modelled by hand or using cores or moulds. Subsequently faience was used throughout the dynastic period to manufacture brightly decorated vessels, as were similar glazed media, such as frit, 'Egyptian Blue' and, later, glass. (An old axiom in Egyptology insisted that glass was brought to Egypt during the 18th Dynasty in the reign of Thutmose III, but glass objects appear already in Middle Kingdom burials and possibly even earlier.) For example, decorative animal motifs, such as the 'gaping' fish, are humorous and attractive as well as ideal for glazed flasks and suchlike, bright vessels which seem to find their natural home in the tomb [219]. The green faience dish with a flaring base and slightly flaring sides may imitate an open lotus and the outside is decorated with flowers [218]. In any event, the inner surface shows three interlocking fish nibbling the marsh plants, on top of which birds are standing. Again, marshes and birds are familiar enough in funerary art and this fish, known locally as *būlti*,

218 Dish decorated with floral images on the outside, and fish and ducks inside. Unknown provenance. Faience. 13 cm (5 in.) diameter. Probably 18th Dynasty.

219 Polychrome ointment vessel shaped as a fish. Found buried under the floor of a house in Akhetaten. Glass. 14 cm (5½ in.) long. 18th Dynasty.

220 Bowl showing a monkey and a lure player, naked but for a wig, collar and jewelry, with a tattoo of a *bes* on her thigh. Faience. 14 cm (5½ in.) diameter. 18th or 19th Dynasty.

221 Partially restored hippopotamus from the burial of a household member in the tomb of the governor Senbi II. Meir. Faience. 20 cm (8 in.) long. 12th Dynasty.

or tilapia in English, is associated in mythology with Hathor and female fertility, perhaps because it seems to swallow its eggs and give birth by regurgitating its progeny. The tilapia also symbolizes the daily circuit of the Sun, and dishes decorated with fish may be shaped as the cartouche, which was used to enclose the king's name in writing and called in Ancient Egyptian the 'great circuit' (*shen wer*). Generally, as we shall see, images of fish are extremely common on small grave goods.

A characteristic of glazes and faience of the New Kingdom is black-painted design on a distinctive deep blue colour made from a natural mix of cobalt and alum. In this example, the woman playing a lute is naked but for her wig, collar and girdle [220]. She is shown next to a pool or perhaps on a mound, beneath a shelter of blossoms or fruit, recalling the tomb of Sennedjem or the pool of Irynefer (see pp. 102–105, 190). The flowering lotuses are a funerary image too, and frame the scene as though bounding a sacred place with the columns of a temple (see pp. 202–203). Finally, a monkey plays at her girdle, and may represent mischief or perhaps some mythological allusion to her sexuality. Is the young lady a carefree companion 'on the shore of intoxication', the goddess Hathor even, or maybe a play-time prostitute? By contrast, the faience hippopotamus, of which some fifty are known today, is bursting with simple charm [221]. However, a second glance indicates he is covered with marsh plants, like the faience dishes. Perhaps we should see in the hippopotamus a 'marshy' horse – not quite a land creature nor a river creature. In this sense, he would be like the marshes themselves – at the boundaries of form. More to the point, perhaps, the hippopotamus in art and mythology is associated with the god Seth, and may be shown harpooned by Horus during his triumph over rebellion and lawlessness (see p. 285), just as the tomb owners typically harpoon fish (see p. 101). So, the happy hippo of the decoration is burgeoning with religious symbolism, whereas the faience vessel itself has no obvious practical value for tomb or home.

Wooden or ceramic models of servants embody many of the themes of reliefs and paintings. However, they are often part of the actual burial, placed either in niches in the burial chamber or with the coffins. In some cases, this may be because they belong to smaller, simpler tombs for which a decorated offering chapel was not practical. On the other hand, perhaps they are intended to bring a (literally) fuller presence than two dimensions do. In any event, models probably constitute a different medium for essentially the same funerary art, their use partly dictated by regional differences or the preferred practices of different workshops (see Chapter 10).

Early examples of such models include the painted limestone butcher and potter from the lost tomb of Nykauinpu, who in a straightforward sense are simply provisioning the offering cult of the deceased [222, 223]. Certainly they cannot be confused with the statues of tomb owners, which are the named subjects of an offering cult (see Chapter 9). Unlike the slaves of Ahmose, son of Abana, or the household of Khu discussed in Chapter 13, most of these tomb models are anonymous – almost generic

222 Model of a potter. Giza. Painted limestone. 13 cm (5 in.) high. 5th Dynasty.

223 Model of a butcher. Giza. Painted limestone. 37 cm (14½ in.) high. 5th Dynasty.

224 Model of a girl balancing a dish on the head of a monkey. Probably from Thebes. Ebony. 15.5 cm (6 in.) high. 18th Dynasty.

characters. Of course, we cannot be sure that they are not somehow modelled on individuals from life, and very occasionally they are named. Typically models are not restricted by the formal conventions of art, though even this butcher, hard at work, has a vertical centre-line at right angles to the baseline. Three of the bull's legs are tied as the butcher flips him over by the fourth leg. From the front, the butcher has a strikingly determined countenance, precisely delineated features and a broad nose, while he deftly wields the knife at the animal's throat. Moreover, his body with powerful legs conforms to the Old Kingdom canon of proportion. However, the potter, spinning the wheel with his left hand as he works the clay with his right, seems emaciated, his ribs protruding and his cheekbones pronounced, whereas his facial features are less well defined and his painted hairline is receding. He still maintains an erect position and we may wonder whether he is the victim of straitened circumstances, worn down in service to a demanding lord, as a first glance would suggest, or whether he is an 'elder' – in other words a master of his trade – or, for that matter, whether the sculptor did model him after a real-life character.

During the 18th Dynasty a marvellous flowering of these model servants, often shown carrying boxes and dishes, brought with it the kinds of sensuality and humour we otherwise associate with pharaonic tomb art. Several have been found still with traces of solid unguents, possibly the type of oil we see used by the queen in the scene on Tutankhamun's gold throne (see pp. 231–31). An ebony container from Thebes naming Amenhotep II, inlaid with ivory and electrum studs, and decorated with the characteristic image of a type of imp known as *bes*, may well be an instance of a jar intended for such unguent. A striking example of a servant model is the ebony girl with a monkey bought in Cairo (but reportedly from Thebes), which stands about 15.5 centimetres (6 inches) tall, not including the stand [224]. The great pioneer of Egyptian archaeology, Flinders Petrie, described it as:

> one of the supreme pieces of carving of the early XVIIIth dynasty. The modelling is superb, full and muscular without losing anything in dryness or hardness, the suppleness – the grace – the movement of it, with the back foot half raised, and the sweetness of the expression, are beyond any of the carvings that I remember … It is a perfect joy to look at the silhouette of it in any direction, for its elasticity and expression.

She has the same eyes and hairstyle as the girl on the mirror handle above, and holds a dish emulating one made of incised bronze or perhaps blue faience, with a marguerite or daisy pattern covering the upper surface and a zigzag incised along the rim. Her tied hair indicates she is still a youth, which would be consistent with her plump curves, but she too is naked and has developing breasts, so there is an intrusive sexuality about her. Of course, the monkey may recall the bowl with the naked lute player above.

The serving-girl model from the reign of Amenhotep III, reportedly found in the tomb of a high priest Meryptah, is made of boxwood, and also stands about 15 centimetres (6 inches) without the (modern) stand [225]. She is not so plump as the previous servant and has barely developed breasts, but she too is unabashedly sexual – naked but for a gold girdle and a charm in the form of a *bes*, she wears facial cosmetics and an earplug, and the artist has painted her pubic hair. The sockets on the sides of

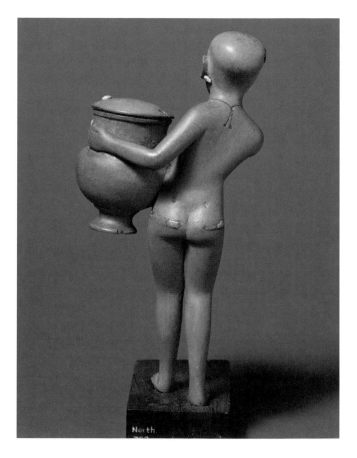

225 Model of a serving girl, reputedly from the tomb of Meryptah, High Priest of Ptah, at Saqqara. Boxwood, with gold and ivory inlay and some gilding. 15 cm (6 in.) high. 18th Dynasty.

226 Flask in the shape of a reclining man. Unknown provenance. Pottery. 15 cm (6 in.) high. 18th Dynasty.

her head indicate that she wore a heavy wig, which in pharaonic literature was often an invitation to sex. (The wig is now lost but would have covered her 'missing' ear.) The jar, carved out of the same original piece of wood, is positioned on her left hip and she is bent away to compensate for the weight. Therefore, her centre-line has left the vertical in a manner which recalls the 'sexy' musicians in Nebamun's tomb, or the ostracon with the gymnast, or, of course, Rekhmira's serving girl (see pp. 121, 122, 256).

The ceramic flask shaped as a heavy man is a different matter, though again it is roughly the same height [226]. Unlike the serving girls, the man himself is the container, and the spout an integral feature of his head. He wears a kilt on which he has unrolled a scroll as though to write, while his right leg is raised and the left foot trapped behind it, so superficially the composition may recall the statue of Harwa (see p. 245). However, this fellow is leaning away from the vertical without the influence of any heavy weight except perhaps his own extraordinary bulk, and he brings none of the dignity of Harwa, seeming instead to be unusually relaxed or awkward. We may even suppose he is the worse for alcohol – an impression heightened by his wry smile – and wonder whether this is an indication of the intended contents of the flask. Perhaps

227 Shabty for a high-status lady, Satti. Probably Saqqara. Faience. 25 cm (10 in.) high. 18th Dynasty.

the flask is about intoxication, perhaps about literacy, perhaps good humour, and these are all familiar themes in the art of pharaonic tombs.

Originally the well-known Egyptian shabty figures may also have been a form of tomb model. However, in their developed forms shabtys are usually identified in writing with the tomb-owner, who is thereby represented as Osiris, wrapped in linen with only his or her head or a mask showing [227]. Early examples from the Middle Kingdom made of wood, stone or unfired clay, and later 'stick' or 'peg' shabtys may even have their own coffins, such as Thuty's [228]. Occasionally shabtys were deposited in temples, especially at Abydos, as though they were a statue of the deceased, and an example such as that of Wepwawetmose is an exquisite piece of miniature art in its own right [229]. On the other hand, groups of shabtys are shown in Theban tomb scenes being carried in a funeral procession, along with a mummy mask and a collar for the deceased, so they seem to have had a prestigious role in burials. Of course, king Taharqa was buried with more than a thousand, which may suggest that part of the prestige of shabtys in some instances was the prospect of being accompanied en masse. So we may well be wrong to assume shabtys had a single function. Even the name has caused confusion because modern scholars have suggested various etymologies, such as *shabty* (stick) or *ushebty* (respondent) or *shawebty* (persea wood), all of which may be supported by different ancient writings.

The notion of 'respondent' does seem consistent with the so-called 'shabty spell', often inscribed on the shabty's body and originally taken from the Book of the Dead Spell 6, which begins: *'O, said shabty, if the deceased [Name here] be allocated to any work that is done there – in the cemetery, that is, and getting through physical labour there – as a man appointed for his duties, so you shall say, "Look, here I am"'*. In keeping with the tenor of Spell 6, most shabtys hold agricultural implements, though after the Amarna Period many also appear in fine clothes – as inappropriate for working in the fields as linen mummy wrappings would be, or the clothes of

228 Shabty for a man named Thuty, presented in a coffin. West Thebes. Pottery. 24 cm (9 in.) high. 17th or 18th Dynasty.

229 Shabty for Wepwawetmose, deputy controller of a temple's rowers. Saqqara. Painted ebony. 26 cm (10 in.) high. 19th Dynasty.

Sennedjem and his wife for farming (see p. 103). From the New Kingdom on, shabtys were often mass produced from moulds in faience or glazed steatite, and the richness of specific details allows scholars to date most of them on the basis of typology. For example, a distinctive 'Deir el-Bahri blue' colour, derived from cobalt, is typical of the early 1st millennium, whereas a vivid green or yellow, derived from antimony, is characteristic of the 26th Dynasty and after. However, the essential distinctions in the actual forms of shabtys remain whether or not the figure holds agricultural implements, and whether the figure is wrapped as a mummy or wearing fine apparel.

A type of shabty wearing fine clothes and holding a stick is occasionally inscribed with the title 'boss of ten', and accompanied by a group of mummiform 'workers'. Tutankhamun's tomb yielded 413 shabtys – along with 1,800 miniature agricultural implements made of copper, faience or wood, held in twenty-four boxes – and the number of shabtys has been explained as 365 'workers' plus 36 'bosses' (or 'overseer' shabtys) along with 12 'monthly bosses'. On the other hand, Tutankhamun's largest shabty is made of wood and stands fully 50 centimetres (19½ inches) tall; others are made in a variety of forms from limestone, quartzite, granite and faience, and some were donated by family members. So the assumption that the king's shabtys form a single coherent group – along with any explanation of the number and specific forms on that basis – is provisional.

Ancient jewelry has certainly been the subject of books in its own right, but here we can usefully note again that most of the jewelry on display in modern museums is not only from tombs, but also probably from the bodies of the deceased or their immediate

230 Pectoral from the tomb of the king's daughter Sathathoriunet, composed with falcons flanking the name of king Senwosret II standing on hieroglyphs spelling 'millions of years'. Lahun, in the Faiyum region. Gold, inlaid with carnelian, garnet, lapis lazuli and turquoise. 8 cm (3 in.) wide, with a beaded necklace 82 cm (2 ft 8 in.) long. 12th Dynasty.

231 Some of the high-quality artefacts from a royal burial discovered in 1908 by Flinders Petrie, including the four-stranded gold collar at bottom right. Qurneh, West Thebes. 18th Dynasty.

burials, like the pectoral of Sathathoriunet [230] or the pendant of Osorkon II (see p. 233). Necklaces, bracelets and girdles made from beads or charms of stone, faience or metal are common in burials at all social levels in all periods. However, the appearance of gold and precious objects again raises the problem of discerning what was prepared for the grave and what was taken from life. For example, a royal burial from the early 18th Dynasty discovered by Flinders Petrie in 1908 included a woman's gilded coffin, which is a tall, slender counterpart to the kings' coffins of the era (see p. 275). The jewelry found with her, according to Petrie, was (and still is) 'the largest group of goldwork that had left Egypt', including a girdle of thirty-eight electrum beads threaded on a double string, and a pair of hooped gold earrings. Most impressive of all, she wore a collar that consists of four strands threaded with 1,699 gold rings, each made from wire of gold up to 95% pure [231]. Examinations under an electron microscope indicate that the beads of the girdle are deformed in a manner consistent with the girdle having been worn, but not so the collar and earrings, which were unused at the time of the woman's burial.

In 1913 the archaeologist Rex Engelbach, excavating on the slopes of a cemetery at el-Haraga, discovered three burial chambers at the bottom of a shaft some 7 metres (23 feet) deep, then another shaft dropping 2 metres further to the burial of a young girl, whose mummy still lay in its ruined coffin. The grave goods surviving from this anonymous tomb included five gold pendants in the shape of fish, the finest of which is a masterpiece of the goldsmith's art [232]. Although just 4.1 by 1.9 centimetres (1½ by ¾ inches), it is actually one of the largest examples known.

232 Fish-shaped pendant from el-Haraga, in the Faiyum region. Sheet gold on an unidentified core. 4 cm (1½ in.) long. 12th Dynasty.

Two halves have been formed by pressing sheet gold into moulds, before they were soldered together over a (clay?) core, with the fins and a suspension ring slotted in, so the fish's final appearance gives the impression of solid gold. The details have been added by chasing in such detail that the species can be identified. It is not a tilapia, in this case, but a fish known locally as *shāl*, or the 'upside-down catfish', because it often floats belly up against a rock or a plant. Of course, the shape of the pendant recalls the decoration of glazed dishes discussed above, and fish-shaped pendants were so significant they had their own name (*nekhaw*) in Ancient Egyptian. One tale from the late Middle Kingdom tells how the old king Snofru went on a pleasure-cruise rowed by a score of busty virgins, who wore only fish-nets. When one rower lost a turquoise fish-pendant from her hair, the chief priest Djadjamankh was obliged to fold over the waters of the lake to recover it from the bottom before the women would 'Carry On' rowing. Such evocations of pleasure and sexuality, along with a hint of magic, seem entirely consistent with the art of pharaonic tombs, and the tale certainly employs imagery from the Book of the Dead.

Since this discussion of the minor arts keeps leading back to the tomb, we must not overlook the fact that coffins too may be a

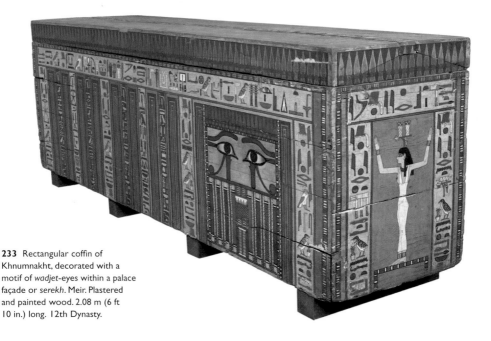

233 Rectangular coffin of Khnumnakht, decorated with a motif of *wadjet*-eyes within a palace façade or *serekh*. Meir. Plastered and painted wood. 2.08 m (6 ft 10 in.) long. 12th Dynasty.

234 Embalmed body of a treasurer Ukhhotep, wrapped with a mask to create the appearance of Osiris (cf. pp. 186–87). Meir. 12th Dynasty.

235 The Osiris-shaped coffins of two obscure kings named Inyotef, with *rishi* ('feathered') decoration. West Thebes. 1.88 m (6 ft 2 in.) and 2 m (6 ft 6½ in.) high. 17th Dynasty.

rich source of figurative art from ancient Egypt [233]. In a peculiar sense, there may be little in one's life more personal than the coffin in which one is laid forever, and likewise nothing could be more specifically funerary. The earliest, dating back to the dawn of the pharaonic era, are simple boxes decorated as shrines to hold the contracted body after the fashion of the gods' statues, which seems consistent with 'adoration' and the beliefs discussed in Chapter 9. During the late Old Kingdom, mummies tended to be embalmed first and so were buried in extended postures, while coffins grew longer and were decorated with texts requesting the usual funerary offerings and invoking the mythology of Osiris. By this time painted *wadjet*-eyes were added, human eyes combined with the external markings of a falcon's eyes, which might have let the corpse, laid on its left side, look out to the sunrise.

From the early Middle Kingdom, Osiris-shaped coffins begin to appear as an extra container inside these rectangular coffins [234, 235]. At Thebes, in the late Middle Kingdom, these coffins developed a style of decoration that showed the deceased smothered in the elaborately feathered wings of a kite, a decorative style known in Egyptology by the Arabic word *rīshi* or 'feathered'. In temple scenes at Abydos the kite represents Isis simultaneously protecting the dead Osiris and conceiving his child (see p. 38). This 'feathering' remained the decorative tradition for royal coffins in the Valley of the Kings but, from the reign of Amenhotep III, so-called 'yellow coffins' became typical elsewhere and remained in use for more than half a millennium. This was a lavishly coloured style, employing a background of vivid yellow or more properly gold, often enhanced by resin varnish (see pp. 102–105). The identification with Osiris was usually emphasized by adding a king's arms crossed over an elaborate collar. The decoration of 'yellow coffins' usually incorporates scenes analogous to contemporary tomb paintings, including the mythology of Osiris and the voyage of the Sun through the night sky. As a rule the number of these scenes increased through time, until coffins underwent another transformation in decoration in the 10th century BC, when the background colour reverted to white and the density of the decoration was drastically reduced. None the less, the symbolism of Osiris remains explicit in the overall form of the coffin and the now-standard depiction of Ptah-Sokar-Osiris on the inside (see pp. 212–15).

Scarabs are a unique phenomenon among the minor arts, insofar as they are a specifically Egyptian art form that spread widely abroad. They originate in the collections of small amulets placed within, or on top of, the linen wrapping of an embalmed body, and the distinctive beetle shape is simply the hieroglyph that writes the word 'becoming' (see p. 157). However, the underside of the beetle also provides a cartouche-shaped space suitable for inscribing the identity of the deceased or funerary texts. As early as the mid-2nd millennium BC we find scarabs in places such as Palestine and Greece, often inscribed with 'stock' names of Egyptian kings, images of gods, or hieroglyphs spelling out simple 'lucky charms'. The migration of scarabs to non-Egyptians suggests

236 The 'weighing of the heart' illustrated on an extract from a Book of the Dead made for the king's scribe Any. West Thebes. Painted papyrus. 42 cm (1 ft 4½ in.) high. 19th Dynasty.

they could be used in ways that somehow allowed them to be seen, and occasionally abroad they do appear strung as beads or mounted in finger-rings. By the early 1st millennium BC demand for scarabs was such that factories in Egypt were producing glazed steatite or faience scarabs specifically for export, while factories in places such as Rhodes produced 'fake Egyptian' scarabs. Following the trade routes of the Phoenicians in particular, scarabs have since turned up in places as far across the Mediterranean as Algeria, Spain, Turkey and Cyprus.

However, in Egypt scarabs continued to be used almost exclusively for embalming and burial. The largest and finest examples were typically laid over the heart of the mummy, and inscribed with the 'scarab spell', taken from the Book of the Dead Spell 30B, which begins: '*O, my will from my mother, O, my will from my mother, O, my heart of my changing forms: Do not stand against me as a witness. Do not strike at me in the Council. Do not be the opponent against me in the presence of the Keeper of the Balance.*'

The 'Keeper of the Balance' is a reference to a final judgment, in which the deceased would be asked to give an account of his or her conduct before Osiris in the so-called 'weighing of the heart' ceremony, famously illustrated in the Book of the Dead [236]. The deceased (in this instance, a king's scribe named Any) stands before the first gods of Creation, his heart weighed on the Balance against a feather, which is the hieroglyph that writes the word 'Truth' (see pp. 16, 242). Horus presents the deceased to Osiris with the words, '*I have come before you, O, Wenennefer, bringing you the deceased Any because his will, which has come through the Balance, is true.*' Then Horus asks that the deceased receive the wherewithal of an offering cult, saying, '*Let the bread and beer that are distributed in the presence of Osiris be given to him. He now exists like those who follow Horus for all time*'. The deceased also speaks up, saying to Osiris, '*There is no wrongdoing in my belly. I do not knowingly lie. No, no! Let me exist like the praised ones who are following you.*' At last Thoth, god of wisdom, pronounces the judgment: '*His soul is standing as witness to him, and his moment on the Great Balance is true.*' Thus eternity may hinge on the sentiment of the simple 'scarab spell': let your heart be in accord with Creation and all will be well, even in death.

Masterpiece
Crown of Khnumet

237 Gold crown of the king's
daughter Khnumet. Dahshur.
12th Dynasty.

In February 1895, at Dahshur in the ruinous pyramid complex of Amenemhat II, Jacques de Morgan set to work. In his previous season of excavation, the French-born Director of Antiquities for the Egyptian government had found boxes of personal treasures in the burials of two women, Sathathor and Meret, laid to rest beside the pyramid of Senwosret III. The princesses' dazzling jewelry was characterized by gold openwork frames inlaid with semi-precious stones to create brilliant polychrome effects. Now, in his second season, de Morgan had exposed the burials of Amenemhat's daughters, Khnumet and Ita, in a single tomb built within a vast rock-cut gallery alongside his pyramid. He was able to make a brief final sketch of the women's mortal remains, still – barely – preserved inside granite sarcophagi.

Collected in a small side-chamber beside her sarcophagus, Khnumet's treasures included collars, pectorals, rings, several bead necklaces, and numerous pendants. The Frenchman declared the jeweler responsible 'incomparable' in any age. A gold crown was formed in a pattern of stylized lotuses, inlaid with lapis lazuli, carnelian and turquoise, topped by a gold falcon and a slender 'reed' draped with delicate leaves. Khnumet had another crown too, so delicate that de Morgan supposed the slightest breath might snap it, though ironically Jaromír Málek describes the delicacy as 'breathtaking'. A network of interlaced gold wires entangles nearly 200 tiny flowers, each with a carnelian eye and five turquoise-inlaid petals, recalling the hieroglyphic stars that write the word 'adoration' (see p. 149). The wires are anchored to three pins on either side of five inlaid 'Maltese crosses', which are actually clusters of lotus blossoms – the ubiquitous image of rebirth in a funerary context – and terminate at a pair of rings on the back of a sixth 'cross'. The curator W. Stevenson Smith noted that 'the airy lightness of the goldwork must have allowed … the flowers to appear as though scattered through the hair of the wearer', while the art historian Arielle Kozloff goes so far as to suggest 'it conjures up the image of a lovely young girl as she pads barefoot through the palace or dances in the Audience-Hall with the wreath jingling and rustling on her head'. However, for the moment we may wonder whether Khnumet ever once put it on – or whether we are discussing something specifically funerary. More recently, the Egyptologist Wolfram Grajetzki has suggested that elements in the treasure hoards of the 12th Dynasty princesses correspond to elements in the funeral rites of Osiris himself, as described in the ancient Pyramid Texts.

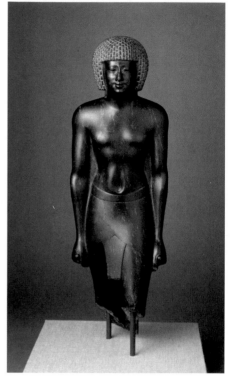

238 Statue of Darius. Susa.
Greywacke. 2.46 m (8 ft) high.
522–486 BC.

239 Statue of an anonymous
priest of Amun-Ra. Presumably
from Karnak, near Thebes.
Diorite. 0.51 m (1 ft 8 in.) high.
30th Dynasty.

Chapter 15 'I Shall Bring No More Offerings For You': The Latest Art of Pharaonic Egypt

As noted at the end of Chapter 12, following more than 2,000 years of pharaonic civilization, the atrocities of the Assyrian invasion of 664 BC were not about to extinguish the spiritual heart of Egypt. Likewise, a century of Persian rule from 525 BC left little trace on Egyptian art and architecture. Ironically, a colossal limestone statue of the Persian emperor Darius the Great (522–486 BC), which sat beside a palace doorway at Susa in Iran, is immediately recognizable as a pharaonic statue, down to the hieroglyphic inscriptions identifying the king with Atum and Ra-Horakhty [238]. Though the king himself is modelled in Persian dress, the pleats of which have been inscribed in three of the languages of the Persian empire, the statue is unequivocally Egyptian, more than likely sculpted in Egypt under the supervision of Darius' contemporary 'overseer of works', Khnemibra. In effect, it shows the foreign ruler offering a pharaonic interpretation of himself to his own people, instead of presenting an occupier's face to Egypt.

In the second half of the 1st millennium BC the ongoing search for inspiration in the art of earlier generations created renewed interest in polished hard stones for statues, an emphasis unseen since the first two dynasties of kings. Perhaps this emphasis arose partly from the stones' own aesthetic properties, perhaps from the magisterial presence of genuinely ancient statues now devoid of their colouration, and perhaps from an awareness that the most ancient models were indeed made in hard stones (cf. [97, 100]). (There is no unequivocal evidence for the regular adoption of iron tools in Egyptian stone-working before the 3rd century BC, so a simple technological change is apparently not the appropriate explanation.) A statue of a 30th Dynasty priest has a plain, powerful physique and a simple kilt, comparable to the modelling of king Menkaura (see pp. 51, 59) in the 4th Dynasty, along with a beaded wig that would not be out of place on a 5th Dynasty statue [239]. The use of lead cladding on a purported royal statue from the 4th century BC may be one instance of innovation during this time, but only in material, not in form.

The art of royalty

The increasing simplicity of relief decoration at this time, especially in the treatment of hieroglyphic inscriptions, may also reference the simplicity of origins. At the start of the 30th Dynasty, a distinctive group of temple reliefs of Nectanebo I (380–362 BC) [240] exhibits the 'feral' excesses of the human form in early Amarna art – Nectanebo's 'jutting chin and nose seem to close like pincers,' notes Stevenson Smith – as well as the fleshy torso and heavy jowls of Ankhhaf and his Old Kingdom peers, not to mention the skull-tight cap and elevated uraeus-cobra associated with images of Kushite kings (see pp. 242–43). Such reliance on old times might well have been connected with political uncertainty, of course, but it is not at all out of step with traditional practice, which had always sought inspiration in archetypes. In fact, Nectanebo's reliefs are examples of a genuine architectural innovation – that is, a stone screen now fitted between the columns at the far side of hypostyle halls (that is, at the junction with the colonnaded Sun-court) in preference to a full-length wall, which had been the New Kingdom standard.

Indeed, with regard to royal imagery temples as ever provide the most pertinent illustrations, while very little has survived from – or is even known about – the burials of the kings in Egypt after the 22nd Dynasty. For much of the 1st millennium BC, most building essentially maintained the development of New Kingdom

240 Section of a wall showing Nectanebo I offering bread to the goddess Edjo. Obtained near Alexandria, originally from elsewhere. Greywacke. 1.23 m (4 ft) high. 30th Dynasty.

temples, and the activity of the era is best exemplified at Karnak and on the west bank at Thebes. That said, the additions of 26th Dynasty kings to temples elsewhere, including Memphis and the cities of the Delta – where an extraordinary granite shrine of Amasis (Ahmose III, 570–526 BC) stands 8 metres (26 feet) above the ruins of the ancient temple at Mendes – witness the fact that ancient patterns of royal conduct still continued throughout the country [241]. The principal new foundation surviving from the Persian era is a temple built for Amun-Ra beyond the Nile Valley at Hibis in the western oasis of el-Kharga, where again Darius the Great is shown as a traditional pharaoh in the company of Egyptian gods. The sanctuary of the temple includes a sequence of scenes illustrating the original act of Creation by Amun-Ra – scenes seemingly adapted variously from Sety I's temple at Abydos and the New Kingdom tombs in the Valley of the Kings.

The overthrow of Persian rule and the establishment of the 30th Dynasty in 380 BC, then the conquest of Egypt by Alexander the Great in 332 BC and subsequent rule by the descendants of his general Ptolemy, ushered in a new era of temple-building, not based on innovation so much as the opposite – the determination of the new regimes to establish themselves firmly within pharaonic tradition. From the 30th Dynasty temples were developed or built on old sites or new – from Philae and Elephantine in the Nubian borderlands to the far north in Heliopolis, Tanis and the new city of Alexandria on the Mediterranean coast [243]. In its present form, the splendid avenue of sphinxes approaching Luxor Temple through the modern town dates from the reign of the first 30th Dynasty king, Nectanebo I –

241 View of the only granite shrine surviving from a series erected by king Amasis at Mendes to accommodate images of the gods in the sequence Ra, Shu, Geb and Osiris (see pp. 37–38). 26th Dynasty.

242 View through the colonnaded Sun-court to the entrance of the hypostyle hall in the temple of Horus at Edfu.

283

243 Statue of the god Horus with Nectanebo II. The composition is a writing of the king's name. Heliopolis. Greywacke. 0.72 m (2 ft 4½ in.) high. 360–343 BC.

244 Scene on a wall in the temple of Hathor at Dendera, showing Cleopatra VII and Ptolemy XV offering to the gods. 44–30 BC.

245 Statues of Ptolemy II and Arsinoë II, removed to the Sallustian Gardens in Rome by the emperor Caligula (AD 37–41), who probably commissioned the third statue to commemorate his late sister, Drusilla (died AD 38). Probably originally from Heliopolis. Granite. Each about 2.7 m (8 ft 10 in.) high. c. 280–260 BC.

and so do the extant avenues at many other temples. At Naucratis in the Delta, a stela from the temple of the goddess Neith records Nectanebo's stated intention of *'protecting and augmenting the temple-offerings'*. To this commitment, the Ptolemies – a foreign dynasty, at least to begin with – added the need to be seen as legitimate pharaohs, which perforce required temple-building (see pp. 20–21). The extant shrine of Amun-Ra in Luxor Temple was added for Alexander the Great (332–323 BC), while the shrine in Karnak was built for his ill-starred half-brother, Philip III (323–317 BC). During the 3rd century BC and, in particular, the middle of the 2nd century BC the relationship between the Ptolemaic kings and the priesthoods fostered a productive synergy between the economics of temple-building and the dynasty's authority. Texts of this period, especially in the temple at Edfu [242] – which Ptolemy III Euergetes began rebuilding in 237 BC – remain the most detailed accounts we have of the whys and wherefores of building temples, typically inscribed above the traditional images

of marshland as though to affirm the continuing reality of 'the Risen Earth' (see p. 46).

With hindsight this was the last great age of pharaonic temple-building, and many temples exist today in the form in which they were built, decorated or redeveloped under Ptolemaic rule. These include iconic sites such as Debod (though the temple is now in Madrid), Philae, Kom Ombo and Dendera, as well as less familiar sites at Kalabsha, Elephantine, el-Kab, el-Tod, Coptos, Karnak, Medinet Habu, Deir el-Medina, Deir el-Bahri, Medamud, Thebaid Ptolemaïs, Hermopolis, Medinet Maadi, Hibis and, of course, Memphis and Saqqara. Today Edfu remains the best place to experience the architecture and decoration of an Egyptian temple as they would have been in ancient times, not as sanitized ruins. Many of these temples have survived because of the increasing distance of the south of the country from the major population centres, which by this time were concentrated in the north because of political and geographical shifts. Though the archaeology is much less well preserved in the Nile Delta, sites there from this era, such as Athribis and Alexandria, are the subject of ongoing investigation.

In the context of international politics, the Ptolemies developed the policy of presenting themselves as 'king' (*basileus*) in the Classical tradition of conspicuous 'indulgence' (*tryphē*). As has often been remarked, this policy may be reflected in the soft, fleshy forms of their Egyptian temple reliefs – round cheeks and deep-set eyes, 'golf-ball' chins, the rounded musculature of men, the heavy breasts of women. On the other hand, these characteristics are far from unknown in pharaonic art, whether in the decades preceding Ptolemaic rule or long before then. More pertinently for the present discussion, the Ptolemies essentially presented themselves within Egypt as traditional pharaohs [245]. To take a single well-known example, the reliefs of Cleopatra VII (51–30 BC) and her infant son Caesarion (Ptolemy XV) in the temple of Hathor at Dendera conform to the usual conventions of art, formally as well as in subject matter, including the infant king shown as an adult offering to the gods [244]. Indeed, much of what we know today about, for example, royal festivals or the cult of Osiris and Horus is detailed in temples of this period, including celebrated scenes of the primeval conflict of Horus and Seth (see p. 38) [246]. In belief, the king and queen remain the incarnations and chief officiants of the gods, so that even texts written in Greek refer to offerings made on their behalf. The model for architecture remains the New Kingdom temple, devoid of intrusive foreign architecture. Both

246 Scene in the temple of Edfu, showing Horus as pharaoh harpooning the hippopotamus that is Seth, his father's brother and murderer.

247 Bronze statue of Horus in Roman ceremonial armour and conforming to Roman artistic conventions, presumably associated with a Roman imperial cult. Unknown provenance. 49 cm (1 ft 7 in.) high. 1st to 3rd century AD.

248 Sphinx of one of the early Ptolemies, from the temple of Serapis at Alexandria. Granite. 2.2 m (7 ft 2½ in.) high. 4th or 3rd century BC.

the 30th Dynasty and the Ptolemies employed the best available native masons and sculptors to a large-scale, open-ended building programme, which returned both elegance and complexity to temple decoration, exemplified by 'composite columns' whose capitals incorporate various plant forms in a mesmerizing, extravagant and colourful new interpretation of ancient imagery. From the reign of Nectanebo I onward, temples were often provided with a new element, a *mammisi* or 'birth place' (a name derived from the Ancient Egyptian language but coined by Egyptologists), but this is simply a smaller, complementary temple where scenes of the queen's insemination, or the royal heir suckled by Isis and dandled by Horus, are obviously analogous to the birth-scenes in the great New Kingdom temples at Luxor and Deir el-Bahri (see p. 197).

Statues of the Ptolemies and, much more especially, the Roman emperors who succeeded them after Cleopatra VII, do sometimes appear in Egypt in forms that adopt the artistic traditions of Greece and Rome – but these statues are from theatres, forums, temples and all kinds of buildings associated with Hellenistic urbanism and governance [247]. Meanwhile, statues from native temples steadfastly maintain the artistic conventions of the previous three millennia [248] so, as Elizabeth Brophy has helpfully summarized, 'Egyptian, Greek, and Roman royal statues belong in recognisably Egyptian, Greek, and Roman spaces'. A handful of Greco-Roman temples, particularly those dedicated to the hybrid Greek–Egyptian god Serapis [251], include both Hellenistic and Egyptian architecture and decoration side by side, but they do not mix. Likewise, a complex of artists' workshops at Athribis during the 3rd and 2nd centuries BC has revealed traditional working practices and materials – from ceramics to faience to Egyptian stones to gold – employed side by side with imported materials such as marble, which were specifically for the production of sculpture in the Hellenistic tradition.

The art of officials

With regard to the statues of private individuals, the anonymous 30th Dynasty priest at the start of this chapter clearly ought to belong to the offering chapel of a tomb [239]. Actually it has no known provenance, and statues of this era do tend to be discovered in temples more often than in tombs. This may indicate an increased emphasis on a cultural phenomenon known from earlier times, and many examples do exhibit the seated-scribe pose of statues of Amenhotep, son of Hapu, or of Harwa, originally

249 Door jambs from the tomb chapel of Tjaiseimu, an overseer of works. On one jamb he is suckled by an obscure goddess (cf. [144]). Saqqara. Plastered and painted limestone. 1.26 m (4 ft 1½ in.) high. 30th Dynasty.

from the same temple context (see pp. 64, 245). The connection between temples and tombs, especially during the gods' festivals, was both ancient and fundamental, and officials of this era may even be shown making offerings – a pose hitherto usually reserved for kings. However, the preponderance of examples from temples is also a function of the discovery of caches, which in turn reflects chance finds of statues collected together at some indeterminate date rather than systematic archaeological excavation. In fact, the picture we have of the tombs of Egypt after the Persian invasion in 525 BC is certainly skewed by a dearth of undisturbed cemeteries, a fact attributable partly to the reuse of earlier cemeteries for later burials and partly to the tendency of earlier generations of archaeologists to rifle through Greco-Roman sites to 'get at' earlier periods. For example, there are few statues of married couples of this era, which may reflect a genuine shift away from the practice of placing cult statues in tombs or simply the dearth of adequately excavated cemeteries. Sites less badly affected by early archaeology, such as Karanis or Tebtunis, have since added a great deal to our understanding of urban archaeology during these centuries, but rather less to our knowledge of the sacred precincts that typically furnish pharaonic art.

Nonetheless, the limited information available does not suggest that tombs fundamentally altered at this time, and there are a handful of magnificent examples at familiar sites, including Thebes and Saqqara, and even Giza and Abusir. A relative increase in the use of painted and plastered wooden stelae in preference to inscribed stone is notable at this time, though formally they adhere

250 Statue of the troop-commander Horsatutu (or Horus, son of Tutu). Apparently obtained in Alexandria, but probably from elsewhere in the Nile Delta (perhaps Sais or Saft el-Hina). Diorite (?). 2nd century BC.

251 Rock-cut galleries beneath the Ptolemaic temple of Serapis at Alexandria. Subterranean galleries for burying mummified animals were a traditional devotional practice that proliferated during the Ptolemaic era.

to familiar conventions. Moreover, where there is relief work this continues to conform to earlier models and is often of excellent quality, exemplified by the door jambs of Tjaiseimu, 'overseer of works' for Nectanebo I [249]. Following one ancient archetype of a royal official, he is conspicuously corpulent beneath his cloak and carries a staff. His clean-shaven head is that of a priest, and the skull is a little distended after the manner of the Amarna Period. His left hand holds his cloak together to reveal the royal seal, which he wears as a ring rather than the typical pendant, while above him is a traditional account in hieroglyphs of his service to the king.

In such images of the Greco-Roman era – more so than with images of kings – there may seem to be an apparent fusion of art styles between Hellenistic or Classical, on the one hand, and pharaonic. However, features sometimes identified as 'Hellenistic naturalism' – just like the corpulence noted in royal reliefs – are probably not far removed, if at all, from traditional Egyptian forms. For example, the statue of Horsatutu is notably ageing and wrinkled but as such stands in the tradition of Ankhhaf and Harwa [250]. The figure maintains a frontal pose because it is a tomb statue, but its striding legs have been lost so the disproportionate visual influence of the contemporary hairstyle and dress may lead a modern observer towards interpretations more or less removed from its original function. What is most seemingly 'Greek' or 'Roman' about Horsatutu? First, the pleated drapery of his mantle – though, leaving the specific stylistic details aside, both pleats and fine linen are traditionally Egyptian. Secondly, his tightly curled wig, which again is a contemporary interpretation of a standard Egyptian feature – the more noticeable here because, typically of this time, the curls of hair have been left unpolished in contrast to the statue's overall sheen.

During the 20th century, any suggestion of Hellenistic or quasi-Classical features in Egyptian art tended to be interpreted as prima facie evidence of the inevitable evolution of 'ancient' art into (more progressive) 'Classical' art. However, 'Hellenism' is not such a simple matter. In an obvious sense, the culture of even the Egyptian social elite under Greek-speaking rulers is still Egyptian: a Greek-speaking Egyptian serving the Ptolemies or the Roman emperors would have had less in common with, say, fellow Greek-speakers St Paul (born in Turkey) and St Luke (born in Syria) than a fellow Egyptian who happened not to speak Greek. Though the effect of Greek education may be significant, in the 1st century AD the historian Josephus noted that in his culture, among Aramaic-speaking Palestinians, learning Greek was

252 View of the colonnaded entrance to the tomb chapel of Petosiris (cf. [242]). Tuna el-Gebel, near Hermopolis. 4th century BC.

considered 'common' (*koinos*). Meanwhile, letters from Ptolemaic Egypt written in Greek applaud men for learning Egyptian because they were likely to increase their exposure to pharaonic values as a result. So the cultural development of Greco-Roman Egypt need not be a simple matter of Egyptians being obliged to copy (more progressive) Greek-speaking masters. In fact, statues of this era may reveal or conceal complex artistic identities, both in respect of the subject (ethnically Egyptian, Greek or otherwise) and the sculptural form (pharaonic, Hellenistic or otherwise). Like Darius the Great at the start of this chapter, Greek subjects and Hellenistic gods may just as well be 'Egyptian-ized' as the other way round, and this certainly seems to be the case with funerary practice among indigenous and immigrant communities, as we shall see. Generally, however, in life as well as art, 'among the classic parameters of cultural interactions, language, education, literature, religion and the like,' writes Jean Bingen, a distinguished scholar of Egypt under Ptolemaic rule, 'in most respects what prevailed was several centuries of relative opaqueness, impossibility or refusal of excessively visible cultural borrowings.' In respect of art, this conclusion seems all the more reasonable when we remember art's specific uses in Egyptian tradition.

More importantly, perhaps, the extent to which Egyptian and Hellenistic ideas and practices interact in a given context may be specific to individuals rather than subject to general principles of historical development. In this regard, the most famous instance is perhaps the most challenging – the decoration of the tomb at Tuna el-Gebel of Petosiris, a priest in Hermopolis [252]. Here several scenes on the lower walls and screens of the hypostyle hall have

253 Traditional scenes in the tomb chapel of the priest Petosiris, showing the purification of the soul above and the fecundity of Egypt below (cf. [27, 141]). Hermopolis. Plastered and painted limestone. 4th century BC.

254 Scene of a vineyard and wine press in the entrance colonnade of the tomb chapel of Petosiris (cf. [27]). Painted limestone. 4th century BC.

been interpreted by generations of scholars as straightforwardly Hellenistic in appearance, though the tomb itself has a standard Egyptian form, the scenes in question are arranged in canonical registers, and the subjects are traditional [253, 254]. Looking more closely, the 'Classical naturalism' of the figures is actually little different from the dynamic poses of minor figures in the tombs of the Old and New Kingdoms discussed earlier in this book (see pp. 121, 122). Stevenson Smith has suggested that the colouration of these scenes was more akin to contemporary Greek art than Egyptian, but he also noted the problem of knowing what the original colours might have been before the pigments faded in the Sun or changed their chemical composition. Actually, as with Horsatutu's statue, the least Egyptian aspect of the minor figures' appearance is simply the contemporary style of their clothing and hair. Inside the tomb chapel, where the principal characters in the offering cult are presented, the decoration is typically Egyptian; the dead man's son, Djedthutefankh, makes the requisite offerings, accompanied by speeches from gods including Atum and Osiris-Khentyimentu. The possibility of 'hybrid' decoration in the hypostyle hall seems the more remarkable because Petosiris was a near contemporary of Tjaiseimu in the 30th Dynasty, and his death dates to the very start of the Ptolemaic era, so we ought not to underestimate the essentially Egyptian character of his tomb nor ascribe the art style to 'creeping' Hellenization. In part, perhaps, the scenes are the distinctive work of a local artist; in part they may simply reflect the specific dress and culture of whoever commissioned the relevant tomb scenes, whether Petosiris or Djedthutefankh. In any event, modern observers must consider whether their interpretation of the scenes as 'Hellenistic', 'naturalistic' or otherwise is a simple observation or has been coloured by their own expectations of what art in Egypt ought to be like under Greco-Roman rule.

As a final note, before presuming to use the tomb of Petosiris as a model for its age, we must not underestimate its personal, almost individual character. In this instance a lament for his dead son, Thutrekhu, inscribed in Ancient Egyptian, brings home the individual stories within the edifice: '*Whoever hears my words, his heart may break as a result. Because I am a child snatched by force, cut short in years without cause, suddenly snatched as an infant like an old man taken away in sleep.*' Interestingly, more than 400 years later in the reign of the Roman emperor Hadrian (AD 117–138), in the same cemetery at Tuna el-Gebel, a man built a tomb still in the traditional Egyptian style, but this time inscribed in Greek with two poems for his own child, Isidora, tragically drowned. '*This is for you,*' he says. '*The offerings made each year, the ceremony like that for the immortal gods. But I shall bring no more offerings for you, my daughter, because of the weeping.*' What do we make of this ostensibly Egyptian father's poetry in Greek: an affectation, a sophisticated commission or the most personal aspect of the whole tomb?

In the rock-cut complex of officials' tombs at Kom el-Shuqafa in Alexandria, mostly dated to the 2nd century AD, more than one Egyptologist has suggested we finally encounter reliefs and paintings 'which can no longer be identified as truly ancient Egyptian art' [255, 256]. However, we may also recognize this unfamiliar and disorientating subterranean complex as a local adaptation to traditional practice. Perhaps the burials of animal mummies in vast subterranean galleries – a religious phenomenon that proliferated and thrived under Greco-Roman rule – might have influenced the design here [251], but probably the main factor was the need to develop a cemetery inside a populous coastal city that stands on waterlogged ground. Inside the complex, a communal area for funeral ceremonies and subsequent offerings

255 Traditional scene from a vaulted tomb chapel at Kom el-Shuqafa, showing Anubis preparing the deceased for burial, on a lion-shaped bed, in the presence of Horus and Thoth (see pp. 275–76). Probably 2nd century AD.

256 View of the colonnaded entrance to the same tomb at Kom el-Shuqafa, exhibiting standard architectural forms. The crowned uraeus-serpents and Sun-discs flanking the door originate in traditional Egyptian iconography but have been adapted to incorporate references to Classical mythology.

257 Sarcophagus of the senior royal official Horkhebit, with Isis spreading her protective wings across his chest. Saqqara. Greywacke. 2.57 m (8 ft 5 in.) high. 26th Dynasty.

at the top of the complex gives way to a lower-level network of individual tomb chapels and niched galleries for large numbers of burials. The chapels are decorated with relief scenes familiar from the traditional offering cult, though the hairstyles and clothing may reflect contemporary styles and there are occasional details taken from Roman religious symbolism. Elsewhere in Alexandria there are certainly tombs of the same date that have little or no traditional Egyptian decoration, but doubtless these serve to indicate that, in imperial Alexandria, it was not so much the case that native art was evolving but that the urban demography of the Eastern Mediterranean was morphing.

In fact, subtly shifting emphases in Egyptian art during these centuries may best be illustrated in coffins, where painting on wood may occur alongside hard stone sculpture. In paintings especially, specific forms may seem more familiar to modern eyes and 'less Egyptian', though the underlying beliefs remain essentially unchanged and the imagery of Osiris still predominates. Clothing and jewelry may seem naturalistic and certainly contemporary but, in a funerary context, they actually relate to the concept of 'adoration' and recall the elegantly dressed denizens in the age-old tombs of Sabni or Ramose (see pp. 101, 116, 120). Again, there is no simple equation of traditional Egyptian art with stereotypes and Greco-Roman art with Hellenistic naturalism.

The most prominent development in the form of coffins during this period – which was, in fact, a tendency since the late New Kingdom – is the increased prominence of faces [257]. In the most

258 Mummy board with the face of a woman on each side. Faiyum region. Encaustic painted wood. 38 cm (1 ft 3 in.) high. 2nd century AD.

259 Elaborately wrapped mummy of a girl aged 5 to 7 years, with painted and gilded cartonnage mask. Her bare breasts may emulate the iconography of the goddess Nut, usually shown inside coffins of this time. Hawara. 0.92 m (3 ft) long. 2nd century AD.

obvious manifestation of this development, faces tend to become relatively larger and broader, until they may seem grossly out of proportion with the overall figure. Of course, a mummy with an uncovered face, a wig and a collar is the ancient image of Osiris, but the increased prominence of the face presumably also relates to the meaning of the Book of the Dead Spell 151 inscribed on the gold mask of Tutankhamun (see pp. 213–14). Recognizing this emphasis on faces, we can also appreciate the indigenous Egyptian aspect of the phenomenon of the 'Faiyum portraits', dating from the 1st to the 3rd century AD. They are so called because they have been collected mostly from sites in the Faiyum region, especially Hawara, and formally the portraits are obviously related to the Hellenistic tradition of painting in three-quarter view, often with naturalistic shadows and highlights. On the other hand, the portraits were painted on wooden boards, then fastened into the linen wrappings of mummies over the face, a custom that is definitively Egyptian. Though the clothing, hairstyles and jewelry illustrate fashions common across the whole Roman empire, the appearance of these items in Egyptian funerary art is entirely to be expected. Perhaps some of the principals among the Faiyum communities in question were Greek-speaking immigrants, at least by descent, who adopted Egyptian beliefs, rather than Egyptians for whom 'Classical art' seemed to be the way forward. For example, the face of the woman shown on either side of a portrait board in the Ashmolean Collection has been interpreted as more 'Roman' (that is, more naturalistic) in presentation on one side, more 'Egyptian' on the other [258]. However, we may simply see in the faces portraits at different ages, in line with an indigenous tradition exemplified by the statues of Amenhotep, son of Hapu or, more pertinently perhaps, the stela of the lady Khu (see p. 249).

Undoubtedly another type of mask used with mummies at this time has a more traditionally Egyptian appearance, like the three-dimensional face of a wooden coffin but modelled in clay or plaster. Some of these masks are entirely stylized, whereas others are moving evocations of real human beings. A poignant example is the mummy of a girl excavated by Flinders Petrie in a shallow pit, also at Hawara [259]. The wrappings are arranged in lozenges with gilded studs and a gilded plaster foot-case, and, though she was little more than five years old when she died, following Egyptian artistic conventions her gilded mask shows her as a mature woman with prominent breasts. Her hair and jewelry seem fashionable, though formally the mask is very different from the contemporary 'Faiyum portraits'. Once interred her mummy was covered with a linen sheet, and copper mirrors were placed on her breasts and belly (see p. 263), and she was accompanied by items including a faience statuette of the infant Horus and a statue of a lion. A wooden board or stela found beside her head is painted on each side with a figurative scene conforming to Egyptian conventions: one shows a naked woman or goddess giving birth; the other a seated man holding some shears over a brazier – perhaps a doctor? The Classicist Véronique Dasen has suggested that the imagery of the burial conveys the hope that the girl's destiny to be a mother may be fulfilled in the afterlife, though we may also speculate whether the meaning lies closer to traditional Egyptian mythology, perhaps in the relationship between Osiris and Isis.

The advent of Christianity

The girl from Hawara passed away in the 2nd century AD, as did Isidora at Tuna el-Gebel and most of the folk interred at Kom el-Shuqafa. By then international politics were already hastening the demise of pharaonic culture. Mighty, ruthless Rome, having disposed of the Ptolemaic dynasty in 30 BC, sought to appropriate the authority of pharaonic Egypt by transporting its monuments to imperial Alexandria or to Rome and the Egypt-themed gardens springing up on the estates of Italy's wealthiest politicians and land-owners. Today more Egyptian obelisks stand just in the city of Rome than in their original locations in Egypt. Even the obelisks of Thutmose III in London and New York travelled overseas after first being removed to Roman Alexandria. The whole nation is portrayed on coins of the conqueror Octavian (who became the emperor Augustus, 30 BC to AD 14) beneath

260 Unfinished statue of a pharaoh, identified as Caracalla by comparison of the face with those of named statues. Mendes. Quartzite. 1.42 m (4 ft 8 in.) high. AD 198–217.

261 Scene showing the emperor Tiberius being presented as pharaoh to the god Khnum, in the Sun-court of the temple at Esna. AD 14–37.

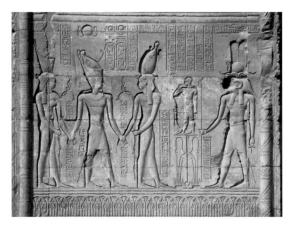

262 A 19th-century watercolour showing the shrine of the temple of Amun-Ra at Luxor as discovered in its final form, plastered over and decorated for a Roman cult in favour of the emperors Diocletian and Maximian.

the legend 'Aegypto capta'. Ironically Egypt is here represented as a crocodile, the very image once used by Ankhtyfy to symbolize Egyptian national unity (see p. 185). Many high priesthoods were effectively abolished in the aftermath, including the office of 'greatest of directors of craftsmen', which was as old as written history (see p. 76). Under Roman governance, Greek-speaking entirely displaced the Ancient Egyptian language in administration – even in personal correspondence – and by the 2nd century AD an inability to write in Greek was defined as illiteracy. A sequence of emperors from Commodus (180–192) to Decius (249–251) on one wall of the hypostyle hall in the temple of Khnum at Esna may be the last procession of kings in traditional temple decoration [261]. However, the bloody Roman soap opera entailed in the succession from Septimius Severus (193–211) to Caracalla (198–217) and Geta (209–211) has no relevance here, where the priesthood was investing its worship in absentee 'pharaohs'. When Caracalla did actually visit Egypt in 215, he ordered the expulsion of all Egyptians from Alexandria and the execution of all the city's young men for treason. A statue discovered near the shrine of Amasis in the temple at Mendes seems almost to superimpose the fearful, alien countenance of Caracalla on the primordial image of the pharaoh [260], and may serve in this book as the closing statement of pharaonic art, the bookend to Narmer's palette (see p. 22).

In this context, the Christian call to 'give to Caesar the things that are Caesar's, and give to God the things that are God's' defined the gulf between domains of faith and authority that in Egypt had previously been one and the same for millennia [262]. Effectively the subject of this book ends when a hermit named Antony walked into the forum in Alexandria about AD 305, anticipating judicial execution for his beliefs but obtaining instead an Egyptian-speaking Christian Church, for which the artistic embers of pharaonic authority had no meanings left other than either Rome or Christ. Astoundingly, in Egypt the pharaohs had become the essence of impropriety and foreign oppression – Antony and his fellow Christians were celebrated for defying Diocletian (284–305) and Maximian (286–305), '*lawless and degenerate kings*'. By the middle of the 4th century, possibly half the population of Egypt was openly Christian, and the overwhelming majority would be so before its end. In 371 Egypt became a separate diocese of the Roman empire divided into four separate regions, but an alternative national authority emerged in the form of the Coptic Church – 'Coptic' being simply the Greek word for 'Egyptian'. To reclaim the use of their own language in writing the Coptic community adapted the Greek alphabet to translate holy scripture, philosophy and biography into Egyptian. Hence on Coptic funerary stela the *crux ansata* ('cross with a handle') had become a Christian symbol, whose meaning as a hieroglyph was now lost [263]. In cultural terms, however, a boat evidently evokes religious festivals and beliefs in life after death whose models were the most ancient pharaonic ideas and practices [264].

At Philae a historic grant by Ptolemy II Philadelphus (285–246 BC) of taxes from a 12-mile (19-kilometre) district south of Aswan (the *dodecaschoenus*) had allowed the temples there to flourish, partly at the expense of the more ancient temples at Elephantine [265]. Philae endured even while briefly occupied by

263 Coptic stela in the form of a 'false door', though the characteristic shape, lack of decoration and open 'doorway' indicate that it originates in the Roman era and is probably not a reused pharaonic monument. The inscription records the death of a church elder named Matay. West Thebes, probably Medinet Habu. Painted granite (?). 0.6 m (2 ft) high. 5th to 8th century AD.

264 Stela roughly inscribed for a monk named Peter, with a processional boat adapted from pharaonic iconography. Unknown provenance. Limestone. 38 cm (1 ft 3 in.) high. 5th to 8 th century AD.

265 View of the temple of Isis on the island of Philae, probably the last pharaonic temple to function other than as a Christian church. Now relocated to Agilqiya, near Aswan.

the Meroitic king Arqamani as early as 207 BC because, of course, he still maintained the pharaonic traditions of the 25th Dynasty (see Chapter 12). His successor Adikhalamani founded the temple at Debod (see p. 285), while the latest known inscriptions in Egyptian hieroglyphs and the indigenous cursive script appear at Philae alongside inscriptions in Meroitic. Typically, the inscriptions in both languages summarize the contributions of kings and officials to the cult of Isis and her procession to the temple of Osiris on a neighbouring island. However, they come to an end in AD 452 and the temple itself was shut for the last time by order of the emperor Justinian in 543.

As early as 385 the Roman prefect Maternus Cynegius had arranged the closure of the other pharaonic temples in Egypt but for many of them this was far from the end. Once again Thebes provides the best example, where we see the descendants of the villagers from Deir el-Medina still living at Medinet Habu 1,800 years after the Valley of the Kings had been closed, in a town still named Djeme (see p. 198). Here the mighty temple of Ramesses III continued in service as a Christian church, while the Ptolemaic temple at Deir el-Medina became the Church of St Isidore the Martyr. The people of these communities were prosperous – in some instances remarkably wealthy – with business interests extending through the length of the country, until they were evicted under Islamic rule in the late 700s. Today these places are tourist destinations but after AD 385 they had remained homes for villagers and priests, when the Christian centuries at Thebes breathed life and service back into the ancient sacred spaces, conveniently exemplified by a Christian stela inscribed on a pharaonic false door.

Masterpiece
The Tazza Farnese

266 The interior of the Tazza
Farnese incised in cameo with a
scene set in Egypt. Agate. 20 cm
(8 in.) diameter. Ptolemaic era.

267 Gorgon shown on the base
of the Tazza Farnese.

The magnificent, enigmatic Farnese Cup (Tazza Farnese) is made by cameo from a rich sardonyx agate featuring yellow and black striations. The 'cup' is presumably in fact a libation dish, 20 cm (8 inches) in diameter, reputedly manufactured in Alexandria. If so, its assimilation of Egyptian mythology to the Hellenistic art tradition seems undeniable, and the cup stands as an outlier in the present book – an Egyptian masterpiece of the pharaonic age manufactured entirely apart from the indigenous art tradition. On the interior surface, figures carved from a stratum of white and gold include the central trio of an old man, a crowned lady and a young man. In an Egyptian context, indicated by the sphinx below them, such a trio may be interpreted as a family of gods, in this case presumably Osiris (or Serapis), Isis and Horus. However, the art style is Hellenistic, so accordingly the forms of the putative Osiris and Isis are those of the Greek gods Pluto and Demeter together with the agricultural god Triptolemus. The cornucopia in Pluto's hand may evoke the Nile Inundation, which from the planting of the seed in Triptolemus/Horus' bag brings forth the harvest, here held by Demeter. Perhaps the two figures at bottom right holding out a cornucopia and a dish (this very 'cup'?) represent the consumption of the harvest in its traditional Egyptian aspects of bread and beer.

In other words, the mythology and geography of the principal scene could well be Egyptian, or at least Egyptianizing, but the artistic interpretation and treatment is Hellenistic or Classical. The exterior base of the cup is completely filled by the head of a Gorgon with locks of snakes, drawn straight from Greek mythology. On the other hand, the uniqueness of the cup is such that various scholars have dated the piece to each one of the Ptolemaic centuries, or suggested links to historical events right down to the reign of Cleopatra VII or the victory of Octavian (Augustus). The recorded history of the cup actually begins in Persia in the 15th century, from where it reached the Aragonese court of Naples, and latterly the celebrated collection of Lorenzo de' Medici. In Naples, the specific imagery on the cup, including two figures in the sky representing seasonal wind and rain, might have become part of the inspiration for Botticelli's celebrated *Birth of Venus*.

Masterpiece
Statue of the priest Pasherbastet

Though conventionally dated to the 1st century BC, a smaller than life-size statue of the priest Pasherbastet seems essentially traditional in form, made in basalt, one of the characteristic hard stones used for statuary at the end of the 1st millennium BC. The priest strides forward onto his left foot with one hand gripping the nub of a 'staff', according to the age-old archetype from the tomb chapel. He wears a vest, kilt and fringed cloak gathered in his left hand, so in pose and costume Pasherbastet in three dimensions recalls the image of Tjaiseimu in relief (pp. 287–88), while his cloak alone is reminiscent of that in the ivory of an early king (see p. 130). More obviously than is the case with Tjaiseimu, the image of this man has a bulbous, enlarged cranium after the 'Amarna' style, leaving the mouth and jaw disproportionately small, though his nose and eyes are proportionate – and noticeably large in profile as a consequence. The apparent traces of a beard and moustache have been caused by the deterioration of the stone surface, and in fact his clean-shaven head is a more characteristic indication of his priestly depilation (see p. 262). This statue has a powerful, 'young torso' rather than the heavy physical presence of an archetypal 'older' man, such as Tjaiseimu. However, the shape of the head, together with the lines in his face, heavily lidded eyes and careworn expression evoke familiar virtues, such as experience, responsibility, serenity and wisdom. In fact, his downturned mouth and round eyes are characteristic of late Ptolemaic royal statues, though the typical uncertainty of this era applies regarding the specific provenance and dating of Pasherbastet's statue.

Masterpiece
Wooden portrait board of woman wearing jewelry

269 Mummy board of anonymous woman. Hawara. Encaustic painted wood. 44 cm (1 ft 5½ in.) high. 2nd century AD.

The so-called 'Faiyum portraits' represent a specific phenomenon rather than a historical artistic trend, but formally many are obviously related to the Hellenistic tradition of portrait painting (see p. 293). These mummy boards are often described as encaustic portraits, that is to say, painted using hot wax or resin – using the Greek word 'burnt in' (*en-causticos*; compare the English word 'caustic') – though in Egyptology encaustic has come to mean any method of decoration using pigments mixed with wax. Nonetheless, encaustic painting on wood evokes the appearance of oil painting because the pigments could be applied in thick layers with free brush strokes, and are often more vividly preserved than the surface colours of tomb scenes or statues.

This beautiful example, excavated at Hawara in 1911, shows a woman wearing a scarlet dress, and a scarlet cloak with a blue and gold fringe. Of course, it was originally bound into the exterior wrappings of a mummy, which were arranged in lozenges with gilded studs and a gilded foot-case like the young girl's in [259]. The young adult woman portrayed here has her hair arranged into four tiers of curls, with a plaited bun secured by a fancy top-pin and decorated with a gold chain. Her jewelry consists of a pair of earrings, three beaded necklaces round her throat, and a gold collar and pendant. The visual impact of her jewelry and cloak has been enhanced through the use of fine gold leaf, which is entirely typical of 'Faiyum portraits', and perhaps comparable to the traditional gilding of faces in Egyptian coffins. The specific details of the hairstyle, dress and jewelry have been used to date the portrait to the first half of the 2nd century AD, and certainly they each reflect styles worn across the Roman empire generally rather than just this part of Egypt. On the other hand, her face is shown frontally with an 'expressionless' visage after the pharaonic manner, while her elaborate wig with a decorative band may be understood as a contemporary interpretation of the appearance of Nofret (see p. 87) and countless well-heeled Egyptian women of earlier centuries. The use of shadows and highlights does correspond to the Hellenistic tradition, and the three-quarters view across her neck and shoulders creates a naturalistic drop from the 'near' shoulder to the 'far' one. This arrangement seems to have impacted upon the eyes, which stare along the perspective line created, so that the 'far' eye sits below the level of its counterpart, whereas the frontal pose seems to require them to sit on the same horizontal.

Postscript

'He that hath found some fledg'd bird's nest, may know / At first sight, if the bird be flown; / But what fair well or grove he sings in now, / That is to him unknown,' sang the Welsh mystic, Henry Vaughan. However, the art of ancient Egypt represents a committed attempt throughout the centuries to illustrate human lives in a context that does not move on or pass away. In that respect, how can ancient Egyptian art be understood in anything other than pharaonic terms? In pharaonic culture, acts of creating, building and decorating, together with the festivals, rituals and beliefs they illustrate and dignify, became the means both to organize and celebrate human relationships – with one another, with authority, with divinity, with the mere fact of life and Creation and the meaning of things. Those who do not believe in higher authorities or life after death are obliged to dig through such matters to unearth what is left when the art is stripped of its baggage, but they will find no indication that an ancient Egyptian artist ever did so. Our modern interpretation of early history is so bound up with evolution we may casually assume ancient artists were striving to do what artists do today, and their refusal to adopt modern conceptions of the individual or the moment (or iron technology or alphabetic writing) betrays their intellectual inferiority. No doubt we expect progress in the past because we are in a hurry to get to ourselves. In other words, if we assume that what we mean by art is its natural meaning, and that art in antiquity is *bound to be* steps on the way to how we do things, then we can also dismiss the possibility we might have somewhere taken a misjudged turn or two. (It does not follow that we have, but to think in such terms may allow a different point of view.)

On the other hand, should we simply admit that the artists of ancient Egypt were utterly conventional and unwilling to embrace change? Ironically, part of the appeal of pharaonic Egypt is the implication that it stands at the threshold of civilization. Its very essence seems to be a giant leap along the road of progress – the vanguard of social, technological and economic innovation in late prehistory and early history. In Egypt we find many of the earliest towns, the grandest monuments, the oldest books and so on. The suggestion that such a nation conveniently insisted 'this far and no further' shortly after the dawn of written history seems convenient, to say the least. After all, on a writing board in the British Museum, Khakheperrasonb, a Middle Kingdom priest in Heliopolis, pointedly begins his philosophical teaching with the lament, '*If only I had an unknown song and some discovered words;*

270 A 19th-century watercolour showing the second Sun-court of the mortuary temple of Ramesses III at Medinet Habu as discovered. The monolithic sandstone columns with Corinthian capitals, mostly seen fallen, supported the central span of the roof of the 'Holy Church of Djeme' when the site was abruptly abandoned in the 8th century (see p. 198).

a new way of speaking which was not here before; free from what gets repeated or one word from the opinions former generations spoke'. Better perhaps to forego our expectations and appreciate that art itself in ancient Egypt was ordinarily intended to be about sacred things, things that do not change – because the whole vastness of time and Creation cannot be even an infinitesimal fraction of eternity. To the ancients we walk in the glory of god-given meaning, though the patterns and shapes we discern in our lives and in the world around seem distorted and obscure. G. K. Chesterton's shrewd sleuth Father Brown suggested this is because 'we here are on the wrong side of the tapestry', whose design only makes sense when looked at from somewhere else. For 3,000 years, the ancient Egyptians too affirmed that art may offer a glimpse of the view from that somewhere else – or in the words of Ankhtyfy, *'a gateway to the far side of the sky'.*

King-list & Dynasties

Note on chronology

The dates for Egypt are generally considered to be among the most secure in the ancient world – accurate to within two centuries as far back as *c.* 3000 BC, accurate to within two decades during the 2nd millennium BC (i.e. 2000–1000 BC), and generally exact from 664 BC. The Egyptians' own records did not use an absolute dating system, but instead dated events to a specific year in the reign of a specific king (regnal dating). However, a few surviving examples of the Egyptians' own king-lists occasionally state reign lengths in years and months, and summarize the key events of each reign, especially religious festivals. The Greek historian Herodotus, writing around 430 BC, claims that the Egyptians were respected among all nations for having the most accurate records of the past. Of course, we are now able to check this information against archaeological data and other written evidence.

A comprehensive history of Egypt written by the native priest Manetho for the pharaoh Ptolemy II Philadelphus (285–246 BC) – a foreigner, born on the isle of Cos – has not survived, but the gist of it may be deduced from excerpts provided by later historians. Manetho's account established the thirty-one dynasties that still structure our modern chronology of pharaonic Egypt. In his history a 'dynasty' typically corresponds to an era when one family held the throne of Egypt in a single line of succession, but evidently this was not always the case. Consequently modern historians have grouped the dynasties into broader eras based on 'kingdoms', when there was essentially only one king throughout Egypt. Hence we have the Old, Middle and New 'Kingdoms', separated by 'Intermediate Periods', when the rule of the country may be divided. As a final point, there no longer seems any sense in maintaining the conventional distinction between the Old Kingdom pharaohs (3rd to 6th Dynasties) and the kings who, we now know, simply ruled before them during the 'Early Dynastic Period' (1st and 2nd Dynasties).

Unexpectedly, perhaps, an arcane method known as 'Sothic dating' – based on the discrepancy between (a) when a specific observation of the star Sirius (Egyptian name Sothis) ought to

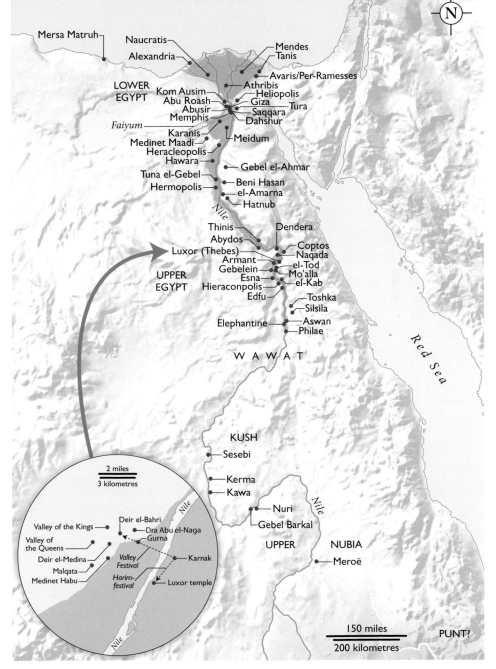

Mediterranean Sea

N

Mersa Matruh

Naucratis
Alexandria

Mendes
Tanis

Avaris/Per-Ramesses

LOWER
EGYPT
Kom Ausim
Abu Roash
Abusir
Memphis

Athribis
Heliopolis
Giza
Saqqara
Dahshur

Tura

Faiyum

Karanis
Medinet Maadi
Heracleopolis
Hawara

Meidum

Gebel el-Ahmar

Tuna el-Gebel
Hermopolis

Beni Hasan
el-Amarna
Hatnub

Nile

Thinis
Abydos
Luxor (Thebes)
Armant
Gebelein
Esna
Hieraconpolis
Edfu

Dendera
Coptos
Naqada
el-Tod
Mo'alla
el-Kab

UPPER
EGYPT

Toshka
Silsila

Elephantine

Aswan
Philae

W A W A T

Red Sea

KUSH
Sesebi

Kerma

Kawa

Nile

Nuri
Gebel Barkal

UPPER   NUBIA

Meroë

PUNT?

150 miles
200 kilometres

2 miles
3 kilometres

Valley of the Kings
Valley of
the Queens
Deir el-Medina
Malqata
Medinet Habu

Deir el-Bahri
Dra Abu el-Naga
Gurna

Nile

Valley
Festival
Harim-
festival

Karnak

Luxor temple

Nile

occur and (b) ancient records of when it actually did occur – has become the established method for dating the 2nd millennium BC in Egypt. Calculations of this discrepancy have produced dates that are widely accepted among scholars, at least in the sense of narrowing dates down to a handful of options which are roughly in agreement. Nonetheless, different books may give different dates for the same event, suggesting that Ramesses II became king in 1301, 1290 or 1279 BC, and so on. Dates before the 12th Dynasty, which essentially means dates for the 3rd millennium BC (i.e. 3000–2000 BC), have to be extrapolated by dead reckoning, so there is much less consensus about these very early dates and they are stated in the following list using round figures. Consequently Narmer might have become the first king of Egypt as early as 3200 BC or as late as 2900 BC according to different books. For this reason, most Egyptologists prefer to discuss pharaonic history by reference to kings' reigns or to dynasties rather than by using calendar years, which may be so uncertain.

Eventually we are able to obtain absolute dates for ancient Egypt by means of synchronisms with other nations who did have absolute dating systems. The earliest such secure date is 664/663 BC, when the armies of Ashurbanipal of Assyria sacked and nearly razed the mighty Egyptian heartland of Thebes, an event which in turn corresponds to the beginning of the 26th Dynasty and the Late Period. In August 30 BC, Egypt formally lost its independence and became established under the jurisdiction of the Roman emperors, which is how it remained (officially under Byzantine government from AD 395) until the nation surrendered to the armies of the Arab Rashidun Caliphate in November AD 641. Throughout the first two centuries of Roman rule, the emperors were usually represented in Egyptian art as though they were pharaohs. However, following edicts of Galerius and Constantine the Great (AD 306–337), Christianity was formally tolerated by the Roman empire and the pharaonic art of Egypt was abandoned in favour of Christian art traditions (see Chapter 15). Hence the list of kings of Egypt given here includes the Roman emperors down to Constantine, whose reign basically corresponds to the end of the period covered by this book.

PRE-DYNASTIC

'Dynasty 0'   c. 3000 BC–c. 2950 BC
Existence uncertain:
Iryhor (?) / Ro (?) / Ka (?) / Scorpion (?)

EARLY DYNASTIC / OLD KINGDOM
One line of kings, 800+ years.

1st Dynasty   c. 2950 BC–c. 2750 BC
Narmer
Aha
Djer
Djet
Den
Anedjib
Semerkhet
Qa'a

2nd Dynasty   c. 2750–c. 2650
Hetepsekhemwy
Raneb
Ninetjer
Weneg (?)
Sened (?)
Peribsen
Khasekhemwy
(one line of kings, 500+ years)
What does this refer to?

3rd Dynasty   c. 2650–c. 2550
Netjerykhet (Djoser)
Sekhemkhet
Khaba
Zanakht
Huni

4th Dynasty   c. 2550–c. 2400
Snofru
Khufu
Radjedef
Khafra
Menkaura
Shepseskaf

5th Dynasty   c. 2400–c. 2300
Userkaf
Sahura
Neferirkara Kakai
Shepseskara Izi
Raneferef
Nyuserra Ini
Menkauhor
Zezi
Unas

6th Dynasty   c. 2300–c. 2150
Teti
Userkara
Pepy I
Nemtyemzaf I
Pepy II

FIRST INTERMEDIATE PERIOD
Eventually two lines of kings, c. 150(?) years.

7th / 8th Dynasty   c. 2150–c. 2100
Nemtyemzaf II (?), then numerous
ephemeral kings

9th / 10th Dynasty   c. 2100–c. 2000
Several kings, including:
Khety I–V
Merykara

11th Dynasty (Thebes only)   c. 2075–c. 2020
Inyotef I–III

MIDDLE KINGDOM
One line of kings, c. 250 years.

11th Dynasty (all Egypt)   c. 2020–c. 1950
Montuhotep II   c. 2020–c. 1970
Montuhotep III   c. 1970–c. 1960
Montuhotep IV   c. 1960–c. 1950

12th Dynasty   c. 1950–c. 1750
Amenemhat I   c. 1950–c. 1920
Senwosret I   c. 1920–c. 1875
Amenemhat II   c. 1875–c. 1845
Senwosret II   c. 1845–c. 1840
Senwosret III   c. 1840–c. 1805
Amenemhat III   c. 1805–c. 1760
Amenemhat IV   c. 1760–c. 1755
Nefrusobk   c. 1755–c. 1750

SECOND INTERMEDIATE PERIOD
Eventually many lines of kings, 200+ years.

13th Dynasty   c. 1750–c. 1630
Traditionally sixty kings, including
(order uncertain):
Sobkhotep I
Amenemhat V
Qemau
Sahorunedjheryotef
Sobkhotep II
Hor
Amenemhat VII
Wegaf
Khendjer
Sobkhotep III
Neferhotep I
Sahathor
Sobkhotep IV
Sobkhotep V
Sobkhotep VI
Ay I
Sobkhotep VII
Neferhotep II

14th Dynasty
Numerous ephemeral kings, wholly
contemporary with other dynasties

15th Dynasty (Avaris only)   c. 1630–c. 1521
Six 'Hyksos' kings, wholly contemporary with
other dynasties, including:
Sekerher (Salitis?)
Sheshi
Khyan
Apophis   c. 1570–c. 1530
Khamudy   c. 1530–c. 1521

16th Dynasty
Numerous ephemeral kings, wholly
contemporary with other dynasties

17th	**Dynasty** (Upper Egypt only)	**c. 1630–c. 1539**
	Numerous kings, wholly contemporary	
	with other dynasties, probably ending:	
	Inyotef V	
	Inyotef VI	
	Inyotef VII	
	Sobkemsaf II	
	Ahmose I	
	Taa	
	Kamose	c. 1541–c. 1539

NEW KINGDOM

One line of kings, c. 450 years.

18th	**Dynasty**	**c. 1539–c. 1292**
	Ahmose (II)	c. 1539–c. 1514
	Amenhotep I	c. 1514–c. 1493
	Thutmose I	c. 1493–c. 1481
	Thutmose II	c. 1481–c. 1479
	Thutmose III	c. 1479–c. 1425
	with Hatshepsut	c. 1475–c. 1458
	Amenhotep II	c. 1426–c. 1400
	Thutmose IV	c. 1400–c. 1390
	Amenhotep III	c. 1390–c. 1353
	Amenhotep IV (Akhenaten)	c. 1353–c. 1336
	Smenkhkara	c. 1336–c. 1332
	Tutankhamun	c. 1332–c. 1323
	Itnetjer-Ay (II)	c. 1323–c. 1320
	Horemheb	c. 1320–c. 1292
19th	**Dynasty**	**c. 1292–c. 1190**
	Ramesses I	c. 1292–c. 1290
	Sety I	c. 1290–c. 1279
	Ramesses II	c. 1279–c. 1213
	Merenptah	c. 1213–c. 1203
	Sety II	c. 1203–c. 1197
	(in dispute) Amenmessu	c. 1203–c. 1200)
	Siptah	c. 1197–c. 1192
	Twosret	c. 1192–c. 1190
20th	**Dynasty**	**c. 1190–c. 1069**
	Sethnakht	c. 1190–c. 1187
	Ramesses III	c. 1187–c. 1156
	Ramesses IV	c. 1156–c. 1150
	Ramesses V	c. 1150–c. 1145
	Ramesses VI	c. 1145–c. 1137
	Ramesses VII	c. 1137–c. 1130
	Ramesses VIII	c. 1130–c. 1126
	Ramesses IX	c. 1126–c. 1108
	Ramesses X	c. 1108–c. 1099
	Ramesses XI	c. 1099–c. 1069

THIRD INTERMEDIATE PERIOD

One line of kings for c. 200 years, then
several lines for c. 200 years.

21st	**Dynasty**	**c. 1069–c. 945**
	Smendes	c. 1069–c. 1045
	Amenemnesu	c. 1045–c. 1040
	Psusennes I	c. 1040–c. 990
	Amenemope	c. 990–c. 980
	Osorkon 'the Elder'	c. 980–c. 975
	Siamun	c. 975–c. 955
	Psusennes II	c. 955–c. 945

22nd	**Dynasty**	**c. 945–c. 715**
	Shoshenq I	c. 945–c. 925
	Osorkon I	c. 925–c. 890
	with Shoshenq II	c. 890
	Takelot I	c. 890–c. 875
	Osorkon II	c. 875–c. 835
	Shoshenq III	c. 835–c. 795
	Shoshenq IV	c. 795–c. 785
	Pimay	c. 785–c. 775
	Shoshenq V	c. 775–c. 735
	Osorkon IV	c. 735–c. 715
23rd	**Dynasty** (Thebes only?)	**c. 840–c. 715**
	Details uncertain, wholly contemporary	
	with other dynasties.	
	Takelot II	c. 840–c. 820
	Pedubast I	c. 820–c. 800
	with Iuput I	c. 800
	Shoshenq IV/VI	c. 800–c. 780
	Osorkon III	c. 780–c. 760
	Takelot III	c. 760–c. 745
	Rudamun	c. 745–c. 725
	Peftjauawybast	c. 725–c. 715
24th	**Dynasty** (Sais only)	**c. 730–c. 715**
	Details uncertain, wholly	
	contemporary with other dynasties	
	Tefnakht	c. 730–c. 720
	Bocchoris	c. 720–c. 715
25th	**Dynasty** (Kingdom of Kush)	**c. 800–664**
	Alara	
	Kashta	
	Piye	c. 747–c. 715
	Shabaka	c. 715–c. 702
	Shebitku	c. 702–c. 690
	Taharqa	c. 690–664
	Tanwetamani	664–657
26th	**Dynasty** (Sais only)	**c. 672–664**
	Necho I	c. 672–664

LATE PERIOD

One line of kings, subject to foreign domination, 332 years.

26th	**Dynasty** (all Egypt)	**664–525**
	Psamtek I	664–610
	Necho II	610–595
	Psamtek II	595–589
	Apries	589–570
	Amasis (Ahmose III)	570–526
	Psamtek III	526–525
27th	**Dynasty**	**525–405**
	(First Persian Regime)	
	Cambyses	525–522
	Darius I (the Great)	522–486
	Xerxes	486–465
	Artaxerxes I	465–424
	Darius II	424–405
	Artaxerxes II	405 (in Egypt)
28th	**Dynasty**	**405–399**
	Amyrtaeus	405–399
29th	**Dynasty**	**399–380**
	Nepherites I	399–393
	(Psammuthis 393?)	

Achoris	393–380	
(or Psammuthis 380?)		
Nepherites II	380	
30th Dynasty	**380–343**	
Nectanebo I	380–362	
Teos	362–360	
Nectanebo II	360–343	
31st Dynasty	**343–332**	
(Second Persian Regime)		
Artaxerxes III	343–338	
	(in Egypt)	
Artaxerxes IV (Arses)	338–336	
Darius III	336–332	

GREEK PERIOD

One line of kings, 302 years.

Macedonian (Argaeid) Regime	**332–310**	
Alexander III (the Great)	332–323	
Philip III Arrhidaeus	323–317	
Alexander IV	317–310	
Ptolemaic Dynasty	**310–30 BC**	
Ptolemy I Soter	305/4 (as pharaoh)–285	
Ptolemy II Philadelphus	285–246	
Ptolemy III Euergetes	246–221	
Ptolemy IV Philopator	221–205	
Ptolemy V Epiphanes	205–180	
Ptolemy VI Philometor	180–145	
Ptolemy VII Neos Philopator	145	
Ptolemy VIII Euergetes	145–116	
with Cleopatra II		
Ptolemy IX Soter	116–110	
Ptolemy X Alexander	110–109	
with Cleopatra III		
Ptolemy IX (restored)	109–107	
with Cleopatra III		
Ptolemy X (restored)	107–88	
Ptolemy IX (restored)	88–80	
Ptolemy XI Alexander	80	
with Berenice III		
Ptolemy XII Auletes	80–58	
Berenice IV (queen regent)	58–55	
Ptolemy XII (restored)	55–51	
Cleopatra VII (queen regent)	51–30	
with Ptolemy XIII Theos Philopator	51–47	
with Ptolemy XIV	47–44	
with Ptolemy XV Caesar	44–30	

ROMAN EMPIRE

Succession of foreign rulers, 670 years (not all listed here).

Augustus Caesar	30 BC–AD 14
Tiberius	AD 14–37
Caligula	37–41
Claudius	41–54
Nero	54–68
Galba / Otho / Vitellius	68–69
Vespasian	69–79
Titus	79–81
Domitian	81–96
Nerva	96–98
Trajan	98–117

Hadrian	117–138
Antoninus Pius	138–161
Marcus Aurelius	161–180
with Lucius Verus	161–169
Commodus	180–192
Pertinax / Didius Julianus /	193
Clodius Albinus / Pescennius Niger	
Septimius Severus	193–211
with Caracalla	198–211
Caracalla	198–217
with Geta	209–211
Macrinus / Diadumenianus	217–218
Elagabalus	218–222
Severus Alexander	222–235
Maximinus II	235–238
Gordian I & Gordian II /	238
Balbinus & Pupienus	
Gordian III	238–244
Philip	244–249
Decius	249–251
Trebonianus Gallus	251–253
& Volusianus	
Aemilianus	253
Valerian	253–260
with Gallienus	253–260
Gallienus	260–268
Claudius II 'Gothicus'	268–270
Quintillus	270
Aurelian	270–275
Tacitus / Florianus	275–276
Probus	276–282
Carus	282–283
Numerian & Carinus	283–284
Diocletian	284–305
with Maximian	286–305
Galerius	305–311
with Constantius I	305–306
Constantine I	311–337

Notes

All translations from texts in ancient Egyptian, Coptic and Classical Greek are the author's own. So too is the translation from Hermann Hesse's *Demian* on p. 217.

Chapter 2
35 'It took the whole of Creation to produce my foot, my each feather' from 'Hawk Roosting' by Ted Hughes, *Lupercal* Faber and Faber Ltd, 1960.

38 'What comes from the heart takes the shape of Atum...' from British Museum stela EA 498 ('The Shabaka Stone'), line 53.

Chapter 3
46 'which has given birth to the gods, and from which every thing has emerged' British Museum stela EA 498 ('The Shabaka Stone'), line 58.

47 'For, these days, these folk collect their harvest with less trouble than anyone' from Herodotus, *The Histories* Book 2/14.

57 'The town of Pe is sailing upstream to you...' from Spell 412, in a corridor running east from the antechamber of the pyramid of king Teti (6th Dynasty).

Chapter 5
80 'a nation built out of stone' from the title of H. G. Evers, *Staat aus dem Stein. Denkmäler, Geschichte und Bedeutung der ägyptischen Plastik während des Mittleren Reichs* Verlag F. Bruckmann, 1929.

85 'and when the two parts were brought together they fitted so well...' from Diodorus of Sicily, *A Library of History* Book 1/98.

Chapter 6
93 'Say, is there Beauty yet to find?' from 'The Old Vicarage, Grantchester' by Rupert Brooke, *Collected Poems*, John Lane, 1916.

Chapter 8
144 'I beat the rebels away from the sacred-boat...' from Ägyptisches Museum Berlin stela 1204.

147 'an early example of the Egyptian predilection for squaring the circle' from C. Aldred, *Egyptian Art* p. 36 (see Select Bibliography).

Chapter 9
157 '"self-preservation", to coin an Egyptologist's phrase' see J. Assmann, 'Preservation and Presentation of Self in Ancient Egyptian Portraiture' in P. Der Manuelian (ed.), *Studies in Honor of William Kelly Simpson* Vol. I Boston Museum of Fine Arts, 1996.

164 'according to one interpretation, they represent mostly women' see N. Harrington, 'Anthropoid Busts and Ancestor Cults at Deir el-Medina' in K. Piquette and S. Love (eds), *Current research in Egyptology 2003: Proceedings of the Fourth Annual Symposium*, Oxbow Books, p. 85.

Chapter 10
173 'The first of these, Achthôes, harsher than the generations before him...' ascribed to Eusebius by George the Monk, see W. G. Waddell, Manetho Loeb Classical Library 350, 1940, pp. 60–61.

173 'barbaric stelae present many extraordinary attempts to render the half-forgotten signs' from F. Ll. Griffith in W. M. F. Petrie, *Dendereh 1898* The Egypt Exploration Fund, p. 52.

177 'One authority lists at least 150 cemeteries by the end of the Old Kingdom', see D. Kessler, 'Nekropolen. Frühzeit and A.R. 1-6 Dyn.' in W. Helck and E. Otto (eds), *Lexikon der Ägyptologie IV* Otto Harrassowitz, 1982.

Chapter 11
191 'Today death seems to me like a whiff of myrrh...' from Papyrus Berlin 3024 ('The Dialogue of a Man with His Soul').

195 'Now, my person found this very chapel built of bricks...' from Cairo Museum stela CG 34013.

198 'it is, at least in part, distinctly a memorable edifice as the Medici Chapel at Florence...' from A. B. Edwards, *A Thousand Miles Up the Nile* (2nd edn) A. L. Burt, 1888, p. 392.

211 'My person desired to make a commitment for my father Amun-Ra in Karnak...' from Cairo Museum stela CG 34012.

Chapter 12
217 'In fact I saw – I thought I saw or felt – that it was not even a man's face...' from Hermann Hesse, *Demian. Die Geschichte von Emil Sinclairs Jugend* S. Fischer Verlag, 1921, pp. 53–54.

218 'a quest for naturalism and realism' from R. Hari *New Kingdom. Amarna Period* Iconography of Religions XVI, 6, E. J. Brill, 1985, p. 18.

220 'a revision of the written script to more closely reflect the spoken language of the time' from the British Museum website, accessed in October 2016.

220 'at the most revolutionary point in the early part of the reign of Akhenaten...' from W. Stevenson

Smith, *Art and Architecture* p. 312 (see Select Bibliography).

226 'a single obelisk' from the hieroglyphic text of the obelisk now standing in the town square beside the Basilica di San Giovanni in Laterano, Rome.

228 'the innovators of the Amarna period had left intact the foundations of Egyptian art' W. Stevenson Smith, *Art and Architecture* p. 312 (see Select Bibliography).

231 'Now his person happened to be relaxing in the throne-room' from Cairo Museum stela CG 34002.

234 'three centuries which followed the collapse of Egyptian authority constitute one of the most obscure phases of Nubian history...' from J. H. Taylor, *Egypt and Nubia* British Museum Press, 1991, p. 37.

241 'qualities of maturity and experience are valued more highly than youth and promise' from J. Malek, *Egyptian Art* p. 360 (see Select Bibliography).

241 'is in the more realistic and even brutal style of the dynasty' from C. Aldred, *Egyptian Art* page 219 (see Select Bibliography).

243 'Iriketakana's corpulent form' see R. G. Morkot, *The Black Pharaohs. Egypt's Nubian Rulers* The Rubicon Press, 2000, pp. 271–72.

Chapter 13
247 'If you think about burial, it is ripping out the heart...' from Papyrus Berlin 3024 ('The Dialogue of a Man with His Soul').

251 'this "friend" Inyotef may be the same as the house manager in the upper scene' see J.-R. Pérez-Accino, 'Panorama oblato alto de la pirámide (o al cielo por la puerta de servicio)' in *Gérion* 2007 Extra, pp. 80–81.

Chapter 14
267 'one of the supreme pieces of carving of the early XVIIIth dynasty...' see M.S. Drower, Flinders Petrie. A Life in Archaeology University of Wisconsin Press, 1995, p. 230.

273 'the largest group of goldwork that had left Egypt' from W. M. F. Petrie, *Seventy Years in Archaeology* Low, Marston and Co, 1932, p. 212.

279 'The Frenchman declared the jeweler responsible "incomparable" in any age' see J. de Morgan, *Fouilles à Dahchour en 1894-1895* Adolphe Holzhausen, 1903, p. 60.

279 'Málek describes the delicacy as "breathtaking"' see J. Malek, *Egyptian Art* p. 204 (see Select Bibliography).

279 'the airy lightness of the goldwork' from W. Stevenson Smith, *Art and Architecture* p. 203 (see Select Bibliography).

279 'it conjures up the image of a lovely young girl as she pads barefoot through the palace...' from A. P. Kozloff, 'Luxury Arts' in M. K. Hartwig, *Companion* p. 296 (see Select Bibliography).

Chapter 15

282 Nectanebo's 'jutting chin and nose seem to close like pincers' from W. Stevenson Smith, *Art and Architecture* p. 417 (see Select Bibliography).

286 'Egyptian, Greek, and Roman royal statues belong in recognisably Egyptian, Greek, and Roman spaces' from E. Brophy, *Royal Statues in Egypt 300 BC–AD 220. Context and Function* Archaeopress, 2015, p. 56.

289 'in most respects what prevailed was several centuries of relative opaqueness, impossibility or refusal of excessively visible cultural borrowings' from J. Bingen, *Hellenistic Egypt. Monarchy, Society, Economy, Culture* University of California Press, 2007, p. 251.

290 'the colouration of these scenes was more akin to Greek art than Egyptian' see W. Stevenson Smith, *Art and Architecture* p. 421 (see Select Bibliography).

291 'reliefs and paintings "which can no longer be identified as truly ancient Egyptian art"' from J. Malek, *Egyptian Art* p. 396 (see Select Bibliography).

294 'the girl's destiny to be a mother may be fulfilled in the afterlife' see V. Dasen, 'La petite fille et le médecin. Á propos d'une étiquette de momie d'Égypte romaine' in V. Boudon-Millot et al, *Femmes en Médecine. En l'honneur de Danielle Gourevitch* De Boccard Édition-Diffusion, 2008, pp. 57–58.

296 'lawless and degenerate kings' from Codex Pierpont Morgan 590 ('Pope John's Encomium for St Menas'), folio 61v.

Postscript

304 'He that hath found some fledg'd bird's nest' from 'They Are All Gone Into the World of Light' by Henry Vaughan, Silex Scintillans Part 2, 1655. 'If only I had an unknown song and some discovered words...' from British Museum writing board EA 5645 recto ('The Lament of Khakheperraseneb').

305 'we here are on the wrong side of the tapestry' from 'The Sins of Prince Saradine' in G. K. Chesterton, *The Innocence of Father Brown* Cassell & Co, 1911.

Select Bibliography

Background history
A. M. Dodson and D. Hilton, *The Complete Royal Families of Ancient Egypt* Thames & Hudson, 2004.
A. B. Lloyd, *A Companion to Ancient Egypt* (2 vols) Wiley-Blackwell, 2010.
R. Schulz and M. Seidel, *Egypt. World of the Pharaohs* Könemann UK, 1998.
I. M. E. Shaw (ed.), *The Oxford History of Ancient Egypt* Oxford University Press, 2000.

Background archaeology
J. E. Baines and J. Málek, *Cultural Atlas of Ancient Egypt* (rev. edn) Phaidon Publishing, 2000.
K. A. Bard, *An Introduction to the Archaeology of Ancient Egypt* Wiley-Blackwell, 2007.
F. Goddio and A. Masson-Berghoff, *Sunken Cities. Egypt's Lost Worlds* Thames & Hudson with The British Museum, 2016.
B. J. Kemp, *Ancient Egypt: Anatomy of a Civilization* (2nd edn) Routledge, 2006.
B. J. Kemp, *The City of Akhenaten and Nefertiti. Amarna and Its People* Thames & Hudson, 2013.
M. Lehner, *The Complete Pyramids. Solving the Ancient Mysteries* Thames & Hudson, 1997.
M. Lehner and Z. Hawass, *Giza and the Pyramids* Thames & Hudson, 2017.
D. O'Connor, *Abydos. Egypt's First Pharaohs and the Cult of Osiris* Thames & Hudson, 2011.
S. J. Quirke, *The Cult of Ra. Sun worship in Ancient Egypt* Thames & Hudson, 2001.
C. N. Reeves and R. H. Wilkinson, *The Complete Valley of the Kings. Tombs and Treasures of Egypt's Greatest Pharaohs* Thames & Hudson, 1996.
G. J. Shaw, *The Pharaoh. Life at Court and on Campaign* Thames & Hudson, 2012.
S. R. Snape, *The Complete Cities of Ancient Egypt* Thames & Hudson, 2014.
A complete academic listing of Egypt's pharaonic archaeological sites is to be found in B. Porter and R. L. B. Moss, *Topographical Bibliography of Ancient Egyptian Hieroglyphic Texts, Reliefs and Paintings* (7 vols), published by the Griffith Institute of the University of Oxford (see http://topbib.griffith. ox.ac.uk).

Art and Architecture
G. Robins, *The Art of Ancient Egypt* (rev. edn) British Museum Press, 2008.
D. Arnold, *The Encyclopaedia of Ancient Egyptian Architecture* Princeton University Press, 2003.
M. K. Hartwig (ed.), *A Companion to Ancient Egyptian Art* Wiley-Blackwell, 2015.

J. Malek, *Egyptian Art* Phaidon, 1999 (a richly illustrated companion is the same author's *Egypt. 4000 Years of Art* Phaidon, 2003).
D. Wildung, *Egypt from Prehistory to the Romans* Taschen World Architecture Series, 1997.
R. H. Wilkinson, *The Complete Temples of Ancient Egypt* Thames & Hudson, 2000.
Older, influential books include:
C. Aldred, *Egyptian Art in the Days of the Pharaohs 3100-320 BC* Thames & Hudson, 1980.
T. G. H. James and W. V. Davies, *Egyptian Sculpture* Harvard University Press, 1983.
W. Stevenson Smith, *The Art and Architecture of Ancient Egypt* (rev. edn) Yale University Press / Pelican History of Art, 1981.
H. Schäfer, *Principles of Egyptian Art* Griffith Institute, 1974, is a seminal book, originally dating from 1919 but available in an English translation of the 1963 4th edition, which is sparsely illustrated and philosophically obsolescent but still repays close attention.

Specific topics
A long-running series of perennially useful introductions to many specific aspects of ancient Egyptian art and culture has been published by Bloomsbury Publishing under the imprimatur Shire Egyptology. Other suggestions for initial further reading include the following:
Techniques and technical matters
D. Arnold, *Building in Egypt. Pharaonic Stone Masonry* Oxford University Press, 1991.
W. V. Davies, *Colour and Painting in Ancient Egypt* British Museum Press, 2001.
G. Robins, *Proportion and Style in Ancient Egyptian Art* Thames & Hudson, 1994.
I. M. E. Shaw and P. T. Nicholson (eds), *Ancient Egyptian Materials and Technology* Cambridge University Press, 2009.
Coffins, tombs and the Book of the Dead
A. M. Dodson and S. Ikram, *The Mummy in Ancient Egypt. Equipping the Dead for Eternity* Thames & Hudson, 1998.
A. M. Dodson and S. Ikram, *The Tomb in Ancient Egypt. Royal and Private Sepulchres from the Early Dynastic Period to the Romans* Thames & Hudson, 2008.
R. O. Faulkner, *The Egyptian Book of the Dead. The Book of Going Forth by Day* Chronicle Books, 1994.

Iconography
R. H. Wilkinson, *Reading Egyptian Art. A Hieroglyphic Guide to Ancient Egyptian Painting and Sculpture* Thames & Hudson, 1994.

Jewelry and amulets
C. Aldred, *Jewels of the Pharaohs. Egyptian Jewellery of the Dynastic Period* Thames & Hudson, 1971.
C. Andrews, *Ancient Egyptian Jewellery* British Museum Press, 1990.
C. Andrews, *Amulets of Ancient Egypt* University of Texas Press, 1994.
H. W. Müller and E. Thiem, *Gold of the Pharaohs* Cornell University Press, 1999.

'Faiyum portraits'
E. Doxiadis, *The Mysterious Fayum Portraits. Faces from Ancient Egypt* Thames & Hudson, 1995.
P. Roberts, *Mummy Portraits from Roman Egypt* The British Museum Press, 2008.

The Community at Deir el-Medina
A. McDowell, *Village Life in Ancient Egypt. Laundry Lists and Love Songs* Oxford University Press, 1999.
J. Romer, *Ancient Lives. The Story of the Pharaohs' Tombmakers* Weidenfeld & Nicolson, 1984.

Exhibition catalogues
Most of the museums highlighted in this book make their collections of ancient Egyptian art publicly accessible through their websites. Some older and invaluable catalogue publications include:
D. Arnold, K. Grzymski and C. Ziegler (eds), *Egyptian Art in the Age of the Pyramids* Metropolitan Museum of Art, 1999.
E. Brovarski et al. (eds), *Egypt's Golden Age. The Art of Living in the New Kingdom 1558-1085 B.C.* Boston Museum of Fine Arts, 1982.
E. R. Russmann, *Eternal Egypt. Masterworks of Ancient Art from The British Museum* The British Museum Press with American Federation of Arts, 2001.
F. Tiradritti (ed.), *Egyptian Treasures from the Egyptian Museum in Cairo* Harry N. Abrams, 1999.

List of Illustrations

1 James Morris/akg-images 2 Photo Bill Manley 3 Iberfoto/SuperStock 4 Heritage Images/Diomedia 5 British Museum, London 6 Photo Bill Manley 7 Fondazione Museo delle Antichità Egizie, Turin/Photo Scala, Florence 8 Photo Bill Manley 9 Egyptian Museum, Cairo 10 Photo Olaf Tausch 11 Photo José-Ramón Pérez-Accino, Universidad Complutense de Madrid 12 The Metropolitan Museum of Art, New York: Rogers Fund, 1920 (20.2.2) 13 The Metropolitan Museum of Art, New York: Rogers Fund, 1911 (11.215.453) 14 Photo Keith Schengili-Roberts 15 Photo Bill Manley 16 Photo Mbzt, 2011 17, 18 Photo Bill Manley 19 Kenneth Garrett/Danita Delimont/Diomedia 20 British Museum, London 21 Photo Keith Schengili-Roberts 22, 23, 24, 25 Photo Bill Manley 26 Eliot Elisofon/The Smithsonian Museum of African Art, Washington, D.C. 27 Photo Bill Manley 28 Reinhard Dirscherl/Look/Diomedia 29 Museum of Fine Arts, Boston/Bridgeman Images 30 Gianni Dagli Orti/REX/Shutterstock 31 Kenneth Garrett/Danita Delimont/Diomedia 32 Photo Miguel Hermoso Cuesta 34 Gail Mooney-Kelly/Alamy 35 DeAgostini/Getty Images 36 Photo Chip Dawes 38, 39 Egyptian Museum, Cairo 40, 41, 42 Photo Bill Manley 43, 44 Werner Forman/Universal Images Group/Getty Images 45 Photo Bill Manley 46 Fitzwilliam Museum, Uni Bill Manley 49 G. Dagli Orti/DeAgostini/Diomedia 50 Maurice Babey/akg-images 51 André Held/akg-images 52 British Museum, London 53 G. Dagli Orti/DeAgostini/Diomedia 54 The Trustees of the British Museum, London 55, 56 Photo Bill Manley 57 G. Dagli Orti/DeAgostini/Diomedia 58 Kröller-Müller Museum, Otterlo 59 National Portrait Gallery, London 60 National Museums of Scotland 61 Fitzwilliam Museum, University of Cambridge/Bridgeman Images 62, 63 Photo Bill Manley 64 National Museums of Scotland 65 The Trustees of the British Museum, London 66 Christian Decamps/Musée du Louvre, Paris/RMN-Grand Palais 67, 68, 69 Photo Bill Manley 70 The Griffith Institute, University of Oxford 71 James Morris/akg-images 72 Photo Bill Manley 73 British Museum, London 74 Photo Keith Schengili-Roberts 75 Egyptian Museum, Cairo 76 Photo Keith Schengili-Roberts 77, 78 Leemage/Diomedia pp. 128-29 Louie Lea/Shutterstock.com 79 The Trustees of the British Museum, London 80, 81, 82 Illustration Claire Gilmour, East Ayrshire Museums 83 Photo José-Ramón Pérez-Accino, Universidad Complutense de Madrid 84, 85 The Trustees of the British Museum, London 86 The Metropolitan Museum of Art, New York: Rogers Fund, 1907 (07.228.156) 87 The Metropolitan Museum of Art, New York: Rogers Fund, 1968 (68.59) 88 Photo © Toby Wilkinson 89 Photo Bill Manley 90 Photo Rama, Wikimedia Commons, cc-by-sa-2.0.fr 91 DeAgostini Picture Library/REX/Shutterstock 92 Photo Archivo Heracleópolis Magna. Courtesy Spanish Archaeological Mission 94 Iberfoto/SuperStock 95 The Trustees of the British Museum, London 96 Egyptian Museum, Cairo 97 British Museum, London 98 Photo Bill Manley 99 Photo Miguel Hermoso Cuesta 100 Neues Museum, Berlin 101 from Selim Hassan, *Excavations at Giza* 1929-1930, 1932 (Oxford University Press) 102 A. Jemolo/DeAgostini/Diomedia 103 from Selim Hassan, *Excavations at Giza* 1929-1930, 1932 (Oxford University Press) 104 Musée du Louvre, Paris 105 Kelsey Museum of Archaeology, University of Michigan 106 Kunsthistorisches Museum, Vienna 107 Photo Einsamer Schütze 108 The Metropolitan Museum of Art, New York: Rogers Fund, 1948 (48.111) 109, 110 Museum of Fine Arts, Boston. All rights reserved/Scala, Florence 111 Egyptian Museum, Cairo 112 Werner Forman Archive/Heritage Images/Diomedia 113 Christian Larrieu/Musée du Louvre, Paris/RMN-Grand Palais 114 Brooklyn Museum, New York: Charles Edwin Wilbour Fund (39.602) 115 The Trustees of the British Museum, London 116 G. Dagli Orti/DeAgostini/Diomedia 117 Egyptian Museum, Cairo 118 Museum of Fine Arts, Boston. All rights reserved/Scala, Florence 119 The Trustees of the British Museum, London 120 The Metropolitan Museum of Fine Art, New York: Rogers Fund, 1920 (20.2.29) 121 Museum of Fine Arts, Boston. All rights reserved/Scala, Florence 122 G. Dagli Orti/DeAgostini/Diomedia 123, 124, 125 Photo Bill Manley 126 The Metropolitan Museum of Art, New York: Gift of J. Lionberger Davis, 1966 (66.123.1) 127 Photo Archivo Heracleópolis Magna. Courtesy Spanish Archaeological Mission 128 The Metropolitan Museum of Art, New York: Rogers Fund, 1926 (26.3.29) 129 Egyptian Museum, Cairo 130 from G. Maspero, *Recueil de Travaux* 32, 1910 (Paris) 131 The Metropolitan Museum of Art, New York: Rogers Fund, 1925 (25.2.3) 132, 133, 134, 135, 136 Photo Bill Manley 137 Alfredo Dagli Orti/REX/Shutterstock 138 National Museum of Antiquities, Leiden/Werner Forman Archive/Diomedia 139 Photo Keith Schengili-Roberts 140, 141 Photo Miguel Hermoso Cuesta 142 Photo Gunter Schmidt 143 age fotostock/SuperStock 144 Gianni Dagli Orti/REX/Shutterstock 145 from Giovanni Battista Belzoni, *Narrative of the Operations and Recent Discoveries in Egypt and Nubia*, 1820 (London) 146 Alfredo Dagli Orti/REX/Shutter stock 147 Photo Bill Manley 148 Werner Forman Archive/Diomedia 149 Photo Bill Manley 150 Martin Child/Robert Harding/Diomedia 151 University of Memphis 152 from Pierre Lacau, *Catalogue général des antiquités égyptiennes du Musée du Caire*, 1909 (Paris) 153 Photo Bill Manley 154 Photo © Ad Meskens/Wikimedia Commons 155 from Uvo Hölscher, *The Excavation of Medinet Habu*, 1934 (Chicago) 156 Photo Bill Manley 157 Photo José-Ramón Pérez-Accino, Universidad Complutense de Madrid 158 Werner Forman Archive/Diomedia 159 The Theban Royal Mummy Project 160 Travelshots/SuperStock 161 The

Metropolitan Museum of Art, New York: Rogers Fund, 1916 (16.10.224) **162** The Metropolitan Museum of Art, New York: Rogers Fund, 1931 (31.3.94) **163** A. Jemolo/DeAgostini/Diomedia **164** Photo Bill Manley **165** Egyptian Museum, Cairo/Werner Forman Archive/Diomedia **166** A. Jemolo/DeAgostini/Diomedia **167** Egyptian Museum, Cairo **169** Robert Harding/Diomedia **170** Mike Nelson/EPA/REX/Shutterstock **171** The Metropolitan Museum of Art, New York: Gift of Norbert Schimmel, 1985 (1985.328.15) **172** Photo Bill Manley **173** British Museum, London **174** Photo Bill Manley **175** Neues Museum, Berlin **176** Photo Bill Manley **177** after Norman de Garis Davies, *The rock tombs of El-Amarna, Parts V and VI*, 1905 (London) **178** from Pierre Lacua, *Catalogue général des antiquités égyptiennes du Musée du Caire*, 1909 (Paris) **179** Iglesia de Santo Tomé, Toledo **180** Photo Bill Manley **181** Brooklyn Museum, New York: Charles Edwin Wilbour Fund (66.174.1) **182** Egyptian Museum, Cairo **183** after B.B. Williams, *Excavations between Abu Simbel and the Sudan Frontier*, 1986 (Chicago) **184** Egyptian Museum, Cairo/Werner Forman Archive/Diomedia **185** G. Dagli Orti/DeAgostini/Diomedia **186** Photo Aidan Dodson **187** Magica/Alamy **188** Universal Images Group/Diomedia **189, 190** The Trustees of the British Museum, London **191** Heritage Images/Diomedia **192** The Walters Art Museum, Baltimore: Acquired by Henry Walters, 1924 (22.398) **193** Staatliche Museen zu Berlin **194** Photo Bill Manley **195** Musée du Louvre, Paris **196** British Museum, London **197** Museum of Fine Arts, Boston/Bridgeman Images **198, 199** Photo Bill Manley **201** The Trustees of the British Museum, London **202, 203, 204, 205, 206** Photo Bill Manley **207** Christian Decamps/Musée du Louvre, Paris/RMN-Grand Palais **208** Photo Martin Dörrschnabel, Wikimedia Commons, cc-by-sa-2.5 **209** Egyptian Museum, Cairo **210** Fondazione Museo delle Antichità Egizie, Turin/Werner Forman Archive/Diomedia **211** Brooklyn Museum, New York: Charles Edwin Wilbour Fund (37.440E) **212** Brooklyn Museum, New York: Charles Edwin Wilbour Fund (37.40E) **213** Egyptian Museum, Cairo **214** The Metropolitan Museum of Art, New York: Rogers Fund, 1936 (36.3.69) **215** S. Vannini/DeAgostini/REX/Shutterstock **216** The Metropolitan Museum of Art, New York: Fletcher Fund, 1919–1920 (26.8.98) **217** Brooklyn Museum, New York: Charles Edwin Wilbour Fund (60.27.1) **218** The Trustees of the British Museum, London **219** British Museum, London/Werner Forman Archive/Diomedia **220** Rijksmuseum van Oudheden, Leiden **221** The Metropolitan Museum of Art, New York: Gift of Edward S. Harkness, 1917 (17.9.1) **222** Erich Lessing/akg-images **223** Oriental Institute Museum, University of Chicago **224** The Petrie Museum of Egyptian Archaeology UCL, London **225** Oriental Museum, Durham University/Bridgeman Images **226** The Trustees of the British Museum, London **227** Brooklyn Museum, New York:

Charles Edwin Wilbour Fund (37.123E) **228** The Metropolitan Museum of Art, New York: Gift of the Earl of Carnarvon, 1914 (14.10.10a–c) **229** Rijksmuseum van Oudheden, Leiden **230** The Metropolitan Museum of Art, New York: Purchase, Rogers Fund and Henry Walters Gift, 1916 (16.1.3a, b) **231, 232** National Museums of Scotland **233** The Metropolitan Museum of Art, New York: Rogers Fund, 1915 (15.2.2a, b) **234** The Metropolitan Museum of Art, New York: Rogers Fund, 1912 (12.182.132a, b) **235** Gianni Dagli Orti/REX/Shutterstock **236** British Museum, London **237** Egyptian Museum, Cairo **239** National Museum of Iran, Tehran **240** Brooklyn Museum, New York: Charles Edwin Wilbour Fund (52.89) **241** Photo Stuart Jackson **242** Photo Bill Manley **243** The Metropolitan Museum of Art, New York: Rogers Fund, 1934 (34.2.1) **244** Photo Bill Manley **245** Photo Scala, Florence **246** Photo Bill Manley **247** British Museum, London **248** Werner Forman Archive/Diomedia **249** Fitzwilliam Museum, University of Cambridge/Bridgeman Images **250** Photo Miguel Hermoso Cuesta **251** Photo Bill Manley **252** Photo Einsamer Schütze **253** Roger Lichtenberg/akg-images **254** G. Sioen/DeAgostini/Diomedia **255** Gianni Dagli Orti/REX/Shutterstock **256** Marka/SuperStock **257** The Metropolitan Museum of Art, New York: Rogers Fund, 1907 (07.229.1a, b) **258** Ashmolean Museum, University of Oxford/Bridgeman Images **259** National Museums of Scotland **260** Granger Historical Picture Archive/Alamy **261** Photo Bill Manley **262** from John Gardner Wilkinson, *Manners and Customs of the Ancient Egyptians*, 1937–41 (London) **263** The Pushkin State Museum of Fine Arts, Moscow **265** The Coptic Museum, Cairo **265** Photo Bill Manley **266, 267** Museo Archeologico Nazionale di Napoli **268** The Trustees of the British Museum, London **269** National Museums of Scotland **270** Wellcome Library, London **271** Martin Lubikowski, ML Design, London

Masterpiece accession numbers

The Narmer Palette
   Egyptian Museum, Cairo. JE 14716
Label from the tomb of Den, the fourth king of Egypt
   British Museum, London. EA 32650
Greywacke statue of Menkaura
   Egyptian Museum, Cairo. JE 46499
Offering shrine of Ptahshepses
   British Museum, London. EA 682
Life-size statues of Rahotep and Nofret
   Egyptian Museum, Cairo. CG 3 + 4
Sennedjem's burial chamber
   Deir el-Medina, Luxor. Burial chamber of Theban Tomb TT1
Nebamun with his wife and daughter capturing water-fowl
   British Museum, London. EA 37977
Steatite disc of the palace official Hmaka
   Egyptian Museum, Cairo JE 70164
Bust of the vizier Ankhhaf
   Museum of Fine Arts, Boston 27.442
Tomb of Sarenput II
   Qubbet el-Hawa Tomb 31, Aswan.

Limestone chapel, Deir el-Bahri
   Egyptian Museum, Cairo JE 38574+5
Gold mask of Tutankhamun
   Egyptian Museum, Cairo JE 60672
Gold throne of Tutankhamun
   Cairo Museum JE 62028
Sphinx of Amenhotep III from Sulb, Nubia
   British Museum EA 2
Statues of Taharqa at Kawa, Nubia
   British Museum EA 1770
Seated statue of the chief steward Harwa
   Nubian Museum CG 37377
Ostracon of dancing girl
   Museo Egizio, Turin. C.7052
The Tazza Farnese
   National Archaeological Museum, Naples 27611
Statue of the priest Pasherbastet
   British Museum EA 34270
Wooden portrait board of woman wearing jewelry
   National Museums Scotland NMS A.

Acknowledgments

The author is pleased to acknowledge a debt of gratitude to the following at Thames & Hudson: Colin Ridler for commissioning the project; Jen Moore, the editor, for unstinting encouragement; Carolyn Jones for scrupulous, helpful attention to the text; Louise Thomas for painstaking picture research; Adam Hay for thoughtful design work; and Celia Falconer for detailed attention to the illustrations. I would also like to thank Lucia Gahlin (University of Exeter) and Jan Picton (UCL Institute of Archaeology) for bringing to my attention the quote on page 267, to Dr Aidan Dodson (University of Bristol), Dr José-Ramón Pérez-Accino (Universidad Complutense de Madrid) and Dr Toby Wilkinson (University of Cambridge) for supplying photographs from their personal archives, and to Claire Gilmour (East Ayrshire Museums) for preparing the line drawings on pages 132–33.

Index

Names including the Arabic article *'el'* are listed without taking this element into account. Page references in *italics* refer to illustrations.